Foreign Affairs and the Founding Fathers

FOREIGN AFFAIRS AND THE FOUNDING FATHERS

From Confederation to Constitution, 1776–1787

Norman A. Graebner,
Richard Dean Burns, and
Joseph M. Siracusa

AN IMPRINT OF ABC-CLIO, LLC
Santa Barbara, California • Denver, Colorado • Oxford, England

Library of Congress Cataloging-in-Publication Data

Graebner, Norman A.
  Foreign affairs and the founding fathers : from confederation to constitution, 1776–1787 / Norman A. Graebner, Richard Dean Burns, and Joseph M. Siracusa.
    p. cm.
  Includes bibliographical references and index.
  ISBN 978-0-313-39826-1 (hardcopy : alk. paper) — ISBN 978-0-313-39827-8 (ebook)   1. United States—Foreign relations—1775–1783.   2. United States—Foreign relations—1783–   3. United States—Foreign relations—Philosophy.
4. Constitutional history—United States.   I. Burns, Richard Dean.   II. Siracusa, Joseph M.   III. Title.
  E249.G73   2011
  973.3—dc23   2011019817

ISBN: 978-0-313-39826-1
EISBN: 978-0-313-39827-8

15   14   13   12   3   4   5

This book is also available on the World Wide Web as an eBook.
Visit www.abc-clio.com for details.

Praeger
An Imprint of ABC-CLIO, LLC

ABC-CLIO, LLC
130 Cremona Drive, P.O. Box 1911
Santa Barbara, California 93116-1911

This book is printed on acid-free paper (∞)

Manufactured in the United States of America

CONTENTS

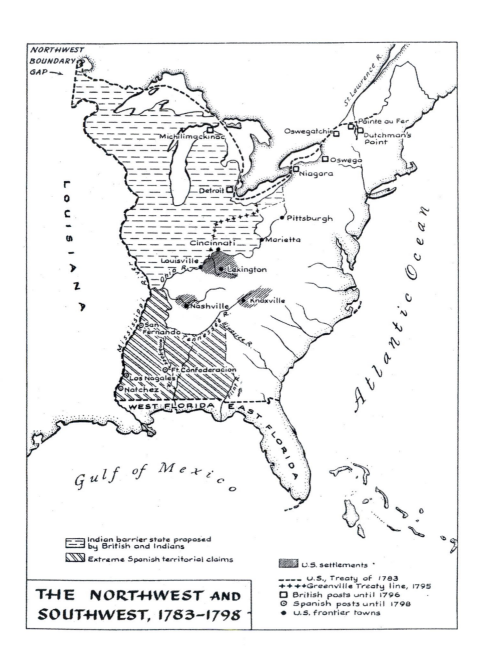

NORTHWEST
BOUNDARY
GAP →

St. Lawrence R.

Pointe au Fer
Oswegatchie
Dutchman's
Point

Michilimackinac

Oswego

Niagara

Detroit

Pittsburgh

Cincinnati

Marietta

Louisville R.
Lexington

Ohio R.

Nashville

Knoxville

San
Fernando

Tenn. R.

Ft. Confederacion

Los Nogales

Natchez

WEST FLORIDA   EAST FLORIDA

L O U I S I A N A

Mississippi R.

Atlantic Ocean

Gulf of Mexico

Indian barrier state proposed
by British and Indians

Extreme Spanish territorial claims

U.S. settlements

---- U.S., Treaty of 1783
++++ Greenville Treaty line, 1795
☐ British posts until 1796
⊙ Spanish posts until 1798
● U.S. frontier towns

THE NORTHWEST AND
SOUTHWEST, 1783-1798

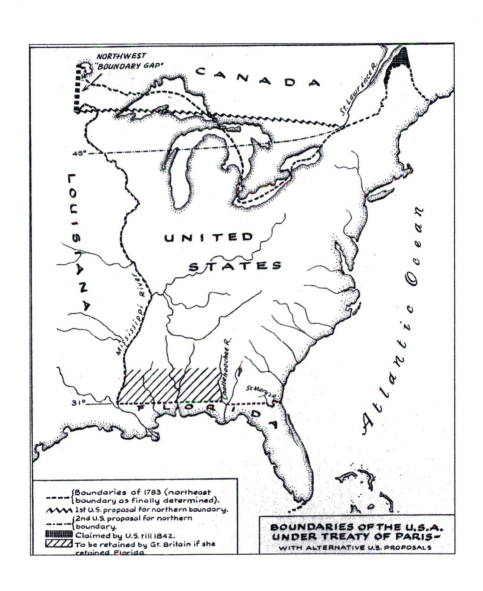

NORTHWEST "BOUNDARY GAP"

CANADA

St. Lawrence R.

45°

LOUISIANA

UNITED

STATES

Mississippi River

Chattahoochee R.

St. Marys R.

31°

FLORIDA

Atlantic Ocean

Boundaries of 1783 (northeast boundary as finally determined).
1st U.S. proposal for northern boundary.
2nd U.S. proposal for northern boundary.
Claimed by U.S. till 1842.
To be retained by Gt. Britain if she retained Florida.

BOUNDARIES OF THE U.S.A.
UNDER TREATY OF PARIS~
WITH ALTERNATIVE U.S. PROPOSALS

PREFACE

In a poll taken in 2007, 72 percent of respondents told Pew researchers that they completely agree with the statement, "If Founding Fathers came back today, they would be disappointed with the way America has turned out."[1] This strikes us as an understatement. They would be astounded to learn of an American empire that boasts 301,000 soldiers based in 38 countries, led by military chiefs who draw comparisons with the Roman empire, inspired by books with such titles as *Empires of Trust: How Rome Built—and America Is Building—a New World.*[2] Immersed in the perspective of 18th-century political realism, putting national interest and security over ideology and moral concerns, the Founding Fathers would have great difficulty coming to grips not only with the state of America in the world today but also with concepts such as "wars of choice," which have driven national foreign policy in the 21st century to the ends of the earth. What doubtless would have impressed them, however, would have been the discovery that the United States is now considered the most powerful nation on the planet, in contrast with their own era, the last two decades of the 18th century, in which the new Republic struggled to establish its very sovereignty in a hostile world dominated by European monarchies. It was a very near thing and should give us pause—and perhaps some modesty—in dealing with the world around us.

It is in this context that we have sought to write a concise diplomatic history of the Confederation era, providing a realist interpretation of how the Founding Fathers responded to the threats and problems associated with America's place in the world, from the aftermath of the Revolution to the new polity under the Constitution in 1787. By focusing on the aspirations, thoughts, and actions of the Founding Fathers during the seminal decades of the American nation, we also hope, in the words of Rebecca Rimel, in a related but different context, to take the reader "backstage, where we can eavesdrop on motives and personally understand the opportunities and challenges of the day almost as the Founding Fathers weighed and determined them."[3] For a revolutionary generation that thought and acted in terms of power and diplomacy, we hope to remind readers of the wisdom of America's Founding Fathers in dealing with the nation's external affairs. The events of recent times suggest that we have yet to fully understand that wisdom. We like to think there is still time.

A prolific essayist, Professor Graebner wrote on a wide range of topics including the Founding Fathers and was a consulting editor for the National Historical Publications and Records Commission's three volumes, *The Emerging Nation: A Documentary History of the Foreign Relations of the United States Under the Articles of Confederation, 1780–1789* (1996), published under the direction of Mary A. Giunta. This study has drawn on those volumes as well as Graebner's vast collection of archival materials and earlier essays. We wish to thank the following organizations for extending the courtesy of reprinting portions of some of his previous endeavors: "Adams and Jefferson in Europe, 1783–1788," a lecture delivered at Mary Baldwin College on October 12, 1962; "Foreign Affairs and the U.S. Constitution," from the *Proceedings of the Massachusetts Historical Society* 98 (1986): 1–20; "Isolation and Antifederalism: The Ratification Debates," *Diplomatic History* (October 1987): 337–54; and "The Illinois Country and the Treaty of Paris of 1783," *Illinois Historical Journal* 78:1 (1985): 2–16.

This book on the foreign policy of the Founding Fathers is also the final installment in our "trilogy" of salient episodes of the American diplomatic experience, from the unique perspective of political realism, by three generations of diplomatic historians, which began with *Reagan, Bush, Gorbachev: Revisiting the End of the Cold War* (2008), followed by *America and the Cold War, 1941–1991: A Realist Interpretation* (2010). It has been a remarkable journey.

PROLOGUE: THE CHALLENGE OF EXTERNAL RELATIONS

Traditions rest lightly on the American people. With the founding of the Republic more than two centuries ago, Americans, contemplating the rich Continent before them as well as the possibilities afforded by their new Constitution, could anticipate one long experiment in democratic government, economic progress, and freedom from war, unrestrained by the lessons of history. Amid changes that crowded one another with unprecedented rapidity, what could one generation say to the next that mattered, especially when the challenges that confronted each generation scarcely seemed to exist in the previous one? It is not strange, then, that the country's citizens generally detected little need for historic guidance in the formulation of attitudes, purposes, and policies. Even intellectual conservatives have often revealed little respect for the nation's past.

Still, there is often a widespread lament, shared by writers, scholars, and political leaders, that the country lacks a tradition in foreign affairs commensurate with its power and responsibilities. Many have regarded the use of power and diplomacy, the central historic presumption of international relations, as an unacceptable, even immoral, foundation for the country's external policies. Those who reject this approach to international affairs often express regret over the absence of a countering American tradition that might serve as a more effective and realistic guide to national action abroad.

This is strange. Experience had taught the Founding Fathers that the major forces of international society tended simultaneously toward stability and change. Individual nations ranged themselves on one side or the other of this equation in accordance with their immediate or long-term interests, as they understood them. It was the uncertainty, the lack of precision, in the international system that rendered assessments difficult. Decisions, once made, soon engaged the interests and preferences of other countries. For the Founding Fathers, no less than for Europe's statesmen, the central task of diplomacy was that of limiting the behavior of the ambitious in a fundamentally anarchical international environment to what they regarded acceptable. What preserved Europe's remarkable stability and the general outlines of its international boundaries, despite the continuing wars, was the existence of an equilibrium or balance of power. Writers on the balance of power assumed that one or more ambitious countries would always seek to enhance, if not to maximize, their power. Nations checked such recurrent aggressiveness with counterchecks composed of opposing combinations of power. Indeed, every state, in its own interest and in the interest of the equilibrium, carried the obligation to prevent any one country from becoming too powerful. On the day that one country became strong enough to challenge all others combined, the balancing system would cease to exist. The Founding Fathers discovered early that the European equilibrium would be the essential source of American security. Even as colonists, the American people achieved major victories over Europe's two most powerful nations by managing to throw British power against France to drive the French from the North American Continent, and, then, within 20 years, to drive the British out of the 13 colonies by utilizing the power of France.[1]

John Adams, representing the young Republic in Europe during the 1780s, understood clearly that as long as Britain and France, occupying the two poles of the European equilibrium, emerged from the war strong and antagonistic toward one another, the United States was safe. In his tardy acceptance of the French alliance, Adams could foresee no future American war except against Britain and Britain's allies. "The United States...," he concluded, "will be for ages the natural bulwark of France against the hostile designs of England against her, and France is the natural defense of the United States against the rapacious spirit of Great Britain against them. France is a nation so vastly eminent...that united in close alliance with our States,...there is not the smallest reason to doubt but both will be a sufficient curb upon the naval power of Great

Britain." At the same time Adams recognized Britain's importance to the European equilibrium. A Dutch merchant in Paris informed him "that they in Holland had regarded England as the Bulwark of the Protestant Religion and the most important Weight in the Ballance of Power in Europe against France." "I answered," Adams reported, "that I had been educated from my Cradle in the same opinion...."[2] Adams knew that Britain would leave the war as an essential element in the European equilibrium and a defense against French ambition in the New World.

The Founding Fathers were the creatures of tradition, steeped in the political and diplomatic wisdom of the age. Overwhelmingly they accepted the philosophic conviction of Edmund Burke that society comprised a continuing compact between the dead, the living, and the yet unborn. The living might be masters of their immediate destiny, but they would, if they were wise, take cognizance of those traditions that had the sanction of wisdom and common sense and transmit that heritage to those who would follow. In fulfilling that obligation to themselves and to posterity, such early American leaders as George Washington, Thomas Jefferson, James Madison, Alexander Hamilton, John Adams, in their voluminous writings, drew on the European past and those who had analyzed it so brilliantly—Grotius, Hobbes, Fenelon, Vattel, and Burlamaqui—to create for the United States a realistic diplomatic tradition, from which subsequent generations could draw.

*****

Thus for America's Founding Fathers the European state system was never a mystery, nor were the brilliant 17th- and 18th-century writings that described the system and defined the rules that governed it. The Peace of Westphalia (1648), with its recognition of the sovereignty of nations and the optimum conditions for their security and survival, had reorganized the European system. That treaty redistributed western Europe among its several rulers, with the intention that the new status quo would be permanent. The Westphalian system underwrote Europe's emerging stability by establishing the independence of states and the notion of religion and freedom and tolerance, imposing order and continuity on the disparate, sovereign elements that comprised its complex political structure. Assuming the inevitability of war, the system emphasized the ending of conflicts under conditions best suited to limit change and reimpose the necessary forms of order. What preserved Europe's post-Westphalian stability, despite the continuing wars, was the concept of equilibrium or balance. The system sought to check the universal selfishness of men and nations with counterchecks composed of opposing combinations of power. Thus Friedrich von Gentz, the noted Prussian diplomat, defined such balance of power as "that constitution which exists among neighboring states more or less connected with each other, by virtue of which none of them can violate the independence or the essential rights of another without effective resistance from some quarter and consequent danger to itself."[3]

Fundamentally, the objective in maintaining an equilibrium among the powers was the preservation of Europe's international community. The balancing system assumed that each major power formed an essential element within the system. The second objective, then, followed logically from the first: to assure the survival of such individual states by preventing the ascendancy of one over the others with the power to encroach on their sovereignty and ultimately to destroy them. To fulfill their obligations to defend the established distribution of power and territory, nations maintained standing armies and endless diplomatic negotiations, requiring permanent legations in the important capitals. Cardinal Richelieu, who introduced the classic approach to international relations based on the nation-state and motivated by national interests as its ultimate goal, devised this scheme in the 17th century to protect France's superiority over its Hapsburg rivals in Spain and Austria.[4] That small states on occasion ceased to exist demonstrated both the subordinate role of independence to the general equilibrium and the predominant role of the great powers as the custodians of international society.[5]

European statesmen recognized movement in history as reflected in the rise and decline of national power and ambition. The constant change in the relationship of nations to the balance of power demanded the vigilance necessary to detect the predominant tendencies within international society and to judge their consequences in terms of the general good. Emmerich de Vattel, the influential author of *The Law of Nations* (1758) and the chief authority of American leaders, argued that the effort to curtail the internal development of any nation would be futile and unjust. It was preferable, he wrote, to overcome discrepancies in power and to counterbalance the growing weight and ambitions of states by forming alliances. The incessant changes in the power and purposes of nations placed a premium on diplomatic flexibility. As the Abbé de Pradt suggested, in any threat to Europe's equilibrium it was imperative that "enemies come together for common defense, and allies momentarily separate for the same reason." There was no room in a balanced system for partiality. Maintaining the equilibrium was more important than peace, pledges, treaties, and friendships. In practice, nations generally supported the causes of others with less energy than they supported their own. Even with such limitations, the balancing system sustained Europe's international order. To prevent the unnecessary enlargement of war and the excessive uses of power, writers on the balance encouraged neutrality; the more widespread the neutrality, the more confined the war and the less its impact on international stability. Neutrality would not necessarily please the warring parties. To avoid unwanted involvement in war, a country required sufficient power to make its neutrality effective.

After Westphalia, five closely related and generally equal nations—Great Britain, France, Russia, Prussia, and Austria—dominated the European state system. Europe contained a number of secondary and lesser nations, including Turkey, which often played definable roles in the European equilibrium, but the Big Five managed the system and determined its fundamental policies. What contributed to the success of this balancing system was Europe's common culture and the concept of a common destiny, which gave the nations a certain unity of outlook despite their continuing differences. G. F. Von Martens, in his *Summary of the Law of* Nations (1795), stressed this essential unity when he wrote that

> the resemblance in manners and religion, the intercourse of commerce, the frequency of traders of all sorts, and the ties of blood between sovereigns, have so multiplied the relations between each particular state and the rest, that one may consider Europe (particularly the Christian states of it) as a society of nations and states, each of which has its laws, its customs, and its maxims, but which it cannot put in execution without observing a great deal of delicacy towards the rest of society.

Europe, furthermore, was tied together by common experience and common institutions. All member states within the system shared similar diplomatic and economic practices, similar military organizations, and a group consciousness that gave all a mutual interest in the perpetuation of the balance of power structure itself. European civilization was unique, and its perpetuation was the goal of wise statesmanship.

Europe's cosmopolitanism reinforced the equilibrium by encouraging moderation in war. It was an 18th-century maxim that victors never crush an aggressor nation in the interest of stern justice but rather perpetuate that country's capacity to play its traditional role in the general balance. "You must take care," argued Fénelon, "that the engagements you lay yourself under, do not reduce your enemy too low, and prove too beneficial to your ally; which may lay you under a necessity either to suffer what may be ruinous to you, or to violate your engagements."[6] Montesquieu once asserted that the "law of nations is naturally founded on this principle, that different nations ought in time of peace to do one another all the good they can and in time of war as little injury as possible, without prejudicing their real interest." In practice, governments limited violence in war by demanding sacrifices from opponents small enough to provoke only limited responses. The smaller the political objective in war, the less would be the resistance and the needed exertion of force to gain it. Thus the political objective, the original motive for war, determined the nature of the resulting conflict and the levels of power that the contestants would unleash. Pursuing limited goals, the aggressor might readily give up the effort rather than escalate the costs beyond the value of the objective. To contain the scope of war, nations sought to avoid international animosities that might turn the slightest quarrel into an explosion disproportionate in magnitude to the issues at stake.[7] It was not strange, therefore, that nations generally sustained their contacts with their enemies even in time of war, the more easily to retrieve a mistaken policy. The essential purpose of the balance of power was to confine national ambition by encouraging moderation. Within the limits imposed by existing moral and political restraints, each nation was free to pursue its own interests as it chose to define them."[8]

Before the Peace of Westphalia, two rival dynasties, the French Bourbon and the Austrian Hapsburg, dominated European politics. The region of controversy had been central and southern Europe, but Westphalia established France's dominance on the Continent. Great Britain's subsequent triumphs over the Dutch gave it command of the seas and the power to confront French ambitions in western Europe and in the Atlantic. Long before the end of the 17th century, the burgeoning rivalry between Britain and France replaced France's older competition with the Hapsburgs as the central feature of European politics. If British leaders recognized the importance of the European balance of power, they could not agree on the need of an active British policy to maintain it. Some argued that Britain's insular position offered that country sufficient security, whatever the lack of equilibrium on the Continent.[9] In time France's Continental ambitions denied Britain the luxury of isolation from European politics.

*****

The United States, as an independent nation, would necessarily exist in a fundamentally anarchical world of sovereign states, each struggling to enhance its security, assure the integrity of its political life, expanding its economic opportunities and protect the well-being of its citizens through the exercise of power and diplomacy. John Adams engaged the world of power politics as critic and practitioner during the decade that followed his first European venture in 1778. He understood, for example, that specific conditions and environments could influence effective use of a nation's power. Military advantages, he knew, could assume a variety of forms: some geographic, some demographic. In October 1780, he explained to a Dutch correspondent why Britain would never defeat the rebelling colonies. A hundred thousand British troops, he acknowledged, might gain and preserve a royal government in three provinces of the Confederacy, but no more. The States, he wrote,

> are at such distances from one another, there are such difficulties in passing from one to another by land, and such a multitude of posts are necessary to be garrisoned and provided in order to command any one Colony, that an army of a hundred thousand men would soon find itself consumed in getting and keeping possession of one or two States....Such is the nature of the country, and such the character of the people, that if the English were to send ever so many ships, and ever so many troops, they never would subdue all the Americans. Numbers, in every State, would fly to the mountains, and beyond the mountains, and there maintain a constant war against the English.[10]

Like his contemporaries, Adams had accepted the notion that international politics comprised an amoral struggle in pursuit of interests and power, and that all countries should calculate their goals accordingly. He readily engaged the European state system, with its evolving rules and traditions, as the only available structure for maintaining a reasonable peace and security in a fundamentally anarchic world of sovereign nations. His observation that some European powers were at war every 10 or 15 years eliminated any engagement in international reforming enterprises.[11] Adams, possessing an acute sense of the role of power in international affair, recognized the existence of an international equilibrium and the persistent effort of nations to sustain it. For him, as well as other American leaders, that balance of power underwrote North America's security. Adams knew that Britain, even after American independence, would be an essential element in the European equilibrium and a defense against French ambition in the New World. One day, he predicted, the European system would encompass the United States as an active and powerful participant, with the authority to serve its own interests as well as those of others.[12] Adams accepted Europe's mercantilism no less than its system of international politics. America had prospered under it and would continue to do so.[13]

Yet the acceptance of such a seemingly forbidding worldview, based on the politics of power, was scarcely universal. Some Americans adopted the more reassuring notion that the United States, in separating from England, had escaped the world of power politics. Thomas Paine had argued in *Common Sense* (1776) that America's attachment to Britain alone had endangered its security. It was the British connection that had tended "to involve this Continent in European wars and quarrels, and set us at variance with nations who would otherwise seek our friendship, and against whom we have neither anger nor complaint." More specifically, Paine predicted that France and Spain, both New World powers, would never be "our enemies as *Americans,* but as our being *subjects of Great Britain.*" An independent United States of America would have no cause to defy other countries with demanding foreign policies. "Our plan," he wrote, "is commerce, and that, well attended to, will secure us the peace and friendship of all Europe; because it is the interest of all Europe to have America a free port. Her trade will always be a protection, and her barrenness of gold and silver secure her from invaders." Paine advocated a navy adequate to protect American shores. Such naval power would effectively reinforce a policy of military and political isolation from Europe.[14] Paine's assumption that independence from England had freed America from the vicissitudes of European politics or that commerce, especially that conducted by Republics, and had eliminated the danger of war.

Alexander Hamilton questioned this assumption. "Have republics in practice," he asked, "been less addicted to war than monarchies? Are not the former administered by men as well as the latter? Are there not adversions, predilections, rivalships, and desires of unjust acquisitions that affect nations as well as kings? Are not popular assemblies frequently subject to the impulses of rage, resentment, jealousy, avarice, and of other irregular and violent propensities? Has commerce hitherto done any thing more than change the objects of war? Is not the love of wealth as domineering and enterprising a passion as that of power or glory? Let experience, the least fallible guide of human opinions, be appealed to for an answer to these inquiries." Carthage, a commercial Republic, was the aggressor in the very war that terminated its existence. Holland, another commercial Republic, played a conspicuous role in the wars of modern Europe. Britain's marked addiction for commerce never prevented that country from engaging in war. Public passions could draw a country into war as readily as monarchial ambitions. "There have been....almost as many popular as royal wars," Hamilton concluded. "The cries of the nation and the importunities of their representatives have, upon various occasions, dragged their monarchs into war, or continued them in it, contrary to their inclinations, and sometimes contrary to the real interests of the state."[15]

For the Founding Fathers, competition and conflict were the normal conditions of international life. "To look for a continuation of harmony between a number of independent, unconnected sovereignties in the same neighborhood," Hamilton observed in *The Federalist No. 6*, "would be to disregard the uniform course of human events, and to set at defiance the accumulated experience of ages." For Hamilton the causes of hostility among nations were innumerable. The rivalry for markets among trading nations remained high on the list, but he noted also "the love of power or the desire of preeminence and dominion.... the attachments, enmities, interests, hopes, and fears of leading individuals in the communities of which they are members." Too often, Hamilton warned, such men, whether favorites of the king or the people, had "abused the confidence they possessed; and assuming the pretext of some public motive, have not scrupled to sacrifice the national tranquility to personal advantage or personal gratification."[16]

Alexander Hamilton rushed to the defense of the Washington administration with a series of brilliant essays, published in 1793 and 1794 under the names "Pacificus" and "Americanus." These writings constituted the most pervading examination of the diplomatic principles guiding the young Republic to come from the pen of any of the nation's early leaders. The country's pro-French legions had anchored their demands for a strong national allegiance to France on the assumptions that the United States must be faithful to its treaty obligations, show gratitude for previous assistance, and underscore its affinity for republican institutions in a monarchical world. Hamilton attacked these notions head on. He argued in "Pacificus" that the country's first obligation was to itself. Without sea power the United States carried no obligation even to the French islands in the West Indies. There could be no balance, enjoying the sanction of common sense, between the damage that the United States would inflict on itself by opposing Britain and the advantages that it might bring to France. "All contracts," wrote Hamilton, "are to receive a reasonable construction. Self-preservation is the first duty of a Nation; and though in the performance of stipulations relating to war, good faith requires that the *ordinary hazards* of war should be fairly encountered,...yet it does not require that *extraordinary* and *extreme* hazards should be run...." From engaging in a naval war with Great Britain, without a navy or coastal fortifications, he concluded, "we are dissuaded by the most cogent motives of self-preservation, no less than of interest."

What troubled Hamilton especially was the popular plea that the United States owed a debt of gratitude to France. Hamilton reminded his readers that the conduct of external relations was purely a governmental function, one not belonging to individuals or the people. Thus the commitment to moral obligations by a government, acting as an agent and not a principal, could not be the same as that of an individual. "Existing millions and for the most part future generations," he wrote, "are concerned in the present measures of a government: While the consequences of the private actions of an individual, for the most part, terminate with himself or are circumscribed within a narrow compass. Whence it follows, that an individual may on numerous occasions meritoriously indulge the emotions of generosity and benevolence; not only without an eye to, but even at the expense of his own interest. But a Nation can rarely be justified in pursuing [a similar] course; and when it does so ought to confine itself within much stricter bounds." It was essential that governments contemplate the long-term interests of society and not moral impulses shared only by some of its members.

Rather than follow the dictates of partiality toward other countries, the United States, believed Hamilton, should seek the best possible relations with all. In defending the Jay Treaty with his remarkable "Camillus" papers of 1795—a primer on Vattel—Hamilton argued that peaceful arrangements, even when not totally satisfactory, would serve the nation's interests far better than war. Nor did he believe that concepts of national honor or moral disapprobation should eliminate efforts at compromise. Seldom in history, he noted, did national outrages upon others render negotiations dishonorable. "Nations," he wrote, "ought to calculate as well as individuals, to compare evils, and to prefer the lesser to the greater; to act otherwise, is to act unreasonably; those who advocate it are imposters and madmen."[17]

With the achievement of peace in 1783, John Adams believed the European balance of power sufficiently stable to guarantee America's future independence. "[T]here is a Ballance of Power in Europe," he assured James Warren in March. "Nature has formed it. Practice and Habit have confirmed it, and it must forever exist. It may be disturbed for a time, by the accidental Removal of a Weight from one Scale to the other; but there will be a continual Effort to restore the Equilibrium." Before the war, the nations of Europe had regarded Britain too powerful; now they accepted the diminution of British power with pleasure. With Europe's equilibrium restored, neither London nor Paris could cross the Atlantic with sufficient force to endanger the territories, much less the independence, of the United States without facing an overwhelming coalition of countering power in Europe itself.

None of the nation's early leaders matched Thomas Jefferson in his persistent concern for the European equilibrium. During his years as minister to France, he commented often and brilliantly on Europe's shifting balance of power and its significance for European and Atlantic stability. For Jefferson it was essential that the United States judge its interests and manage its policies in accordance with the vicissitudes of the European equilibrium. "While there are powers in Europe which fear our views...," he observed in December 1787, "we should keep an eye on them, their connections and oppositions, that in a moment of need we may avail ourselves of their weakness with respect to others as well as ourselves, and calculate their designs and movements on all the circumstances under which they exist." Later, with the outbreak of the Napoleonic wars after 1803, with the full might of Napoleon's France confronting that of Britain and the rest of Europe, Jefferson feared a victory of either France or Britain over the other.[18]

With independence a vital challenge to the United States in 1783, the question arose as to whether its government had the ability to project the necessary power to effectively employ diplomacy to serve its national interests. For the Founding Fathers, these immediate interests involved favorable commercial arrangements, establishing the nation's boundaries and gaining international respect. Could the state-oriented Articles of Confederation organize the nation's real and potential power to gain these ends? Or would a substantially modified Constitution be required to provide the nation success in foreign affairs?

Chapter 1

AMERICA ENTERS THE
INTERNATIONAL COMMUNITY

As Americans sought to gain their independence from Britain, most leaders understood that success would require far more military power and financial resources than the colonies possessed. For that reason, the movement for independence was never separable from the international environment in which it occurred. The Declaration of Independence was not simply a symbolic effort of the United States to escape the demands and vicissitudes of European politics but rather the necessary precondition to the alliance with France. It was the affirmation of a widespread conviction that the interests of the English settlers in the New World required a deeper involvement in the affairs of Europe than membership in the British Empire permitted. Even in the 18th century, the appreciation of geographic isolation and its advantages were lesser determinants of American behavior than the quest for commercial empire and the direct, purposeful reliance on Europe's power structure. Whatever differences from the European standard actually existed in early American diplomatic practice resulted less from conceptual uniqueness than from the greater freedom of action permitted by the absence of contiguous nations that possessed the power to challenge the American people at every turn.

Yet colonial Americans frequently had found themselves caught up in the Anglo-French struggle for leadership in world affairs. Indeed, where British and French colonies met in a vast wilderness in North America, their rivalries would often spark conflict.

****

Following La Salle's overland journey in 1682, the French built a series of posts that followed the arc of their claims through the

Great Lakes country and down the Mississippi River to the Gulf of Mexico. Already the contest for the Great Lakes fur trade focused on western New York where the powerful Iroquois, dominating the other tribes, penetrated the lake country and diverted much of the lucrative fur trade from Montreal and Paris to Albany and London. Facing an unwanted conflict in the North American wilderness, Britain and France signed the Treaty of Whitehall in November 1686. This agreement pledged the two nations to live in "peace, union, concord, and good correspondence" in the New World. Should any rupture occur in Europe between them, they agreed additionally that "true and firm peace and neutrality shall continue in America...as if no rupture had occurred in Europe."[1] The treaty had little effect simply because the stakes of empire in North America were too high. The War of the Spanish Succession (1701–1713) was preeminently a war to reestablish Europe's equilibrium by preventing a union between France and Spain. Despite its importance, the British victory would not resolve the contest in America for control of the back country.

During Britain's continuing wars with France, the seaboard colonies from Massachusetts to Virginia recognized the French challenge to their interests in the region of the Ohio and the Great Lakes. English colonies claimed the great inland empire, regarding the French as intruders. Many anticipated the time when Britain alone would control the vast wealth of North America. To avoid further conflict over the fur trade, Britain and France agreed not to molest the Indians residing within the dominions of the other, but after the War of the Spanish Succession, the two powers penetrated the Indian buffer zone with additional forts in preparation for an eventual showdown. The French added Fort Niagara in 1720, and New York, on its own initiative, countered with the erection of Fort Oswego on Lake Ontario. The Indian barrier itself now became the area of friction and strife, with the bitter skirmishes along the frontier creating a violent reaction in New England, New York, and Virginia. For colonial leaders determined to secure their borders and control the fur trade, it seemed essential that the English colonies break the French hold on the St. Lawrence and the Great Lakes trading routes.[2] Thus, the struggle for the wilderness was primarily an issue between the English and the French residing in the New World. Not until its final stages did this contest become part of the global imperial competition between the two great European rivals.

French officials, conscious of the colonial threat to their empire, prepared for the inescapable British-American assault on their New World possessions. American traders established a post on the Great Miami River that the French destroyed in 1751. Then, in 1754, the French erected Fort Duquesne at the forks of the Ohio to strengthen their claims to the Ohio watershed. Virginia accepted the challenge by dispatching George Washington and a small military force to persuade the French in withdraw; instead, the French drove Washington and his men from the region. This threat to the British position in America was too patent to be ignored by the London government that sent General Edward Braddock with an army to drive the French from the Ohio Valley. The dismal failure of his campaign did not end the struggle; French ambition simply exceeded what the British would tolerate. For American imperialists, only British power could now resolve the contest for the North American continent. To their immense satisfaction, London fully committed itself to the struggle for the American wilderness with the outbreak of Europe's Seven Years' War in 1756.

During the subsequent years of fighting in America, which culminated in the British capture of Louisbourg in 1758 and the fall of Quebec in 1759, colonial spokesmen argued the American case for the total removal of the French from North America. In 1757, John Mitchell, a British botanist and cartographer who had spent many years in Virginia, declared that France had no rights on the North American continent. At stake in the war, wrote Mitchell, was control of the entire Continent with all its wealth and commerce. If Britain failed to eliminate the French from its New World domain, it would eventually lose it all. Benjamin Franklin attacked the popular notion that Britain should retain Guadeloupe rather than Canada lest the American people, no longer fearful of French encroachment, become dangerous to Britain itself. Only by acquiring Canada, he warned, would the British avoid future wars in defense of their New World empire.[3] In December 1762, Lord Shelburne proclaimed his conviction in Parliament that Britain had fought the war for the security of its American colonies; that purpose required the exclusion of France from North America. What gave Britain its leverage in the peace negotiations to deprive France of its North American empire were the successes not only of its armies in the New World but also those of its European ally, Frederick the Great of Prussia, which compelled France to waste its energies in a futile war on the Continent.

American imperialists had their way. The Peace of Paris (1763) transferred Canada and all French territory east of the Mississippi River, with the exception of New Orleans and the fishing islands of St. Pierre and Miquelon south of Newfoundland, to Great Britain. This treaty marked the ultimate triumph of the first American venture into international affairs. With good reason, the war years from 1754 to 1760 provoked an unprecedented burst of goodwill and patriotism toward the British Empire. Franklin expressed the feeling well when he wrote to an English friend in 1760:

> No one can more sincerely rejoice than I do, on the reduction of Canada; and this not merely as I am a colonist, but as I am a Briton. I have long been of [the] opinion, that the foundations of the future grandeur and stability of the British empire lie in America; and though, like other foundations, they are low and little seen, they are nevertheless, broad and strong enough to support the greatest political structure human wisdom ever erected. All the country from the St. Lawrence to the Mississippi will in another century be filled with British people. Britain itself will become vastly more populous, by the immense increase of its commerce; the Atlantic sea will be covered with your trading ships; and your naval 'power, then continually increasing, will extend your influence round the whole globe, and awe the world![4]

*****

With the conclusion of the Seven Years' War in 1763, Great Britain commanded the greatest empire since the fall of Rome. For their part, Americans emerged from the war generally content with their position in the British Empire. They shared Franklin's deep satisfaction with British policy that had freed the frontiers from French encroachments. The Navigation Acts, which confined colonial trade to the ports and ships of the empire, were not onerous; those that might have been troublesome, the British tended to neglect. During the Seven Years' War, colonial merchants profited handsomely from both their trade with the enemy and their expanded smuggling operations. In 1760 the London government ordered the colonial governors to tighten up the customs service, but without success. Americans had become adept at subverting any imperial regulations that the

British sought to enforce, employing techniques of obstruction and delay to defend their commercial interests. Assured access to both British markets and defense, Americans agreed that the advantages of membership in the British Empire far outweighed the liabilities.

Unfortunately, the long war against France had overextended Britain's financial needs and the burdens of empire. The British national debt had doubled during the war; the carrying charge alone absorbed more than half the annual budget. The London government, moreover, assumed the responsibility for keeping an army in America to enforce the Proclamation Line of 1763 along the ridge of the Appalachians that was designed to guarantee the Indians the possession of their lands on the frontier. To relieve British taxpayers and control American commerce, the George Grenville ministry secured passage of the Sugar Act in 1764.[5]

Suddenly cords of empire that seemingly appeared indestructible began to unravel. Parliament's new regulatory and taxing policies, backed by more effective methods of enforcement, came with such speed and force that they rendered the older colonial strategies almost totally obsolete and required the search for new ones. Whether the new program was fair was scarcely the issue. For a people accustomed to the benefits of empire with relatively little obligation, any controls or taxes would have set dangerous precedents. When London again discovered that its controls were no match for the new refined techniques of smuggling in America, it turned to the Stamp Act, an internal tax on newspapers, legal documents, and other items. This time the reaction went beyond boycotts and the refusal to cooperate. Soon, argument drifted into physical violence, reducing the act to a nullity. Convinced that the strategic advantage had passed to America, British leaders advised an end to all parliamentary impositions, and in 1766 Parliament repealed the Stamp Act. One year later, the Townshend Acts—a body of external taxes—faced the customary resistance. Before the end of the decade, Parliament had lifted most regulations, permitting the profitable empire trade to resume much of its traditional pattern. In the colonial resistance to all British efforts at taxing and regulation, the Americans revealed little feeling of gratitude toward Britain for having driven the French from North America.[6]

Why Parliament could no longer resolve its quarrel with the colonies was already obvious. At issue in London's postwar commercial and taxing policies were infringements not only on American interests but also on American authority. Sir Francis Bernard, the Massachusetts governor, detected the nature of the confrontation when he wrote to Lord Barrington, the secretary at war, on November 23, 1765: "All the political evils in America arise from the want of ascertaining the relation between Great Britain and the American colonies. In Britain the American governments are considered as corporations empowered to make bye-laws, existing only during the pleasure of Parliament...In America they claim...to be perfect states, not otherwise dependent upon Great Britain than by having the same King; which having compleat legislatures within themselves, are no ways subject to that of Great Britain. In a difference so very wide who shall determine?"

Parliament, in its Declaratory Act of 1766, asserted that it had the full power to bind the colonies in all cases. Such claims to sovereignty provided the colonies with no legal defense against unjust legislation and thus rendered parliamentary authority a potential danger to liberty itself. For colonial spokesmen, the challenge was clear: How could they limit Parliament's legal jurisdiction in colonial matters without denying its historic supremacy in the British constitutional system? To divide authority left unresolved the question of sovereignty. Governor Thomas Hutchinson of Massachusetts carried the debate to its logical conclusion in 1773 when he declared that there was "no line that can be drawn between the supreme authority of Parliament and the total independence of the colonies: it is impossible there should be two independent legislatures in one and the same state for...two legislative bodies will make two governments as distinct as the kingdomes of England and Scotland before the Union."[7]

This confrontation over constitutional principles might have drifted on indefinitely had not a handful of Boston citizens in December 1773 chosen to defy Parliament's remaining tax on tea by dumping 342 chests of East India Company tea into the harbor. In England, Parliament viewed the Boston Tea Party for what it was—a direct assault on its authority. Lord North informed Parliament that the question was no longer one of legislation or taxation but "whether or not we have any authority there; that it is very clear we have none, if we suffer the property of our subjects to be destroyed." The ministry's opposition suggested that Parliament show its goodwill be repealing the tax on tea. "If you give up this tax," Solicitor General

Alexander Wedderburn stormed back, "you will be required to give up much more, nay, to give up all." In the debates on the repeal of the tea tax, Edmund Burke declared that "they tell you that your dignity is tied to it... This dignity is a terrible encumbrance to you for it has of late been ever at war with your interest, your equity and every idea of your policy." Parliament buried the tea tax repeal by a vote of 182 to 49.[8] For Britain, then, the choices that the Americans offered were narrow and narrowing. Parliament would now exert its will or yield a portion of the empire. In March 1774 it voted overwhelmingly to punish Boston and then imposed the Quebec Act, which placed the lands to the west of Pennsylvania under the control of the Catholic province of Quebec.

To answer the British challenge, colonial leaders assembled the First Continental Congress in Philadelphia on September 5, 1774. Joseph Galloway, leader of the Conservatives, argued that the colonies could not expect to enjoy the privileges of membership in the British Empire without showing some allegiance to it. In the crisis, some colonists advocated royal authority in imperial affairs, assuming that the king would be more restrained and accommodating than Parliament. This was scarcely an alternative, as Parliament would not compromise its long-established authority, nor would the king request it. For Americans, as for the British, the choices were narrow: they would accept parliamentary authority or prepare for war. As King George III wrote to Lord North on September 11, 1774, "The dye is now cast, the colonies must either submit or triumph." Lord Mansfield, Britain's chief justice, agreed that there could be no division of authority in the empire. "We are reduced," he declared, "to the alternative of adopting coercive measures, or of forever relinquishing our claim of sovereignty or dominion over the colonies.... [Either] the supremacy of the British legislature must be complete, entire, and unconditional or on the other hand, the colonies must be free and independent."[9] Parliament made its final decision in February 1775 when it adopted Lord North's resolution upholding parliamentary authority.

In Philadelphia the Second Continental Congress adopted the war that began at Lexington and Concord in April 1775. In rejecting Lord North's final resolution of February 20, the Congress reminded the British ministry that it could not accept parliamentary supremacy merely on the assurance that Parliament had no intention of misusing its power.[10] In response the king accused the colonists of planning a general revolt, leaving London no choice but "to put a speedy end to these disorders by the most decisive exertions." What sustained British as well as American leaders in the crisis, and ruled out any last-minute compromises, was the conviction that war assured the final triumph of their purposes. Many of Britain's political and military leaders assumed that Great Britain would win quickly and easily. In time, declared one member of Parliament, Americans loyal to the king would join the British army, Americanize the war, and permit the British soldiers to return home. Americans were equally conscious of the role of force in international affairs; for years, however, they had insisted that British power rested on the wealth and people of America. To young Alexander Hamilton writing in February 1775, it seemed strange that Britain would risk war to uphold Parliament's claims. "The consequences to Great Britain," he predicted, "would be too destructive to permit her to proceed to extremities, unless she has lost all just sense of her own interest."[11] The American mood of rebelliousness after 1775 simply reflected such convictions of power and importance. "I do verily believe," wrote Richard Henry Lee of Virginia in April 1776, that "N. America will give law to that proud imperious Island."[12]

American leaders. in their quest for independence, quickly recognized their need for an alliance with France. They understood that Europe's endless search for equilibrium dictated the need for some new coalition to offset the power and prestige of Great Britain. On May 2, 1776, David Hartley advised the House of Commons that "it is next to infatuation and madness, for one moment to suppose that we can have an American without a French and Spanish war."[13] His predictions were not wrong. The French minister Comte de Vergennes, after 1774, was determined to employ all means at hand to retrieve the fallen glory of the French monarchy. "The deplorable peace of 1763," he reminded the king, "the partition of Poland, and in fact, other causes equally disastrous, have struck the greatest blows to the respect for your crown." The restoration of French prestige required the humiliation of England.[14]

Not all Americans anticipated with elation the internationalization of the war. Loyalists argued that America should not entrust its future to the European balance of power but rather to British protection. Others saw immediately that without France's help, the Americans would never win the victories necessary to establish their rights within the British Empire. John Adams readily acknowledged the French interest in the American cause and recorded his arguments in favor of a mission to France: "Interest could not lie.... The Interest of France was so obvious, and her motives so cogent, that nothing but a judicial infatuation of her councils could restrain her from embracing US."[15] But Adams feared that the lack of coercive power in the colonies would render France the dominant partner in any alliance. For that reason, he argued against a political or military connection with France, preferring only a commercial arrangement. At the same time, Lee advocated a more venturesome approach to Europe. France, he knew, would not break its formal peace with England merely to assure Americans a more favorable status in the British Empire; therefore, the colonies could obtain the needed help from France only by fighting for their independence. On June 2, 1776, he reminded his fellow Virginian, Landon Carter, that only "by a timely alliance with proper and willing powers in Europe" would colonial leaders "secure America from the despotic aims of the British Court.... But no State in Europe will either Treat or Trade with us so long as we consider ourselves Subjects of G.B.... *It is not choice then but necessity that calls for Independence, as the only means by which foreign Alliance can be obtained.*"[16] On July 2 the Congress declared the United States an independent nation.

*****

Even as American leaders adopted Thomas Jefferson's Declaration of Independence, they were aware of their reliance on France and the need for involving that country in American affairs. Robert Morris reminded John Jay of this on September 23, 1776: "It appears clear to me that we may very soon involve all Europe in a War by managing properly the apparent forwardness of the Court of France; it's a horrid consideration that our own Safety should call on us to involve other nations in the Calamities of War. Can this be morally right or have Morality and Policy nothing to do with each other? Perhaps it may not be good Policy to investigate the Question at this time." Members of Congress anticipated a vigorous European response to the threatened breakup of the British Empire. Elbridge Gerry wrote in November: "It is acknowledged on all hands that now is the Time for France and Spain to destroy the Balance of power which has been heretofore said to be preserved in Europe, but considered as preponderating against them."[17] Samuel Adams added in a letter of February 1777 that "the war between Britain and the United States of America will affect the Balance of Power in Europe. Will not the different Powers take different sides to adjust the Balance to their different Interests?" Writing again in April, Adams said: "When it suits the Interest of foreign Powers they will aid us substantially."[18] From the moment of its inception, then, America entered the world of diplomacy and power as an active and willful participant.

Franklin reached Paris in December 1776 to negotiate an alliance with Vergennes. He carried Congress's treaty plan of September 1776, which asserted America's claim to the lands beyond the Alleghenies; indeed, revolutionary leaders anticipated the acquisition of Canada, Nova Scotia, Florida, and all other British possessions on the North American continent. While Congress officials pursued an alliance with France, they also proposed one with Spain. In return for Spanish aid, the United States would assist Spain in capturing Pensacola, provided the Americans would receive "the free and uninterrupted navigation of the Mississippi and the use of the harbour of Pensacola." Encouraged by Vergennes, Franklin raised the prospect of an alliance to Count d'Aranda, the Spanish minister in Paris, offering essentially the same terms as the Congressional plan.[19] To Count d'Floridablanca, Spain's minister of state, this and earlier proposals indicated that the Americans intended to acquire the east bank of Mississippi and thereby threaten Louisiana. In January 1778, he clarified this country's objectives in any war against Britain as the recovery of "Gibraltar, Minorca....the Gulf of Mexico, the Bay of Honduras, and the coast of Campeche." Clearly Spain could not dominate the Gulf of Mexico unless it controlled the traffic on the Mississippi.[20]

Behind Franklin's success with the French lay the American promise of full military exertion until the conclusion of the war, the decisive American victory at Saratoga, and the growing French interest in severing Britain from its power base in the New World. Moreover he offered France a guarantee of all its possessions in the West Indies; in return he asked the French to renounce all claims on the continent of North America. Vergennes did not object. Although France had no ambitions on the mainland, Vergennes preferred that Canada remain in British hands to maintain some balance of power and perpetuate the new republic's dependence on France. Already, French involvement in American affairs had become so extensive that France either had to turn back ignominiously or fully commit itself to the American cause, even at the risk of war. General Burgoyne's surrender at Saratoga, in October 1777, stirred the French court to action. "We must now either support the colonies or abandon them," Vergennes informed the French minister in Madrid. "We must form the alliance before England offers independence, or we will lose the benefit to be derived from America, and England will still control their commerce."

French and American officials in Paris signed treaties of commerce and alliance on February 6, 1778. The alliance bound the two countries to behave as good and faithful allies, with Article II designed to maintain effectually "the liberty, Sovereignty, and independence absolute and unlimited of the said United States, as well as in Matters of Government as of commerce." The two allies agreed to conclude neither a truce nor peace with Great Britain without the consent of the other; they agreed, in addition, not to lay down their arms until Britain recognized the independence of the United States.

In March, Britain and France broke diplomatic relations; and within days, both countries were at war. John Adams quickly deserted his earlier doubts and accepted the alliance with France as a promising response to the challenges of 1778, persuaded that the French interest in American independence was sufficient to render France a trustworthy ally. France, having given up all pretension to territory in North America, was not likely to harbor jealousy or animosity toward the new American Republic; thus, Adams foresaw no future American wars except with Britain and its allies. "The United States," he concluded, "will be for ages the natural bulwark of France against the hostile designs of England against her, and France is the natural defense of the United States against the rapacious spirit of Great Britain against them. France is a nation so vastly eminent... that united in close alliance with our States, and enjoying the benefit of our trade, there is not the smallest reason to doubt but both will be a sufficient curb upon the naval power of Great Britain." As an American commissioner, Adams wrote from Paris in August 1778 that "the longer I live in Europe, and the more I consider our Affairs, the more important our Alliance to France appears to me. It is a rock upon which we may safely build."[21]

Although France and Spain shared a mutual interest in tilting the European balance of power against Britain, their conflicting purposes elsewhere seemed to render a pact against Britain improbable. France's minister in Philadelphia, Conrad Alexandre Gérard, sought to persuade Congress to forgo its demands for western lands and rights to the Mississippi. Congress's special committee on foreign affairs' initial report on February 23, 1779, doomed his efforts. This report delineated a northern line running from Nova Scotia to Lake Nipissing, then west to the Mississippi. The southern boundary of the United States would separate Georgia from East and West Florida; the western boundary would be the Mississippi. Additionally, Congress demanded the right not only to navigation of the Mississippi to the southern boundary of the United States but also to free commerce and some port below the boundary. While Southern and Western members argued the United States should have complete control of the Mississippi, troubled pro-French members such as Maryland's representative was the American defiance of French and Spanish preferences on such matters as the Mississippi. "We must not aim at too much," he cautioned, "lest we risk the losing of all." During March, Congress accepted a boundary that included the Great Lakes, the Mississippi River to the Thirty-first Parallel, and the northern boundary of Florida. But now Congress denied the South and West their claims to navigation on the Mississippi.[22]

European diplomacy assumed that interests alone determined the objectives and guided the behavior of nations. Mutual interests, not affection, underwrote the Franco-American alliance. Washington gave this central principle of international politics classic form when he observed in November 1778: "Hatred of England may carry some to excess of Confidence in France; especially when motives of gratitude are thrown into the scale.... I am heartily disposed to entertain the most favourable sentiments of our new ally and to cherish them in others to a reasonable degree; but it is a maxim founded on the universal experience of mankind, that no nation is to be trusted farther than it is bound by its interest; and no prudent statesman or politician will venture to depart from it."[23] When a British general argued before the House of Commons in May 1780 that distance, tradition, language, and religion rendered the Franco-American alliance unnatural, Adams retorted: "I know of no better rule than this,—when two nations have the same interests in general, they are natural allies; when they have opposite interests, they are natural enemies. [But] the habits of affection or enmity between nations are easily changed as circumstances vary, and as essential interests alter."[24] Like all alliances, the one with France could be temporary. While earlier, France had posed a danger to the English colonies in America, in 1780 common interests rendered it a natural friend.

No less than Adams and Washington, members of Congress welcomed the French alliance because they assumed the existence of strong mutual interests in the struggle against Britain. "We must expect all nations will be influenced by their own interest," wrote William Whippie of New Hampshire in July 1779, "and so far we may expect the Friendship of any power that inclines to form an alliance with us, but if we expect more, we shall certainly be disapppointed."[25] France's decision to entrust its peace efforts to Russia and Prussia as mediating powers in 1781 troubled those who had no confidence in the two continental courts. However, Maryland's Daniel Jenifer noted in June 1781 that France "must procure us tolerable terms, or She cannot expect to keep us long in her interest, therefore I trust more to her policy than her Justice."[26] Unlike Jenifer, Delaware's Thomas Rodney opposed the instructions of June 1781, which required the American commissioners in Europe to govern themselves ultimately according to the advice of the French court. For him, the new orders were dangerous and humiliating. Still, he agreed that the mediating powers would readily consent to American independence because "it will be ever the Interest of France that they should do this lest we should at a future day form an Alliance with Great Britain."[27]

*****

Historians have often viewed the diplomacy of the American Revolution with cynicism, largely because it revealed the intense rivalry of the European powers and their repeated efforts to deny the new American Republic everything that it wanted. That diplomacy demonstrated that even allies might have legitimate interests so much in conflict that no possible settlement can distribute the gains or losses in any equitable fashion. So diverse were the interests of the nations fighting England, so limited their military exertions, that no one could predict the design of the final treaties that would reestablish the peace. At the end, Britain faced the United States, France, Spain, and Holland in something approaching a world war. Spain and the United States were allied with France but not with each other; the Dutch were allied to no one. Whatever the differing purposes for which these nations fought, the search for a settlement conformed to traditional principles. For the American commissioners in Europe—Franklin, Adams, and Jay, dispatched to Spain in late 1779—the wartime diplomacy demonstrated in classic fashion not only the close relationship between military and diplomatic success but also the manner in which each nation placed its interests in hierarchical order, readily giving up secondary objectives to assure the achievement of those that mattered. Every country emerged from the war with a respectable settlement. This was the real measure of the competence, moderation, and goodwill that characterized the negotiations. There were no reparations, no special punishments, no lingering desires for revenge; this was peacemaking at its best.

Throughout the wartime negotiations, France, the dominant member of the coalition fighting Britain, remained faithful to its commitment to American independence. Vergennes reminded the French minister in America in October 1778 that France would never accept a peace proposal that did not grant absolute independence to the United States. On that point, he wrote, "his majesty could not weaken."[28] That commitment rendered France's needed alliance with Spain elusive. Spain's major interest as a declining power—one far outweighing all others—was the perpetuation of its New World empire. For that reason, it had no interest in American independence, surmising accurately that an independent republic in North America would soon endanger the Spanish hold on Louisiana. In the Convention of Aranjuez of April 1779, which brought Spain into the war, the French agreed to support the Spanish claims to Gibraltar, Minorca, Mobile, Pensacola, Honduras, and Campeche.

France added the transfer of Florida to Spain but avoided the question of Spanish control of the Mississippi. The French court was not committed to any specific boundaries for the United States; it was concerned only that its ally, Spain, eventually gain a settlement that protected its interests in America. What distracted Vergennes after the convention was the sudden realization that Spain and the United States were in direct conflict over the future of the American West. Congress, in framing its war aims during the spring and autumn of 1779, insisted not only on the Mississippi River as the western boundary of the United States but also on the free navigation of that river between the Florida border and the Gulf of Mexico. It was not strange that Jay, conveying Congress's demands to the Spanish court, could never gain formal recognition or reach an agreement. The Mississippi, declared the Spanish minister, the Count of Floridablanca, "was an object that the king had so much on his heart that he would never relinquish it."[29]

In addition to contemplating strategies for gaining recognition of America's independence, favorable boundaries and commercial treaties, U.S. diplomats were charged with obtaining loans with which to carry on the war. In a country desperately short of hard currency, Congress pleaded with its diplomats to obtain foreign loans to meet its obligations and purchase much-needed military supplies. While France, and to a much lesser extent Spain, initially extended gifts to aid the colonists, subsequently Franklin and Jefferson obtained loans from France during 1777–1783 amounting to approximately $6,361,500 while Jay obtained a loan of $174,017 from Spain during 1781–1782. Later, Adams, during 1782–1787, negotiated a series of loans from Holland totaling some $3,200,000, and Jefferson obtained a $400,000 one in 1788. Consequently, the new government in 1789 was confronted with a foreign debt, including principal and interest, totaling approximately $11,710,000.[30]

As late as 1782, the London government, with good reason, resisted the granting of independence to the United States. In the American quest for nationhood, the British faced a totally unprecedented challenge to the integrity of their empire. No British official could know where a successful revolution in America might lead. At a minimum, King George predicted in 1779, Britain would lose much of the West Indies as well as Ireland. Still, for British leaders, time ran out; and in November 1781, London learned not only of the French-American triumph at Yorktown but also of the French victories throughout the West Indies and Minorca. Such British disasters toppled the North government in March 1782. The new government under Lords Rockingham and Shelburne, persuaded at last that Britain could no longer withhold the recognition of American independence, opened negotiations in April by sending Oswald to Paris. Vergennes agreed that the Americans should confer directly with the British under their own instructions, provided that the French negotiations proceed at the same pace, and that the United States and France sign treaties at the same time.

Franklin summoned Jay to Paris on April 22. In carrying the burden of American diplomacy because of Franklin's subsequent illness, Jay faced the problem of securing from the British the immediate recognition of American independence; the fisheries along the Newfoundland coast; and the desired boundaries along the Great Lakes, the Mississippi, and the northern border of Florida. At the same time, Jay sought an agreement with the Spanish minister in Paris, the Count d'Aranda, of the question of the Mississippi River boundary and free navigation of that river to the Gulf of Mexico. Aranda, to protect Spanish interests in the West, turned to the French court for support. Versailles still hoped to satisfy the Spanish government. During the summer of 1782, Vergennes's English-speaking undersecretary, Gerard de Rayneval, joined Aranda in proposing a series of compromise boundaries between the Alleghenies and the Mississippi, all of which were designed to keep the United States away from Louisiana.[31] Aranda's line, Jay complained, "would leave near as much country between it and the Mississippi as there is between it and the Atlantic Ocean."[32] France's obvious sympathy for the Spanish position prompted him to ignore Congress's instructions and to seek a solution with Britain without reference to the French court. "We can depend upon the French," he explained, "only to see that we are separated from England, but it is not in their interest that we should become a great and formidable people, and therefore they will not help us to become so."[33]

Jay understood correctly that Great Britain, once committed to American independence, had no desire to keep the United States away from the Mississippi. During the concluding negotiations with Britain, Adams, who had arrived in Paris from Holland on October 26, 1782, observed that the American commissioners would obtain the Mississippi River boundary only because they had negotiated independently of France.[34] The final treaty with Britain, signed in Paris on November 30, conveyed to the United States both independence and boundaries bordered by the Great Lakes, the Mississippi, and Florida. Vergennes, reading the text, was astounded. For two years he had assumed that American terms, totally unacceptable to Spain, would in some measure be unacceptable to Britain as well. "You will notice," he informed Gerard de Rayneval, that the "English buy the peace more than they make it."[35] "Their concessions," Vergennes wrote, "in fact, exceed all that I should have thought possible."[36] With American independence, France achieved its central objective in the war, but beyond that it gained little. Shortly after the Anglo-French negotiations got under way the news of Admiral de Grasse's stunning defeat in the West Indies reached Europe. From then on the British made it clear that they expected the settlement to follow the Peace of Paris of 1763. France received complete control of Saint Pierre and Miquelon, some gains in India and Africa, as well as the promise of a new commercial treaty with Britain. Given the conflicting purposes of Spain and the United States in the Mississippi Valley, French diplomacy could not have been more candid and consistent than it was.[37]

With the Spanish failure to seize Gibraltar in late 1782, France had no choice but to abandon its promise of Gibraltar to Spain, made in the Convention of Aranjuez. Spain received other compensations, including Minorca and Florida, but it could not prevent the extension of the United States to the Mississippi simply because Britain, in control of that decision, was willing to accept that boundary. With control of both banks of the Mississippi below 31°, Spain could compel the United States to negotiate further if it would acquire free navigation and a commercial depot south of that parallel. So complete was the American success in reaching the Mississippi that it left Spain, a cobelligerent, completely distraught. For Spain, the defeat of Britain turned out to be scarcely a victory at all; it all but sealed the fate of Spanish Louisiana, Texas, and the far Southwest. At the end, Aranda could observe, with understandable regret, "this federal republic is born a pigmy. A day will come when it will be a giant, even a colossus, formidable in these countries. Liberty of conscience, the facility for establishing a new population on immense lands, as well as the advantages of the new government, will draw thither farmers and artisans from all nations. In a few years we shall watch with grief the tyrannical existence of this same colossus."

Despite their elation, the three American commissioners could not be sure that their accomplishment would stand. The treaty required the approval of the British government as well as the Continental Congress at home. In London, the arrangement was decidedly unpopular, producing Shelburne's downfall in February 1783. Yet, in the absence of any clear alternative, Parliament accepted the treaty anyway. The commissioners in Paris were troubled by the possibility that Congress might reject their work, but the recently arrived Henry Laurens was scarcely worried. "I cannot think our country," he wrote, "will hang their ministers merely for their simplicity in being cheated into independence, the fisheries, and half the Great Lakes." Congress did rebuke the commissioners for departing from their instructions, but ultimately, on April 15, 1783, approved the preliminary treaty. Hartley, a friend of both Franklin and America, arrived in Paris to negotiate a definitive treaty with the commissioners; the Americans, however, refused to make any further concessions. On September 3 the British and American negotiators signed the preliminary articles at Hartley's lodgings in the Hotel de York, and later that day at Versailles, the British signed definitive treaties with France and Spain.

With the assurance of independence after November 1782, the United States faced the task of defining its proper relationship to a Europe at peace. How could the new nation best defend its independence, as well as its other interests, against the still great powers of Europe? As late as August 1782, Adams revealed a pervading fear of the British. "They hate us, universally, from the throne to the footstool and would annihilate us, if in their power," he wrote to Jay.[38] But by November Adams had changed his mind, saying that the United States could entrust its future to a policy of neutrality toward Europe's competing factions. The balance of power that had secured American independence would now, by keeping Britain and France at opposite poles, guarantee the status quo in the New World. America, he recalled, "had been a Football between contending Nations from the Beginning, and it was easy to foresee that France and England would endeavor to involve Us in their future Wars. I thought [it] our Interest and Duty to avoid [these] as much as possible and to be compleatly independent and have nothing to do but in Commerce with either of them."[39] One week later, he confided to his diary his conviction that the United States should assert its freedom of action in its future relations with Europe:

You are afraid says Mr. Oswald to day of being made the Tools of the Powers of Europe,—Indeed I am says I.—What Powers says he.—All of them says I. It is obvious that all the Powers of Europe will be continually maneuvering with Us, to work us into their real or imaginary Ballances of Power. They will all wish to make of Us a Make Weight Candle, when they are weighing out their Pounds. Indeed it is not surprizing for we shall very often if not always be able to turn the Scale. But I think it ought to be our Rule not to meddle, and that of all the Powers of Europe not to desire Us, or perhaps even to permit Us to interfere, if they can help it.[40]

Adams concluded that Europe's equilibrium placed a premium on American neutrality, that strong ties with some European states would generate animosities in others. "There is a Ballance of Power in Europe," he reminded Warren in March 1783. "Nature has formed it. Practice and Habit have confirmed it, and it must forever exist. It may be disturbed for a time, by the accidental Removal of a Weight from one Scale to the other; but there will be a continual

Effort to restore the Equilibrium. The Powers of Europe now think Great Britain too powerful. They will see her Power diminished with pleasure. But they cannot see Us throw ourselves headlong into the Scale of Bourbon without Jealousy and Terror."[41] For Adams it was essential that the United States grant no exclusive arrangements or form perpetual alliances with the powers in one scale. To do so would inevitably make enemies of those in the other. "Congress," he stressed, "adopted these Principles and this System in its purity, and by their Wisdom have succeeded most perfectly in preventing every Power in the World from taking Part against them."

Unlike Adams, Franklin distrusted Britain too deeply to entrust America's future peace and security to a policy of neutrality toward Europe. "It is our firm connection with France," he wrote in late December 1782, that "gives us weight with England, and respect throughout Europe. If we were to break faith with this nation, *on whatever pretence,* England would again trample on us, and every other nation despise us."[42] In November 1783, Franklin reported that the good disposition of France toward the United States would continue into the new era of peace, but he sustained his strong distrust of Britain. "Tho' it has made peace with us," he admonished Thomas Mifflin, "it is not in truth reconcil'd either to us, or to its loss of us, but still flatters itself with Hopes, that some Change in the Affairs of Europe, or some Disunion among ourselves, may afford them an Opportunity of Recovering their Dominion, punishing those who have most offended, and securing our future Dependence."[43] Franklin understood perfectly that it was the rivalry between Britain and France that had permitted the United States to achieve independence; in some measure, therefore, its continued independence rested on the rivalries and power that had dictated the terms of the recent peace. What disturbed Franklin and others who distrusted Britain was the possibility that France, totally involved on the European continent in some future war, would leave Britain free to deal with the United States alone.

Adams rejected such fears. Nothing disturbed his faith in a policy of neutrality toward the two leading powers of Europe. For him commercial impartiality between them not only would maximize profits but also would reinforce America's political neutrality. He argued in March 1783 that the United States, as an independent country, should extend no trading privileges to either Britain or France. "We are," he wrote, "under no Ties of Honor, Conscience or good Faith, nor of Policy, Gratitude or Politeness, to sacrifice any profits which We can obtain in Trade with Great Britain, merely to promote the Trade of France." It was better, he believed, for the United States to seek the best bargains; the price and quality of goods should be its criterion. "Let the Rivalry of our Trade be free and unrestrained," he concluded. "Let Nations contend which shall furnish Us the best Goods at the cheapest Rate."[44] Adams continued to regard the European equilibrium sufficient to protect American security against the possibility of a major European assault. In his profound disagreement with Franklin, he argued that France had served its own interests admirably in supporting the American cause. Franklin complained that Adams expressed such views openly, sometimes in the presence of English diplomats, and insisted that he could prove French animosity toward the United States with "hundreds of Instances." Franklin feared that Adams's open hostility toward France created the impression in Paris that anti-French views were sufficiently widespread in the United States to endanger the ongoing Franco-American alliance.[45]

Adams cared nothing for France's friendship as he continued to advocate a policy of neutrality. From The Hague in February 1784 he wrote: "May the world continue at peace! But if it should not, I hope we shall have wisdom enough to keep ourselves out of any broil. As I am quite in sentiment with the Baron de Nolken, the Swedish ambassador at St. James's, who did me the honor to visit me, although I had not visited him. 'Sir,' said he, 'I take it for granted, that you will have sense enough to see us in Europe cut each other's throats with a philosophical tranquillity.'"[46] With Europe at peace, nothing in the immediate future, it seemed, would compel the United States to decide whether its interests demanded neutrality or a reaffirmation of the French alliance, the only real choices before it. Whatever course the nation might choose, its leaders, through a remarkably instructive decade of war and diplomacy, had recognized all the elements of power politics that would determine the success or failure of its future ventures abroad.

Chapter 2

THE CHALLENGE OF INDEPENDENCE

With their independence gained in 1783, the American people accepted the advantages of a separate national existence as well as the inescapable risks. No longer members of the British Empire, they could look to London for neither the sources of power nor the experience in world affairs that, through earlier decades, had guaranteed them not only a high measure of security but also an enriching domestic and foreign trade. Convinced at the end that British commercial restrictions had dimmed their economic future, they anticipated independence as the necessary prelude to the creation of an expanding commercial empire. Thomas Paine had argued in *Common Sense* that the American people, much as they had prospered under British rule, would have flourished even more had they been free of European authority. "The commerce by which [America] hath enriched herself," he wrote, "are the necessaries of life, and will always have a market while eating is the custom of Europe."[1] Supported by the appeal of American products, American merchants would regain their British markets as they penetrated those of the whole European continent. One Massachusetts newspaper predicted that American commerce, freed of its former shackles, would now "extend to every part of the globe, without passing through the medium of England, that rotten island, absorbed in debt, and crumbling fast to annihilation." Alexander Hamilton predicted confidently in March 1783 that "the acknowledgement of our independence by Great Britain will facilitate connections and intercourse between these states and the powers of Europe in general."[2] In Paris, the recent diplomatic triumphs, which assured America's independence, merely enhanced the mood of confidence. If the nation was small in population, it was large in territory.

America's relations with Europe appeared promising enough, and its three experienced diplomats in Paris—Benjamin Franklin, John Adams, and John Jay—were prepared to extend their earlier successes in negotiating with leading European powers into a new era of peace. As no war was in the offing, the commissioners were free to concentrate their efforts, not on questions of equilibrium and alliances but on the expansion of American commerce with Europe. Trade with France rested on the wartime Treaty of Amity and Commerce, presumably designed to promote commerce between the two countries; but during the war, that commerce failed to develop. When peace removed all external restraints, American merchants complained that their efforts in France suffered from numerous internal duties and monopolies embodied in French commercial and financial practice. Franklin hoped that France would remove such impediments quickly so that Franco-American commerce would reach the grandeur promised by the destruction of the British monopoly. Elsewhere the immediate prospects seemed bright. As early as April 1783, Franklin negotiated a commercial treaty with Sweden, one based on existing treaties with France and Holland. "The Treaty with Sweden is made," Adams reported to James Warren on April 12, and "Denmark has ordered our Flag to be respected like that of Republicks of the first order. Portugal has done the same. The Emperor has an Inclination to treat with Us but The House of Austria never makes the first Advances." The Swedish king ratified the new treaty in May; Congress did so in July.[3]

In Paris, Danish, Portuguese, Prussian, Austrian, and other European officials assured Franklin that their rulers desired treaties of friendship and commerce with the United States; even English merchants were eager to resume their commerce with the former colonies. From almost all the ports of Europe, Franklin received applications from persons who desired appointments as American consuls. And in a letter to Robert R. Livingston, secretary of foreign affairs, he rejoiced over this burgeoning interest in the nation's trade: "Since our trade is laid open, and no longer a Monopoly to England, all Europe seems desirous of sharing in it."[4]

*****

During the final peace negotiations, Congress hoped to add Britain to the short list of countries with which it had achieved bilateral commercial arrangements. Lord Shelburne, who headed the British ministry that recognized American independence, favored a total rapprochement with the United States, including the restitution of all commercial benefits that Americans had enjoyed in the empire. He was also prepared to grant American goods and ships free access to British West Indian and Caribbean ports. Despite his open acceptance of the principle of commercial reciprocity, Shelburne eliminated a commercial arrangement from the preliminary treaty. His negotiators argued, wrote Franklin, that "some statutes were in the way, which must be repealed before a treaty of that kind could be well formed, and that this was a matter to be considered in Parliament."[5] Shelburne introduced a measure to admit American goods and bottoms at least temporarily into British and West Indian ports on the same terms as British goods and ships. With Parliament's approval, he hoped to negotiate a full commercial treaty with the United States, but unfortunately the American diplomats, after signing the preliminary peace treaty in November 1782, retained no specific powers to negotiate such a treaty. Adams therefore urged Congress to accredit a minister and instruct him "to enter into a temporary convention for regulating the present trade for a limited number of months or years, or until the treaty of commerce shall be completed."[6] Meanwhile, David Hartley, whose sympathies for the United States matched Shelburne's, remained in Paris to negotiate a commercial treaty with the Americans as soon as they received the necessary commission and instructions.

Parliament was debating the issue of trade with America when the Shelburne ministry fell in February 1783, largely because of its generous behavior toward the United States. Conscious of the rising tide of mercantilism in Great Britain, Adams complained to Warren that Shelburne's refusal to embody a commercial arrangement in the provisional treaty had permitted the critical moment for negotiating a treaty of commerce to pass, apparently forever.[7] Britain's shipping interests now controlled British policy, supported by Lord Sheffield's new pamphlet, *Observations on the Commerce of the American States with Europe and the West Indies* (1783), in which he argued that the Americans, as foreigners, should be excluded from their former colonial trade and that British shipping could gain at American expense and compensate Britain for its financial losses in the war. Sheffield assumed a renewal of the former imperial trade on British terms. As he observed, "At least four-fifths of the importations from Europe into the American States are at all times made upon credit; and undoubtedly the States are in greater want of credit at this time than at former periods. It can be had only in Great Britain." With equal assurance he predicted that Congress was too impotent to retaliate: "It will not be an easy matter to bring the American states to act as a nation. They are not to be feared as such by us.... We might as well dread the effects of combinations among the German as among the American states."[8] Parliamentary majorities seemed to agree as they entrusted commercial arrangements to the king in council.

In early May, Congress was urged to issue a special commission to Franklin, Adams, and Jay to negotiate a commercial treaty with Britain.[9] However, it no longer mattered; there would be no commercial arrangement in the final treaty. Free to act, British leadership responded to Parliament's mercantilist preferences by embodying an increased restrictive policy in a series of orders in council. Following colonial practice, these restrictions permitted American raw materials and foodstuffs, but not manufactured goods, to enter the British home islands in American vessels. Finally, on July 2, 1783, an order in council closed the British West Indies to American ships and goods except for an enumerated list that did not include the country's dominant exports. In Paris the American commissioners responded to the British decrees by advising Congress that they would drop all commercial articles from a definitive treaty with Britain and "leave everything of that kind to a future special treaty, to be made either in America or in Europe, as Congress shall think fit to order." Hartley, unmindful of London's commitment to a mercantilist policy, continued to reassure the American diplomats and to quarrel with his superiors in favor of reciprocity.[10]

Sheffield's predictions soon proved to be disturbingly accurate. In June 1783, Henry Laurens had reported from London that the British government, in rejecting commercial reciprocity with the United States, intended to have the American trade without paying any price for it, especially that of granting American shippers the coveted West Indian carrying trade. As early as May, U.S. ports had been open to British ships; the first imports were enough to reawaken among Americans the general ardor for English products so recently denied them by war and proscription. What drew American trade to British ports, other than habit, was the superior ability of the British manufacturers, which resulted in better goods at lower prices, as well as Britain's greater capital resources and credit facilities. Independence in no way curtailed America's capacity to produce a wide variety of marketable foods and raw materials—fish, tobacco, rice, lumber, furs, and whale oil. To generate prosperity and reasonable profits and to protect its shipping interests, the country required access to foreign markets under conditions that assured fair prices and suitable exchange. London's power to dictate the terms of Anglo-American commercial relations from the outset endangered both the Republic's economic welfare and its standing among the nations of Europe. Americans understood that the negotiation of reciprocal commercial arrangements would comprise, in large measure, Europe's final recognition of the United States as an equal among nations. They discovered not only a contemptuous government in London but also commercial barriers and burdensome trade practices in the Continental states of Europe. Having entered the commercial world of the Atlantic in 1783 as a debtor nation with a colonial economy, the United States faced the insuperable challenge of establishing favorable trade relations in a mercantilist world, without the power to counter the hostile measures of the European governments with mercantile policies of its own.[11]

Especially humiliating for the United States was its troubles with the Barbary pirates. Using them not as independent entrepreneurs but as agents of their governments, the rulers of the North African states—Algiers, Tunis, Tripoli, and Morocco—had transformed piracy into a national industry. By capturing merchant vessels, holding sailors and cargoes for ransom, and extorting protection money from nations willing to pay, these petty sultans discouraged European and American sea captains from entering the Mediterranean. Rather than go to war, Europe's maritime powers preferred negotiated arrangements providing for gifts and tribute. As members of the British Empire, colonial merchants sailed the Mediterranean under the protection of British treaties. They had established a lucrative trade with North Africa, averaging generally 80 to 100 voyages per year. With the war of independence, American sea captains lost their access to admiralty passes; now they faced the pirates, without benefit of treaties or adequate naval protection.

In September 1783, Franklin, Adams, and Jay met British negotiators in Paris to sign the definitive peace treaty. The experience of previous months predicted a rough passage from the full establishment of independence to acceptance as a nation among nations. Only with difficulty, Adams warned, would the United States maintain the respect which the exploits of war had excited in Europe. "In the Calm of peace," he wrote, "little will be said about us in Europe unless we prepare for it, but by those who have designs upon us.... It will become us, therefore, to do every thing in our power to make reasonable and just impressions upon the public opinion in Europe." Adams's distrust of Britain was profound; France, he feared, would join Britain "in all artifices and endeavors to keep down our reputation at home and abroad, to mortify our self-conceit, and to lessen us in the opinion of the world."[12] Russia and Austria, as mediating powers, had officiated at the signing of the treaty among Britain, France, and Spain at Versailles. Their signatures on the American treaty, Adams believed, would have made a deep impression in favor of the United States throughout Europe, but the two imperial courts had refused, thereby leaving the other Continental governments in a state of doubt concerning their proper behavior toward the new Republic.

*****

The structural defects of the government under the Articles of Confederation diminished the immediate prospect of establishing an American commercial empire based on reciprocity. The articles—a product of the Second Continental Congress written in 1776 and finally ratified in 1781—granted Congress the power to enter into treaties of commerce but no authority to control the commercial policies of the states or to threaten other nations with retaliation. Additionally, Congress received no taxing power; thus, it had no means to create an army or navy, or to reduce its extensive foreign indebtedness. For countless citizens, the nation's decentralized political structure served a variety of speculative, political, and individual interests and conformed to their notion of an ideal republic. Those who favored the state sovereignty embodied in the Articles of Confederation distrusted political power; they denied that the conduct of foreign affairs required centralized authority capable of mobilizing the nation's power in behalf of common purposes. Relying on independence and geographical isolation to defend the country's needs abroad, they resisted any move to change the form of the U.S. government. Conservatives who advocated greater centralization argued that the constraints on Congress would never enable the United States to defend adequately its external interests. "Every day," Hamilton had observed bitterly in July 1783, "proves the inefficacy of the present confederation, yet the common danger being removed, we are receding instead of advancing in a disposition to amend its defects. The road to popularity in each state is to inspire jealousies of the power of Congress, though nothing can be more apparent than that they have no power."[13]

Older, well-established attachments to Britain and France merely aggravated the new nation's divisions and animosities. Congress, equally divided, possessed no power to counter the jealousy and perversity or to affect a determined course of action. Back in February, Thomas Jefferson had complained to Edmund Randolph:

> I find...., the pride of independence taking deep and dangerous hold on the hearts of the individual states. I know of no danger so dreadful and so probable as that of internal contests....The states will go to war with each other in defiance of Congress; one will call in France to her assistance; another Gr. Britain, and so we shall have all the wars of Europe brought to our own doors. Can any man be so puffed up with his little portion of sovereignty as to prefer this calamitous accompaniment to the parting with a little of his sovereign right and placing it in a council from all the states?[14]

One month later, Hamilton reported the same weakening divisions amidst the American people: "We have I fear (among) us and men in trust who have a hankering afte[r] British connection. We have others whose confidence in France savours of credulity. The intrigues of the former and the incautiousness of the latter may be both, though in different degrees, injurious to the American interests; and make it difficult for prudent men to steer a proper course."[15]

During the first months of independence, that proper course seemed to demand essentially the congressional control of commerce. Accepting the mercantilist principles of the day, Hamilton had argued in April 1782 that commerce could not flourish without the aid and protection of government, pointing out that Britain's imperial trade had achieved its predominance under government care. Only by regulating the movement of goods could the United States preserve a favorable balance of trade, which for Hamilton was the essential aim of national policy. In the absence of any central authority to regulate commerce, no state dared to impose duties of its own because other states, by not doing so, would gain too many price advantages.[16]

Conservatives generally accepted the need of a mercantilist policy for a mercantilist world. In a letter of September 1783, James Madison argued for retaliatory power: "The Conduct of G.B. in the negociation with America has shown great unsteadiness if not insidiousness on the subject of commerce: and the...proclamation of the 2d. of July is a proof that some experiment is intended on the wisdom, firmness & union of the States, before they will enter into a Treaty in derogation of her Navigation Act." In October, Governor Benjamin Harrison reminded the Virginia delegation in Congress that only an American mercantilist policy, adequately designed and enforced, would compel Britain to alter its trade policies toward the Republic. The British understood the value of American trade; if the United States, he wrote, prohibited "their manufactures or west india commodities except when brought by our own vessels or by those of other nations and thereby oblige them to make their purchases in cash they will very soon come to a compromise."[17] With the achievement of independence, Hamilton argued that Congress should have adjourned and informed the nation forthrightly "of the imperfections of the present system and of the impossibility of conducting the public affairs with honor to themselves and advantage to the community with powers so disproportionate to their responsibility."[18]

By the summer of 1783, the move to strengthen the Articles of Confederation was already a year old. In July 1782, the New York legislature had passed a resolution that declared that the continuance of the constituted government of the United States carried dangers for the safety and independence of the states because it exposed the common interests of the American people to the mercy of events over which they had no control. It seemed essential that the nation "unite in some System more effectual, for producing Energy, Harmony and Consistency of Measures, than that which now exists, and more capable of putting the Common Cause Out of Reach of Contingencies." The resolution urged each state to adopt a measure designed to assemble a convention of all the states for the purpose of amending the Articles of Confederation. George Washington shared the concerns of Hamilton and his New York associates. In March 1783 he wrote to Hamilton, saying that "no man in the United States is, or can be more deeply impressed with the necessity of a reform in our present Confederation than myself. No man perhaps has felt the bad effect of it more sensibly; for to the defects thereof, & want of Powers in Congress may justly be ascribed the prolongation of the War, & consequently the Expences occasioned by it."[19] During July 1783, Hamilton prepared his own congressional resolution, which called for a convention to amend the articles, but he withdrew it when he received little support.[20] Finally, in August, Governor George Clinton forwarded the New York resolution to the Continental Congress.

Congress preferred to focus more narrowly on the exclusion of American merchants and shippers from the valuable markets of the West Indies. It postponed action on New York's motion until the states could respond to Madison's resolution of April 18, 1783, which was designed to break the British monopoly in the carrying trade. Under this resolution, Congress would possess, for 15 years, the authority to prohibit the importation and exportation of goods in vessels belonging to the subjects of any country with which the United States had no commercial treaty. Also during this time, Congress could forbid the subjects of another nation, unless authorized by treaty, from importing into the United States goods not produced in the country of which they were subjects.[21] The Virginia legislature adopted the resolution in May 1784; and that month, Jefferson, as a member of Congress, suggested to Madison that Congress suspend its efforts to obtain treaties of commerce until it wielded sufficient authority to convince Europeans that the United States was capable of protecting its commercial interests.[22] Congress never received the assent of the nine states required to establish its control over the nation's commerce, nor did it act on the resolution which granted it limited power to regulate foreign trade. In November, John F. Mercer expressed the universal anxieties of conservatives over the determination of the states to cling to their sovereignty. "In my judgement," he confided to Madison, "there never was a crisis, threatening an event more unfavorable to the happiness of the United States, than the present. Those repellent qualities the seeds of which are abundantly sown in the discordant manners & sentiments of the different States, have produc'd great heats & animosities in Congress now no longer under the restraint impos'd by the war—insomuch that I almost despair of seeing that body unite in those decisive, & energetic measures, requisite for the public safety & prosperity."[23]

Robert R. Livingston of New York resigned as secretary for the Department of Foreign Affairs in May 1783. From the beginning, Congress had restricted his activities, even in matters of administration; it assumed both the initiative and the power of decision in all external matters. At times it ignored the secretary and conducted its own direct correspondence with American and foreign diplomats. Livingston, with little power to shape foreign policy, threatened to resign in 1782. Madison introduced a resolution in November, adopted by Congress, which gave the secretary greater freedom in his correspondence and the selection of information that Congress could demand from him. Still, Livingston remained severely hampered in the formulation and conduct of policy. Not even in his limited role did he, an admirable administrator, please all members of Congress. One complained that the secretary was often secretive when others had a right to information and open when he should have maintained secrecy. Upon his resignation, Congress thanked Livingston for his services and assured him that it entertained "a high sense of the ability zeal & fidelity with which he had discharged the important trust reposed in him." Congress now sought to strengthen the office. It placed the secretary at the head of the diplomatic corps and declared it "to be his duty from time to time to lay before Congress such plans for conducting the political and commercial intercourse of the United States with foreign nations, as may appear to be conducive to the interests of the said states."[24]

*****

Britain exposed American military and diplomatic impotence directly when it refused to fulfill the terms of the peace treaty. Before independence, the British had maintained a string of forts from Lake Champlain along the St. Lawrence River and the southern shores of Lake Ontario and Lake Erie to the head of Lake Huron, with the major posts in this chain located at Oswegatchie, Oswego, Niagara, Presque Isle, Sandusky, Detroit, and Michilimackinac. Article VII of the preliminary treaty stipulated that the British king would "with all convenient speed...withdraw all his armies, garrisons, and fleets from the said United States, and from every port, place, and harbour within the same." Congress prepared to assume command of these frontier posts as early as May 1783 by providing garrisons consisting of Continental troops that had enlisted for three years. However, when Baron von Steuben, the American Revolutionary hero, traveled to Canada to arrange the transfer of the posts, Governor Sir Frederick Haldimand in Quebec insisted that he had received no orders except to cease hostilities. Without specific instructions, he informed Steuben, he would permit no Americans to visit the posts.[25]

The frontier establishments occupied only small patches of wilderness, but they permitted the British to control thousands of square miles with their well-traveled interior routes. Much of the Great Lakes fur trade, valued at £200,000 annually, was a monopoly of the British Northwest Company, with perhaps two-thirds of the fur coming from the American side of the boundary. But the British capital invested in the Western country was not large, nor would the loss of the fur trade to American trappers necessarily diminish British profits. Whether the pelts reached European markets through Montreal or New York, they would bring the major rewards to London's fur merchants.

Of greater concern to the British government than the eventual transfer of its fur trade was its responsibility for the welfare of its Indian wards. Britain had secured the needed cooperation of the Indians on the American frontier by promising them protection from encroaching pioneers. Unfortunately, the British had neglected those Indians south of the Great Lakes in the peace negotiations; any British move to relinquish the posts would deliver, of necessity, these faithful allies into the hands of their dreaded enemies. When Governor Haldimand received a copy of the preliminary peace terms, he voiced his concern at the idea of abandoning the posts. "My own anxiety...," he reported in May, "arises from an apprehension of the effects which the preliminaries will have upon the minds of our Indian allies, who will consider themselves abandoned to the resentment of an ungenerous and implacable enemy."[26] Not without reason, some British officials feared that the Indians, if they discovered the treaty terms, would vent their rage on the British garrisons.

For Haldimand, the immediate challenge lay in convincing the Indians that Britain would not forsake them. The governor hoped to sustain their confidence, at least momentarily, by plying them with food and munitions. At the same time, he prepared to ease the transfer of the posts—an eventual necessity—by encouraging the Indians to come to terms with the victors in the recent war. Neither policy promised any easy successes. Too much reassurance would encourage the Indians to attack American settlements and possibly involve the British in an unwanted war; too much Indian-American reconciliation would terminate Britain's hold on its allies and endanger the fur trade. Sir John Johnson, the British agent for Indian affairs, assured the Six Nations of the Iroquois at Niagara in late July 1783 that, as they entered a new era of peace, they could continue

to rely on the king's protection. He cautioned them, however, to
avoid trouble with American settlers by concentrating their villages
and avoiding acts of hostility.[27] The Indians suspected that London had
betrayed them. Unrestricted military support against the American
enemy might have erased their doubts, but no Canadian official could
offer such aid.

Trapped between its loyalty to the Indians and its obligations to
the United States under Article VII, the British ministry hesitated
to act. Finally, in April 1784, London's Colonial Office responded to
Canadian remonstrances by ordering the governor of Canada to hold
the posts until he received further instructions. This prompted
Madison to speculate on British motivation:

> Some suppose it is meant to enforce a fulfillment of the treaty
> of peace on our part....Others that it is a salve for the wound
> given the Savages who are made to believe that the posts will not
> be given up till good terms shall be granted them by Congress.
> Others that it is the effect merely of omission in the B[ritish]
> Government to send orders. Others that it is meant to fix the
> fur trade in the B[ritish] channel and it is even said that the
> Governor of Canada has a personal interest in securing a mo-
> nopoly of at least the Crop of this season.[28]

For many Americans, British retention of the posts and reported in-
trigue with the Indians simply measured the depth of British hostility
toward the United States.

British occupation of U.S. territory embraced far more than
the frontier posts. In New York, Sir Guy Carleton, the British commander in chief, continued to control an area far more extensive
than Governor Clinton believed necessary to protect the security
of British troops and stores. By mid-July 1783, Carleton had returned portions of Staten Island and Long Island to their owners,
but Clinton still complained that the British held too much territory and, in defiance of the preliminary treaty, had not returned the
public records in their possession. American observers noted, additionally, that British conduct regarding the Negroes under their
control departed from the treaty provisions; the treaty had declared
specifically that British commanders were to evacuate their troops
without carrying away slaves or other property belonging to inhabitants of the thirteen states. Still it was obvious that many Negroes

were escaping from their owners through New York's waterfront just as they had earlier through other British-occupied ports. During the late summer Carleton received orders for the immediate evacuation of the city; thereafter, the British withdrawal, including Negroes, proceeded rapidly despite the large numbers of Tories who chose to accompany the departing troops.[29]

London officials soon discovered that the United States Congress had neither the power nor the will to force British compliance with the treaty provisions. Still, the British government, to avoid an ultimate military confrontation, required a rationale for its decisions that would place responsibility on the new nation. The peace treaty specified that British and American creditors should meet no lawful impediment to the recovery of their debts. During the war, various states, mostly in the South, had confiscated debts owed to British creditors; with the peace, these states failed to provide payment of these obligations. Congress had no authority to coerce the states, nor could it adequately defend Loyalists from the continuing persecutions, confiscations, and assaults of anti-British extremists. Although the initial British decision to hold the frontier posts rested on imperial considerations, London quickly made the resolution of the debt issue a prerequisite for evacuation. Recognizing the full significance of British complaints against the states, a committee of Congress in May 1783 recommended that the state legislatures execute the treaty provisions for the recovery of debts and the protection of Loyalists.[30]

Hamilton pursued the issue, and in June he reminded Governor Clinton of the widespread and intemperate violations of the peace treaty in New York. For such breaches, wrote Hamilton, the state's government could not escape responsibility. Those whose rights were violated cared little that the government claimed good intentions and then denied that it possessed the power, and thus the responsibility, to restrain its subjects. The United States had limited choices; it had secured a favorable treaty, but it could not coerce Britain to fulfill its provisions. "Great Britain without recommencing hostilities," Hamilton noted, "may evade parts of the treaty. She may keep possession of the frontier posts, she may obstruct the free enjoyment of the fisheries, she may be indisposed to such extensive concessions in matters of commerce as it is our interest to aim at; in all this she would find no opposition from any foreign power; and we are not in a condition to oblige her to any thing." The United States could anticipate no aid from France in another war against England.

For British concessions on the posts and the fisheries, the United States could offer the single equivalent of restoring property and avoiding further injury to those protected by the treaty. With their frontier posts in British hands, the people of New York had good reason to furnish Britain no pretext for delaying—or refusing—to execute the treaty.[31]

Hamilton was also troubled by the adverse effect that American failure to control its citizens would have on European opinion. "Will foreign nations," he asked, "be willing to undertake any thing with us or for us, when they find that the nature of our government will allow no dependence to be placed upon our engagements?" In September, Jay wrote from Paris that the reports of American violations in U.S. newspapers were harming the country. "Violences and associations against the Tories," he informed Hamilton, "pay an ill compliment to Government and impeach our good Faith in the opinions of some, and our magnanimity in the opinion of many." In his first "Phocion" letter of January 1784, Hamilton publicly condemned the legislature and citizens of New York for undermining the country's reputation by their refusal to restore confiscated Loyalist property. No treaty, he declared, could bind one side without binding the other. If Britain avoided further compliance with the treaty because of a breach on the part of the American people, Hamilton warned, the nation would sacrifice its interests as well as its character to "the little vindictive selfish mean passions of a few."[32] As late as November 1784, James Monroe reported that Canadian officials defended the British refusal to evacuate the posts by citing violations of the treaty, especially in New York and Virginia.[33] Clearly, Congress would never settle its outstanding issues with Britain until it could control all internal behavior that affected the country's external relations.

*****

Without instructions to occupy them in Paris, Adams and Jay traveled to England—"unordered and uninvited," as Jefferson put it. Jay went to settle some personal affairs and to relax at Bath; Adams went to see the country. After several weeks, Adams moved to The Hague where, in February 1784, he negotiated a large loan to enable Congress to meet its obligations. The interest rates that the Dutch bankers imposed troubled him. "The credit of the United States must be very low indeed, in this Republic," he wrote to his Dutch agents, "if we must agree to terms so exorbitant as those in the plan you have enclosed to me." Franklin agreed, reminding Adams that *"the foundation of credit abroad must be laid at home.* When the States have not faith enough in a congress of their own choosing to trust with money for the payment of their common debt, how can they expect that the congress should meet with credit, when it wants to borrow more money for their use from strangers?"[34]

Delegates from the necessary nine states did not appear at Annapolis until January 1784 to vote on a unanimous ratification of the Definitive Treaty with Britain. Only six weeks remained to meet the deadline for the exchange of treaties in Paris. Not until the end of March, technically too late, did a copy of the ratified treaty reach Paris, at which time the British minister waived the point. On May 12, Franklin and Jay for the United States and Hartley for Great Britain exchanged ratifications. Even these final ceremonies in Paris could not prompt the British government to send a minister to the United States; should London so decide, quipped one British official, it would require not one but thirteen. Following the exchange, Hartley remained in the French capital to negotiate a commercial treaty. Upon hearing of the ceremonies, Adams advised Congress from The Hague that it should address letters to all the sovereigns of Europe, informing them that the United States was a totally independent nation. It was essential, he believed, that the governments of Europe treat all U.S. ambassadors and other public officials as citizens of a sovereign nation in accordance with their status.[35]

Congress agreed in April to seek treaties of amity and commerce with the European countries without waiting for their governments to send ministers. Only special commercial treaties would open new channels of trade, and the accumulating commercial interests of the United States would tolerate no further delay. Early in May, Congress adopted a plan for negotiating the desired treaties with the European states as well as with the Barbary powers. At the same time, it pondered the choice between appointing diplomats to particular courts or naming them to a single commission to negotiate jointly with the European countries. Ultimately, Congress made the latter choice and appointed Franklin; Adams; and Jefferson, who was then a member of Congress, to a joint commission to open negotiations with the powers of Europe through their legations in Paris. John Jay had asked for his recall and Congress agreed to his return, much to the regret of Franklin and Adams.[36] As Franklin awaited Jay's departure, he complained to Laurens that "I shall be left alone, and with Mr. A[dams], and I can have no favourable opinion of what may be the Offspring of a Coalition between my ignorance and his Positiveness."[37] Jay left Paris on May 16 and sailed from Dover on June 1. Before he reached American shores, Congress appointed him its new secretary of foreign affairs. "Wisdom and Virtue have tryumphed, for once," Adams observed. "And I hope and believe, he will give an entire new Cast, to the Complexion of our foreign Affairs."[38]

Jefferson received his appointment as commissioner on May 7. Madison rejoiced at the news and promised to keep his fellow Virginian informed of those developments in America that merited his attention. The appointment pleased Adams as well; he wrote to Warren: "He is an old friend, with whom I have had occasion to labor at many a knotty Problem, and in whose Abilities and Steadiness I always found great Cause to confide."[39] In June, Jefferson traveled to Boston, intending to accompany Abigail Adams to Paris, but he found that she already had arranged passage to London and was leaving the following day. He then sailed from Boston on July 5, also bound for London; the trip was fast, lasting 19 days. At Portsmouth he transferred to another vessel that took him to Le Havre. After a brief stop at Rouen, Jefferson reached Paris on August 6, establishing his residence at the Hotel d'Orléans adjoining the Palais Royal on the Rue de Richelieu.

His reception was cordial; his reputation for enlightenment and integrity, his interest in the arts and sciences, had preceded him. For Jefferson, the timing of his arrival was superb. Paris was alive with new construction—streets, boulevards, bridges, churches, public buildings, and elegant private town houses. It was the private residences that he visited, filling his notebook with sketches, diagrams, floor plans, and additional observations that he would use later in designing houses and other buildings in Virginia. Jefferson's favorite, the new Hotel de Saim located almost directly across the Seine from the Louvre, influenced the design of his own still-unfinished Monticello. "While I was in Paris," he wrote to Madame de Tessé, "I was violently smitten with the Hotel de Salm, and used to go to the Tuileries almost daily to look at it." After several weeks in the city, Jefferson moved to the Hotel de Langeac adjoining the Grille de Chaillot on the Rue de Berri.[40]

After a favorable Atlantic crossing, Abigail Adams reached London on July 20, 1784. When Adams at The Hague learned of her arrival, he set off to meet his wife and daughter, and on August 7 was reunited with them after a separation of over four years.[41] The next day, the family departed for Paris and there took lodgings near Jefferson's Hotel d'Orléans. To escape the city, the Adamses moved to the Hotel de Rouhault in Auteuil, a village four miles west of Paris near the Bois de Boulogne, a location that delighted Mrs. Adams, who wrote of her life in France:

> We have a Beautiful wood, cut into walks, within a few rods of our dwelling, which upon this Day, resounds with Musick and Dancing, jollity and Mirth of every kind. In this Wood Booths are erected, where cake, fruit, and wine are sold....I believe this Nation is the only one in the world who could make Pleasure the Business of Life, and yet retain such a relish for it, as never to complain of its being tasteless or insipid; the Parisians seem to have exhausted Nature, and Art in this Science; and to be *triste* is a complaint of a most serious Nature.[42]

The three commissioners held their first meeting at Passy near Auteuil, where Franklin maintained his residence at the spacious Hotel de Valentinois overlooking the Seine. In deference to his gout, they continued to meet at Passy, although Adams had long resented Franklin and his devotion to everything French, including the French court. Jefferson, more tolerant of his fellowmen, associated freely with both but still preferred the company of John and Abigail Adams, whose domestic life conformed far more to his than did that of the less-conventional Franklin. The Adams and the Jefferson families were often guests at the home of Thomas Barclay, the American consul general in Paris.[43]

The commission and its instructions had reached Paris in July. In preparing the instructions, Jefferson, as a member of Congress, stipulated—in answer to its European critics who insisted that it had no treaty-making power—that foreign nations must treat the United States as one country. These instructions authorized commercial treaties with 16 European as well as the 4 Barbary powers. It was an ambitious undertaking in an effort to convert all Europe to the commercial principles of the American Revolution. "You will see," Franklin wrote to Adams, "that a good deal of business is cut out for us—treaties to be made with..., twenty powers in two years,—so that we are not likely to eat the bread of idleness."[44] The commercial treaties, in principle, would establish the right of each party to carry its own produce, manufactures, and merchandise in its own ships to the ports of the other and then take on the goods of the other, paying duties established by the axiom of the most favored nation. With countries holding territorial possessions in America, the treaties would admit a direct and similar trade, or at least a direct trade between the United States and certain free ports in those possessions.[45]

Following their first meeting at Passy late in August, the commissioners informed Hartley that they were empowered to negotiate treaties of amity and commerce. At the same time, they told the Danish minister of their powers and requested him to notify his court. For Franklin, reconciliation with Britain was the first order of business, and he warned Hartley that "restraints on the freedom of Commerce and intercourse between us can afford no advantage equal to the Mischief they will do by keeping up ill humour, and promoting a total alienation." Hartley, still optimistic, responded that the British court was ready "to receive proposals from the United States for the forming of such regulations as might tend to the mutual and reciprocal advantage of both countries." Because Hartley, now recalled to London, had no power to treat, the commissioners turned to the Duke of Dorset, the British minister in Paris, who advised them that his government was prepared to discuss all the controversies arising from the unfulfilled clauses of the peace treaty.

Jefferson still anticipated no British concessions. "The infatuation of that nation," he confided to Monroe, "seems really preternatural. If anything will open their eyes it will be an application to the avarice of the merchants who are the very people who have opposed the treaty first mediated.... Deaf to every principle of common sense, insensible to the feelings of man, they firmly believe they shall be permitted by us to keep all the carrying trade and that we shall attempt no act of retaliation because they are pleased to think it our interest not to do so." On November 24, Dorset informed the commissioners that the British ministry preferred that the United States send an authorized representative to London to negotiate with British officials there. Franklin assured him that the American commissioners would travel to London, but the British government, he complained in January 1785, appointed no one to negotiate.[46]

Dorset offered the commissioners no encouragement when he inquired by letter whether they had received their powers from Congress or from the states. This distinction was critical because the first assumption, if true, suggested that any state could render an agreement ineffectual. By January the commissioners understood what difficulties they faced. "We do not find it easy to make commercial arrangements in Europe," Jefferson wrote, "there is a want of confidence in us." In February he told Monroe: "Our business goes on very slowly. No answers from Spain or Britain. The backwardness of the latter is not new. We have hitherto waited for favorable circumstances to press matters with France. We are now about to do it tho I cannot say the prospect is good."[47]

By 1785 much of the earlier desire of the European monarchs to negotiate treaties with the United States had abated. This resulted, Franklin believed, from "the Paines Britain takes to represent us everywhere as distracted with Divisions, discontented with our Governments, the People unwilling to pay taxes, the Congress unable to collect them, and many desiring the Restoration of the old Government, etc. The English Papers are full of this Stuff, and their Ministers get it copied into the foreign Papers." As late as March 18, Jefferson reported that the commissioners had not heard from London: "Nothing will bring [the British] to reason but physical obstruction, applied to their bodily senses. We must show that we are capable of foregoing commerce with them, before they will be capable of consenting to an equal commerce."[48]

Adams shared Jefferson's conviction that the commissioners in Paris would not accomplish much. "You will negotiate for reciprocities in commerce to very little purpose," he instructed Jay in April, "while the British ministers and merchants are certain that they shall enjoy all the profits of our commerce under their own partial regulations." Adams looked back on his months in Paris as mostly unpleasurable: "Our negotiations in this place have not answered the ends proposed by congress and expected by the people of America, nor is there now scarcely a possibility that they should....But I presume congress will not think it expedient to renew the commissions, or attempt any longer to carry on negotiations with the rest of the world in this place." For Adams the only remaining possibility of coming to terms with Britain and placing American-British relations on a certain footing lay in the appointment of a minister to London. "Whoever goes," he admonished Jay, "will neither find it a lucrative nor a pleasant employment, nor will he be envied by me....But the measure of sending a minister to England appears to me the corner stone of the true American system of politics in Europe; and if it is not done, we shall have cause to repent it for a long time, when it will be too late." One week later he repeated this advice but warned again that anyone sent to London "will probably find himself in a thicket of briars from which he will hardly get free."[49]

These reports of failure in Paris troubled Congress. The British and Spanish courts, it was clear, had no desire to treat with American diplomats.[50] In December, Monroe informed Jefferson that Congress contemplated the appointment of a minister to London as well as a replacement for Franklin, who for a year had asked to be recalled from Paris. "If I am kept here another winter, and as much weakened by it as by the last," he complained as early as May 1784, "I may as well resolve to spend the remainder of my days here; for I shall be hardly able to bear the fatigues of the voyage in returning."[51]

During June and July, Franklin prepared for his long, difficult voyage back to America; the French king himself furnished the litter that would carry Franklin to the coast. Jefferson cautioned Monroe not to permit his return to pass special notice, explaining later that summer the significance of Franklin's welcome in Philadelphia: "The reception of the Doctor is an object of very general attention, and will weigh in Europe as an evidence of the satisfaction or dissatisfaction of America with their revolution." Shortly before leaving Paris in July, Franklin had signed a treaty of amity and commerce with Prussia. Jefferson added his signature several days later and forwarded the treaty to London for Adams to sign. William Short, Jefferson's trusted secretary, then carried it to The Hague, where on September 10 Baron Thulemeier signed it for Prussia.[52] That treaty measured the one tangible success of the post-independence diplomatic effort in Paris.

Chapter 3

AMERICAN DIPLOMATS ENGAGE BRITAIN AND FRANCE

It was not enough for the former American colonies to gain recognition of their independence, obtain foreign loans, and achieve a peace settlement with Britain. Their diplomats soon found that expansion of U.S. commercial interests and fulfillment of the peace treaty terms had now become the country's major external concern. Linked closely to the issue of international commerce was the lingering matter of honoring the terms of the peace agreement. When the Americans complained that the British had not honored their commitment to withdraw from forts in the Northwest, London objected to the practice of American states passing laws harmful to Tories and foiling the payment of old debts to British merchants to circumvent the 1783 treaty.

With the opening of American ports in the spring of 1783, British merchants quickly reestablished their commercial monopoly. For Southern producers enjoying a good market for their staples, it mattered little that Britain dominated the American carrying trade. Merchants, farmers, and ship owners in New England and middle states would not fare as well. Convinced that the United States possessed no powers of retaliation, the London government imposed its mercantile policies on the new republic in a series of restrictive orders in council. Then on July 2, 1783, London closed the British West Indies to American ships and goods except for an enumerated list that did not include the country's primary exports. Thereafter, British officials were reluctant to compromise its unchallengeable commercial advantages. Similar trade problems existed with the French. Initially, the French government, with its Arret of August

1784, opened seven ports in the French West Indies to American ships and extended the list of approved imports. By the time that the Arret appeared in the Philadelphia press in March 1785, however, French merchants' indignation over this relaxation of French mercantile policy threatened to close the West Indies trade again. What incited the pressures on a generally friendly French government was the narrow and apparently successful conduct of Great Britain's commercial activities in the former colonies.

It fell to American diplomats to seek beneficial commercial arrangements with European states and to negotiate new loans with America's Dutch bankers to meet the interest payment on wartime loans. Faced with these challenges, the United States' principal envoys—John Adams, minister to London and the Netherlands; and Thomas Jefferson, minister to Paris—presented an odd pair. In personality they differed greatly. Later, when Jefferson learned that Adams was returning home, he wrote to William Smith about the man with whom he had conducted the affairs of the United States in Paris and London: "Long habits of doing business together and of doing it easily and smoothly, will render me sincerely sensible to his loss." Jefferson offered his personal judgment of Adams in a letter to James Madison: "A 7-months' intimacy with him here and as many weeks in London have given me opportunities of studying him closely. He is vain, irritable and a bad calculator of the force and probable effect of the motives which govern men. This is all the ill which can possibly be said of him."

At this time, Adams's opinion of Jefferson was quite positive. When Arthur Lee warned that Jefferson's intellect was suspect and his affectation and vanity great, Adams would have none of it. "My new partner," he replied, "is an old friend...whose character I studied nine or ten years ago, and which I do not perceived to be altered....I am very happy with him." In writing to Henry Knox, he was even more positive, "You can scarcely have heard a character[ization] too high of my friend and colleague, Mr. Jefferson, either in point of power or virtues."[1]

*****

On February 24, 1785, Congress appointed Adams to London, a post he greatly desired, and named William Stephens Smith as the secretary of legation. On March 10, Congress unanimously named Jefferson as the new minister to Versailles. For Adams and Jefferson, the commissions to negotiate commercial treaties remained in force, with the two ministers sharing the task: signing treaties in London or Paris, or separately when they could not meet. Specifically, Congress instructed them to negotiate the best treaties possible with the 16 European states as well as the 4 Barbary powers, securing those commercial advantages that the American people were entitled to expect. In Paris, Jefferson informed Foreign Minister Vergennes of his appointment and delivered his letter of credence to King Louis XVI in private audience. At his formal reception by the royal family—the king and queen—Marie Antoinette welcomed him to France in his new role. As a full member of the diplomatic corps Jefferson was entitled to attend the king's levee every Tuesday and join the whole diplomatic corps at dinner. So high was Franklin's reputation at the French Court that Jefferson soon found the task of succeeding him an exercise in humility. "On being presented to any one as the Minister of America," he later recalled, "the common-place question, used in such cases, was 'c'est vous, Monsieur, qui remplace le Docteur Franklin?' 'It is you, Sir, who replace Doctor Franklin?' I generally answered 'no one can replace him, Sir; I am only his successor.'"[2]

Residing in Paris and still assigned by Congress to The Hague, Adams had extended his stay in Europe following the 1783 peace settlement to undertake negotiations with Prussia and other states. Adams noted graciously, upon receiving the good wishes on his new assignment from Vergennes at Versailles, that it was a form of degradation to go to any European court after being accredited to the king of France. Vergennes retorted that it was "a great Thing to be the first Ambassador from your Country to the Country you sprung from."[3] Adams meanwhile had addressed the Duke of Dorset, British minister in Paris, with the accumulating problems raised by the unfulfilled provisions of the peace treaty, especially British possession of the posts along the Great Lakes, the unpaid American debts to British subjects, and the Negroes whom Sir Guy Carleton had carried away from New York at the end of the war. Dorsey, however, scarcely commented on the unresolved issues.[4]

If diplomacy with France and England sought little, the discourse, at least, initially remained cordial. This alone created some prospect for diplomatic progress in Paris and London. On May 27, Adams submitted his credentials to Lord Carmarthen, secretary of state for the Foreign Department in Prime Minister William Pitt's cabinet.

That day the Dutch minister, after reviewing Adams's early experiences in London, assured him that he had received precisely the same official reception accorded to all other ministries. Adams's high reputation as a diplomatist had preceded him, and during his first week in London, Adams received visits from all the ministers and secretaries of the foreign embassies, as well as some English leaders. Although generally well received in London, the Adams presence in London did not meet universal approval as the *Public Advertiser* bitterly commented: "An Ambassador from America!...This will be such a phenomenon in the Corps Diplomatique that tis hard to say which can excite indignation most, the insolence of those who appoint the Character, or the meanness of those who receive it. Such a thing could never have happened in any former Administration, not even that of Lord North."[5]

Carmarthen informed Adams that on June 1 he would meet the king. That day, the British minister accompanied Adams to the palace where he would present his letter of credence. Members of the diplomatic corps had advised Adams to make a brief speech at Court, as complimentary as possible. While waiting for Carmarthen to usher him into the king's chamber, Adams noted that he was the focus of the eyes of the ministers, lords, and bishops who crowded the room. The Swedish and Dutch ministers quickly relieved him of his embarrassment until Carmarthen returned to take him to the king. When Adams was alone with the king and the secretary of state, he informed the king that as the minister of the United States, he had "the honor to assure your Majesty of their unanimous disposition and desire to cultivate the most friendly and liberal intercourse between your Majesty's subjects and their citizens...." It was his hope, Adams continued, to "be instrumental in recommending my country more and more to your Majesty's royal benevolence, and of restoring an entire esteem, confidence, and affection, or, in better words, the old good nature and the old good humor between people, who, though separated by an ocean, and under different governments, have the same language, a similar religion, and kindred blood."[6]

The king, Adams reported, listened with dignity and apparent emotion. "The circumstances of this audience are so extraordinary, the language you have now held is so extremely proper, and the feelings you have discovered so justly adapted to the occasion," ran the king's reply, "that I must say that I not only receive with pleasure the assurance of the friendly dispositions of the United States, but that

I am very glad the choice has fallen upon you to be their minister.... I will be very frank with you. I was the last to consent to the separation; but the separation having been made, and having become inevitable, I have always said, as I say now, that I would be the first to meet the friendship of the United States as an independent power. The moment I see such sentiments and language as yours prevail,... that moment I shall say, let the circumstances of language, religion, and blood have their natural and full effect." After the formal exchange of greetings, the king, Adams reported, asked him if he had last come from France. To Adams's affirmative answer, the king laughingly said: "there is an opinion among some people that you are not the most attached of all your countrymen to the manners of France." Adams was surprised, not by the accuracy of the statement, but by the king's indiscretion. "[T]hat opinion, sir, is not mistaken," Adams replied, "I must avow to your Majesty, I have no attachment but to my own country." The king retorted, "[A]n honest man will never have any other."[7]

After meeting with the queen, Adams wrote Jay on June 10 to say that the audiences revealed only the intention of the royal family to treat the United States like other foreign powers. But no one should infer from this, wrote Adams, that the British would relax their commercial policy. "We are sure of one thing," he observed, "that a navigation act is in our power, as well as in theirs, and that ours will be more hurtful to them than theirs to us." Adams opened his search for accommodation with Britain on June 17. Carmarthen assured him that the British cabinet desired cordial relations with the United States. Adams then listed the unresolved issues that troubled U.S.-British relations: the posts and territories within the United States still held by British garrisons, the exportation of Negroes and other property in defiance of the seventh article of the treaty of peace, the restrictions on American trade, the seemingly unreasonable British demands for the payment of debts contracted before the war, the British captures on the high seas after the time specified by the treaty, and the liquidation of the charges of prisoners of war. Adams admitted that the negotiation of a commercial treaty would be difficult and time consuming; the other issues, all flowing from the peace treaty, appeared easier. British concerns over the unpaid debts appeared reasonable to Adams; but the British, by restricting trade and depriving America of the profits of the fur trade, had made it impossible for such goods to reach England in payment of the debts. The trade had returned to its old patterns, much to the disadvantage of American merchants; relying on British credit, they were going increasingly into debt. "His Lordship heard me very attentively," Adams recorded.[8] Still, Carmarthen, predicting that patience would adjust all issues, reminded Adams that there would be many rubs along the way. He instructed Adams to make his inquiries concerning infringements on the treaty provisions in writing.

*****

As minister to France, Jefferson also faced the challenge of furthering American commercial interests. The continuing American failure to break the restraints of European mercantilism on the country's foreign commerce destroyed Jefferson's interest in the projected system of commercial treaties. For him, American commercial interests in the Atlantic required two specific changes in established policy. The first was broad, permanent access to the West Indies; this would require concessions from the colonial powers. "Yet how to gain it," he wrote to Monroe in June, "when it is the established system of these nations to exclude all foreigners from their colonies. The only chance seems to be this. Our commerce to the mother countries is valuable to them. We must endeavor then to make this the price of an admission into their West Indies, and to those who refuse the admission we must refuse our commerce or load theirs by odious discriminations in our ports."[9]

American policy failed, Jefferson reminded Jay, not in its inability to negotiate treaties with continental Europe but in its ineffectiveness in dealing with the powers that possessed American territory. To coerce these colonial powers, Jefferson argued secondly, required that the Congress regulate the United States' commerce as effectively as the current constitution would permit. In 1785, several states were pushing their own navigation laws against Britain. Jefferson warned, however, that individual state action would merely antagonize the Europeans without coercing them. Recognizing the need for a national policy, Jefferson suggested to Adams in October that the states be compelled to strengthen the Confederacy.[10]

Failing to further American commerce through treaties with either the West Indies or Europe, Jefferson turned to the immediate task of developing the promised Franco-American commercial axis. His new focus on French commerce in 1785 resulted in part from his new position as minister to France, in part from his conviction

that trade with France could break the British monopoly. The anticipation that France would displace Britain in the American market
continued to meet with disappointment. But Jefferson believed that
France might still succeed if it would abolish its internal restraints
and monopolies that prevented a free exchange of goods in the
French market. Jefferson reminded Vergennes of the possibilities of
a direct commerce between France and the United States:

> We can furnish to France (because we have heretofore fur-
> nished to England), of whale oil and spermaceti, of furs and
> peltry, of ships and naval stores,' and of potash to the amount
> of fifteen millions of livres; and the quantities will admit of in-
> crease. Of our tobacco, France consumes the value of ten mil-
> lions more. Twenty-five millions of livres, then, mark the extent
> of that commerce of exchange, which is, at present, practicable
> between us.
> We want, in return, productions and manufactures, not
> money. If the duties on our produce are light, and the sale free,
> we shall undoubtedly bring it here, and lay out the proceeds on
> the spot in the productions and manufactures we want.... The
> conclusion is, that there are commodities which form a basis
> of exchange to the extent of a million of guineas annually; it is
> for the wisdom of those in power to contrive that the exchange
> shall be made.[11]

Lafayette, many of the French physiocrats and philosophes, and
Vergennes himself sympathized with Jefferson's purpose of achiev-
ing the commercial goals of the American Revolution.

In June 1785, Jefferson warned: "The merchants of this country
continue as loud and furious as ever against the Arret of August
1784, permitting our commerce with their islands to a certain degree.... The ministry are disposed to be firm, but there is a point
at which they will give way." When Jefferson pressed Versailles for
new commercial arrangements in the fall of 1785, the French economy was depressed, and the government had difficulty in defending the limited concessions it had made to American trade in the
West Indies. What reinforced French caution was the conviction that
America had become addicted to British trade. Jefferson reminded
Vergennes that if it were a matter of national prejudice, the trade
would come to France. Unable to cut the bonds of credit that tied

American commerce to Britain, Jefferson launched an assault on the French commercial restrictions that gave the British their advantage. Much of his effort centered on tobacco, America's leading export. France imported large quantities of American tobacco but granted a monopoly for its acquisition to the Farmers-General, the giant company to which the French government farmed out the collection of several indirect taxes and customs duties, including that on tobacco. Because the Farmers-General was tied to the entire French system of public finance, any assault on the tobacco monopoly would be hazardous for anyone who undertook it.[12]

Jefferson's case against the monopoly was persuasive. Since the Farmers-General did not engage in commercial exchange but paid in coin, Americans who sold tobacco in France could not really enter the French market. Because they, as a result, generally entered the British market with their money, Jefferson reminded Vergennes that French policy merely supported British industry. As he explained: "By prohibiting all His Majesty's subjects from dealing in tobacco except with a single company, one third of the exports of the United States are rendered uncommercial here. . . . A relief from these shackles will form a memorable epoch in the commerce of the two nations. It will establish at once a great basis of exchange, serving like a point of union to draw to it other members of our commerce. . . . Each nation has exactly to spare the articles which the other wants. . . . The governments have nothing to do but not to hinder their merchants from making the exchange." To make matters for worse for Jefferson, the French government earlier had given Robert Norris, the American financier, a three-year contract to supply France with all of its American tobacco. This second monopoly had an adverse effect on tobacco prices and eliminated many American tobacco merchants from the French trade entirely. Jefferson, supported effectively by Lafayette, convinced Vergennes to appoint the so-called American Committee to study Franco-American trade and make recommendations for its improvement. The committee managed to end the Morris monopoly but not that of the Farmers-General. In October 1786, the French government announced a series of concessions to American commerce and navigation that freed American exports as well as imports both in France and in the West Indies. Not until December 1787, however, did the French government enact these concessions into law.[13]

Jefferson also devoted much effort to obtaining a French market for American whale oil. Britain, through heavy subsidies and duties on American whale oil, managed to build its own whaling industry. France followed the British example only to fail miserably, injuring the American whaling industry to the benefit of Britain. Jefferson, in a long report, noted that French whaling policy again enhanced British sea power at the expense of American strength in the Atlantic. France could serve both the American and the French interest, he argued, by excluding all European oil from France. In December 1788, France adopted Jefferson's formula, granting French and American whale oil a monopoly in the French market. For American rice, the problem was different. Rice growers had lost much of their world market to the British carrying trade, permitting British merchants to dominate the European rice market. What additionally placed American rice at a disadvantage in the French market was the French preference for the Mediterranean variety. Finding it more promising to alter American produce than the French cuisine, Jefferson, on his tour of France's southern ports in 1787, crossed into Piedmont and smuggled rice seeds across the Apennines. Jefferson's limited gains in creating a French market for American rice, however, came less from his smuggling efforts than from his capacity to induce some French firms to enter the Carolina rice trade.[14]

Jefferson's successes in building Franco-American trade never matched his efforts. Between 1785 and 1789, the total volume of that trade changed little; whatever the real advances, they were more in the West Indies than with France itself. Thus Jefferson failed where it mattered; he could never establish a system of fair exchange in the French market. The Anglo-French commercial accord of 1786 flooded the French market with British goods. The resulting depression in French production further negated his effort to create the essential market for French goods in America. Still, Jay lauded Jefferson for the commercial arrangements that he had made. "They bear Marks of Wisdom and Liberality," he wrote in April 1788, "and cannot fail of being very acceptable."[15]

*****

Early in mid-1785, Franklin and Jefferson had sent Adams the draft of a commercial treaty, based generally on the one proposed to Denmark, for Adams to present to the London government. Adams delivered the treaty draft to Carmarthen late in July.[16] Weeks passed without a response. Adams wrote in late August that he did not expect an answer from the British government before spring "unless intelligence should arrive of all the States adopting the navigation act, or authorizing congress to do it...." On August 24, Adams had a long conference with William Pitt. The prime minister acknowledged that Carmarthen had forwarded the papers that he had written. What held up the evacuation of the posts, Pitt informed Adams, was the interference of the states in preventing the payment of the debts. Pitt noted that several states "had interfered, against the treaty, and by acts of their legislatures, had interposed impediements to the recovery of debts." Adams replied that on the critical issue of payment of interest accrued during the war, American courts had declared that the Revolution, as a social upheaval, had broken all previous contracts and engagements; hence, American debtors were not responsible for the interest on their debts during the period of conflict. Adams insisted that the difficulty in paying the debts rose from the British restrictions on American trade. He argued that the United States had the same right as Britain to control its commerce to its own advantage; to this Pitt agreed. Clearly the issue was not one of rights, but one of policy.

Adams had little confidence in Pitt, the ministry or the British public. They all seemed ignorant of the issues in Anglo-American diplomacy. "There is," wrote Adams, "a prohibition of the truth, arising from popular anger. Printers will print nothing which is true, without pay, because it displeases their readers; while their gazettes are open lies, because they are eagerly read, and make the paper sell." British factions seemed to be united only on a punitive policy toward America. For Adams, the king alone possessed the resolution and energy to carry out a positive course of action, but the factional rivalry isolated him from political reality. Those who surrounded him told him only what he wished to hear.[17]

Adams explained repeatedly why he dominated all conversations with the British: they refused to talk, fearful that they might commit themselves to a position not approved by the cabinet. After weeks of official British silence, Adams complained to Jay in mid-October 1785: "I can obtain no answer from the ministry to any one demand, proposal, or inquiry." Several days later, Adams, in conversation with Carmarthen, lamented the decline of confidence between the two countries since the peace. "I paused here," wrote Adams, "in hopes his Lordship would have made some reflection, or dropped some hint, from whence I could have drawn some conclusion, excited some hope, or started some fresh topic; but not a word escaped him." The British, having been unable to determine any new course of action, Adams concluded, "have agreed together to observe a total silence with me until they shall come to a resolution." Again in October, Adams reported to Jefferson: "We hold Conferences upon Conferences, but the Ministers either have no Plan or they button it up, closer than their Waistcoats."[18]

During his temporary residence in London during March and April 1786 to assist Adams, Jefferson, too, experienced the full measure of official British arrogance. At his formal presentation to Lord Carmarthen, the marquis was not insulting, but cold and evasive. The Americans left a draft treaty with him; he did not reply. When they learned accidently that the draft asked too much, they submitted a modified version. This Carmarthen also ignored. Adams and Jefferson's appearance before the king met with a most ungracious reception. According to the Adams family records, the king turned his back on the two Americans in a manner that permitted all surrounding courtiers to take full notice. Later when the Americans informed the British minister that their commissions were about to expire and that Jefferson needed to return to Paris, Carmarthen was not impressed. Even then Jefferson maintained the forms of politeness by asking Carmarthen if he could carry any messages for him. But, as he confessed to Jay, he again found British silence invincible. "With this country nothing is done," he wrote in April, "and that nothing is intended to be done on their part admits not the smallest doubt. The nation is against any change of measures. The Ministers are against it, some from principle, others from subserviency, and the King more than all men is against it." Jefferson complained to Madison that British merchants "sufficiently value our commerce: but they are quite persuaded they shall enjoy it on their own terms. This political speculation fosters the warmest feeling of the king's heart, that is, his hatred to us. If ever he should be forced to make any terms with us, it will be by events which he does not foresee. He takes no pains at present to hide his aversion."[19]

Upon his return to Paris, Jefferson suggested to Abigail Adams that the British king remained one of America's great benefactors because he was still driving its people toward independence: "He is truly the American Messias.... Twenty long years has he been labouring to drive us to our good and he labours and will labour still for it if he can be spared. We shall have need of him for twenty more.... We become chained by our habits to the tails of those who hate & despise us.... He has not a friend on earth who would lament his loss as much and so long as I should." Jefferson's disagreeable experiences in London merely aggravated his deep resentment of the British. A year later, he wrote to William Smith, "Of all nations on earth, they require to be treated with the most hauteur. They require to be kicked into common good manners."[20]

Jefferson, no less than Franklin, and Adams believed that Britain harbored a fundamental hostility toward the United States. He, like Adams, accused it of flooding Europe with adverse reports about America. He complained to Madison on September 1, 1785: "There was an enthusiasm towards us all over Europe at the moment of the peace. The torrent of lies published unremittingly in every day's London paper first made an impression and produced a coolness. The republication of those lies in most of the papers of Europe (done probably by authority of the governments to discourage emigrations) carried them home to the belief of every mind. They supposed every thing in America was anarchy, tumult, and civil war."[21] Jefferson sought to defend the United States against such accusations. He wrote to his German friend, Baron Geismar, in September 1785: "From the London gazettes, and the papers copying them, you are led to suppose that all there is anarchy, discontent, and civil war. Nothing however is less true. There are not, on the face of the earth, more tranquil governments than ours, nor a happier and more contented people. Their commerce has not as yet found the channels which their new relations with the world will offer to best advantage, and the old ones remain as yet unopened by new conventions. This occasions a stagnation in the sale of their produce, the only truth among all the circumstances published about them." Several weeks later, Jefferson again vented his anger toward Britain when he wrote: "England seems not to permit our friendship to enter into her political calculations as an article of any value. Her endeavor is not how to recover our affections or to bind us to her by alliance, but by what new experiments she may keep up an existence without us."[22]

*****

Adams and Jefferson agreed that coercion alone would advance American commercial interests in London. To protect the public interest in foreign commerce, Congress required the authority to issue threats of retaliation against European discriminations. Jefferson wrote Madison in September 1785, that only when Europe detected a growing disposition to invest Congress with the regulation of commerce could he discover "the smallest token of respect towards the United States in any part of Europe." Because commercial rivalry could ultimately lead to personal insult and property violations on the high seas, Jefferson argued that the United States required greater naval strength to punish any aggression. "[A]n insult unpunished is the parent of many oth[ers]," he wrote to Jay in August. "We are not at this moment in a condition to do it, but we should put ourselv[es] into it as soon as possible.... Our vicinity to their West India possessions and to the fisheries is a bridle which a small naval force on our part would hold in the mouths of the most powerful of these countries."[23]

Jefferson would have preferred that there was no commerce to defend. "Were I to indulge my own theory," he wrote in October 1785, "I should wish them [the Americans] to practice neither commerce nor navigation, but to stand with respect to Europe precisely on the footing of China. We should thus avoid wars, and all our citizens would be husbandmen." But such choices, he admitted, lay in theory only, "and a theory which the servants of America are not at liberty to follow." Jefferson favored agriculture to commerce, but he recognized the importance of shipping to his constituents. "Our people," he wrote, "are decided in the opinion that it is necessary for us to take a share in the occupation of the ocean, and their established habits induce them to require that the sea be kept open for them, and that that line of policy be pursued which will render the use of that element as great as possible to them. I think it a duty in those entrusted with the administration of their affairs to conform themselves to the decided choice of their constituents."[24]

Similarly, the inordinate American addiction for British goods and credit troubled Adams. Britain, he admitted regretfully, controlled American commerce. "[T]he superior abilities of the British manufacturers, and the greater capitals of their merchants," he wrote, "have enabled them to give our traders better bargains and longer credit than any others in Europe;...Britain has monopolized our trade beyond credibility."[25] So pervading was American partiality for English goods that British merchants could simply assume their continued dominance of the foreign trade of the United States. "[T]he ardor of our citizens in transferring almost the whole commerce of the country here, and voluntarily reviving that monopoly which they had long complained of as a grievance, in a few of the first months of the peace,"

Adams complained to Jay, "imprudently demonstrated to all the world an immoderate preference of British commerce." Adams wondered whether the British ministry understood that its behavior toward the United States might eventually strengthen America's relations with France and the other powers of Europe. "If we once see a necessity of giving preferences in trade," he observed, "great things may be done."[26]

British merchants and officials reminded Adams that the former colonies could not exist without British commerce, and thus Americans would never unite on any measures of retaliation or any plan to establish their own mercantilist policy. Adams recognized the depth of British conviction. "If an angel from heaven should declare to this nation that our states will unite, retaliate, prohibit, or trade with France," he observed bitterly, "they would not believe it." Threats of American retaliation would remain ineffective, Adams warned, as long as the British regarded such retaliation unlikely. "You will negotiate for reciprocities in commerce to very little purpose," he wrote to Jay, "while the British ministers and merchants are certain that they shall enjoy all the profits of our commerce under their own partial regulations." For Adams, the American people still possessed the power, if not the desire, to break the British commercial monopoly simply by denying themselves the luxuries supplied by British trade and manufactures. "But the character of our people must be taken into consideration," he wrote to Jay resignedly. "They are as aquatic as the tortoises and sea-fowl, and the love of commerce, with its conveniences and pleasures, is a habit in them as unalterable as their natures. It is in vain, then, to amuse ourselves with the thought of annihilating commerce, unless as philosophical speculations.... Upon this principle we shall find that we must have connections with Europe, Asia, and Africa; and, therefore, the sooner we form those connections into a judicious system, the better it will be for us and our children." Adams preferred the disruption of trade to its continuance under Britain's humiliating impositions. "[I]f every ship we have were burnt, and the keel of another never to be laid," he predicted, "we might still be the happiest people upon earth, and in fifty years, the most powerful."[27]

If Americans would not defy British commercial policy by exercising the right not to buy, Adams would confront the foreign impositions with various forms of commercial retaliation. "It is a diplomatic axiom," he reminded Jay, "that he always negotiates ill who is not in a condition to make himself feared." So strong was the mercantile spirit in Britain, he observed in July 1785, that until the states united on a single commercial policy, British officials would never take the threat of American prohibitions seriously. "I really believe, it must come to that…," he continued. "I have no hopes of a treaty before next spring, nor then, without the most unanimous concurrence of all our States in vigorous measures, which shall put out of all doubt their power and their will to retaliate." Adams hoped then Americans would discard their aversion to monopolies and exclusions and adopt the more selfish principles of the European nations, particularly of France and England.[28]

Several weeks later he wrote to Jefferson: "We must not, my Friend, be the bubbles of our own liberal sentiments. If we cannot obtain reciprocal liberalty we must adopt reciprocal prohibitions, exclusions, monopolies, and imposts." Adams argued that nothing less than the monopolization of American commercial policy through navigation acts would protect American rights in English ports. He recommended that members of Congress and the state legislatures study the British acts of navigation and judge the extent to which similar acts would promote the interests of the American people in their commerce with Great Britain.[29] "[Y]ou may depend upon it," Adams wrote to Jay in October, "the commerce of America will have no relief at present, nor, in my opinion, ever, until the United States shall have generally passed navigation acts." Adams asked Jay to consider whether the states should give Congress unlimited authority to control the external commerce of all the states for a number of years. If Congress and the states refused to impose restrictions on British commerce, Adams concluded, there would be no purpose in stationing a minister in London.[30]

In February 1786, Jefferson, who had traveled to London to confer with Adams regarding discussions with the Barbary states, participated in negotiating an ill-fated agreement with the Portuguese minister in London. Eventually he and Adams negotiated a commercial treaty with Chevalier de Pinto, Portugal's minister. It granted the United States no special privileges but removed some existing obstacles to American trade. Yet the effort came to naught, for the Portuguese government refused to accept the treaty.[31]

*****

Early in December 1785, Adams concluded that the United States simply could not achieve a satisfactory arrangement with the present

British ministry. He admitted to Jay that he no longer insisted on the British evacuation of the posts because the British always tied the issue of debts to the evacuation. He had insisted on the withdrawal in conversation but had made no formal requisition in the name of the United States. "If I had done it," he wrote, "I should have compromised my sovereign, and should certainly have had no answer. Whenever this is done, it should be followed up. I shall certainly do it, if I should see a moment when it can possibly prevail." Convinced that he would continue to meet a blank response, he would no longer press the British for a resolution of any of the issues. "In short, sir, I am like to be as insignificant here as you can imagine. I shall be treated, as I have been, with all the civility that is shown to other foreign ministers, but shall do nothing."[32] Congress would need to share his patience. "It is most certain, that what is called high language," he observed realistically, "...would be misplaced here at this time. It would not be answered with high language, but with what would be more disagreeable and perplexing—with a contemptuous silence." With nothing to be done, he would await the next session of Parliament when the British design would become more apparent. "Thus, I find myself at a full stop," he acknowledged. "I shall not neglect any opportunity, to say or do whatever may have the least tendency to do any good; but it would be lessening the United States, if I were to tease ministers with applications, which would be answered only by neglect and silence." If the London government did not give him an answer in the spring, then, he wrote, Congress could not avoid instructing him to demand an answer, to take leave and return to America.[33]

On November 30, 1785, Adams had presented Carmarthen a memorial demanding that the British withdraw their garrisons from the territories of the United States. He explained his reluctant decision to Jay: "I do not expect an answer till summer. But I thought it safest for the United States to have it presented, because, without it, some excuses or pretences might have been set up, that the evacuations had not yet been formally demanded." Carmarthen informed Adams in January that he was preparing an answer to the memorial on the posts; in response he would cite the complaints of creditors to the ministry. "I am glad to have an answer," wrote Adams to his colleague in Paris, "for, whatever conditions they may tack to the surrender of the posts, we shall find out what is boiling in their hearts, and by degrees come together."[34] In his response, Carmarthen justified the British detention of the posts by pointing to the laws of certain states that impeded the recovery of the old British debts. Another memorial on compensation for the Negroes, Adams predicted, would receive the same answer. For Adams the choices were clear. The United States would either await in vain the evacuation of the posts, the payment for the Negroes, a treaty of commerce, restoration of the prizes, or any other kind of relief, or the states would repeal their laws. The old creditors in Britain, added Adams, had formed themselves into society and would not permit Parliament to forget them. "The States, it maybe said, will not repeal their laws. If they do not, then let them give up all expectation from this Court and country," he warned Jay, "unless you can force them to...[invest] congress with full power to regulate trade."[35]

Driven by necessity and a sense of fairness, Adams now pressed the British case on Jay and Congress. He reminded his official and private correspondents in America that there would be no progress in London until states repealed their acts impeding payments to British creditors and terminated their mistreatment of Loyalists. Adams informed Congress in May 1786, "that it was unquestionably true, that by the seventh article the posts should have been evacuated; but that by the fourth and ninth it was also stipulated that there should be no legal impediment in the way of recovery of British debts; that these articles had been violated by almost every state in the confederacy."[36] When the United States complied with the provisions of the treaty, he promised, the king would also. "It will appear to all the world with an ill grace," Adams pleaded, "if we complain of breaches of the treaty, when the British Court have it in their power to prove upon us breaches of the same treaty, of greater importance. My advice, then if it is not impertinent to give it, is, that every law of every State which concerns either debts or royalists, which can be impartially construed contrary to the spirit of the treaty of peace, be immediately repealed, and the debtors left to settle with creditors, or dispute the point of interest at law." He observed to Samuel Adams in June 1786, "When We have done equity We may with good Grace, demand Equity."[37]

If British compliance with the treaty provisions demanded a diplomatic recognition of the London government's case, British attitudes and commercial policy toward the United States did not. Adams's complaints of British behavior and the nature of American policies that would improve it continued to dominate his correspondence in

1786 and thereafter. For Adams the ministry in London continued to view the United States as a rival, and in the British lexicon that meant an enemy to be reduced by every possible means. Adams complained in March 1786 that he had met very few Englishmen—much fewer than he expected when he arrived—who favored commercial reciprocity with the United States. "1 have long informed congress," he wrote in May, "that nothing is to be expected from this country but poverty, weakness, and ruin." Again the answer for Adams lay in Congressional action. "[T]he United States must repel monopolies by monopolies, and answer prohibitions by prohibitions," he advised. If Congress could agree to regulate the commerce of the United States, predicted Adams, England would seek a treaty. "Like Daniel Defoe's game cock among the horses feet," wrote Adams, "it will be, 'Pray, gentlemen, don't let us tread upon one another."[38]

For Adams his negotiations in London had long ceased to have a future. In August and September 1786, he traveled to the Netherlands to exchange ratifications of the Prussian treaty—that had been under consideration since early 1784—with the Prussian minister. The trip offered him the opportunity to pay his respects to officials in Holland, a country to which he was still accredited and one which Mrs. Adams, who accompanied him, had never seen. Soon thereafter Adams pressed Congress for permission to return to the United States. During the early months of 1787, Adams's routine office duties no longer involved any diplomatic business with the British government. On February 3 he reported to Jay: "Parliament opened with uncommon loom and has been sitting in mournful silence." He noted "a dead taciturnity prevails about America." What troubled him even more was his discovery that Britain spent many times the profits of the fur trade to maintain its frontier posts in America. He acknowledged his dejection: "[A] life so useless to the public, and so insipid to myself, as mine is in Europe, has become a burden to me, as well as to my countrymen." Still his diplomatic burdens continued.

During the summer of 1787, Jefferson and Adams faced the task of negotiating another loan with the country's Dutch bankers, Willink and Van Staphorst. Jefferson learned in June that his secretary, William Short, had recommended him for the money negotiations in Holland. Jefferson balked at the thought of going. "On the contrary," he wrote to Madison, "it is a business which would be the most disagreeable to me of all others, and for which I am the most unfit person living. I do not understand bargaining nor possess the dexterity requisite to make it."[39] Jefferson had long argued that the United States should pay off its French debt and transfer its entire indebtedness to Holland. With France on the verge of bankruptcy in 1787, Jefferson believed this transfer all the more necessary; the debt to France, he reported to Madison in August, was injuring the standing of the United States in that country. That month Jefferson learned that Adams had traveled to Amsterdam alone and had negotiated another large loan with Willink and Van Staphorst because the Dutch bankers had insufficient funds on hand to pay the interest on the American loan. On Adams's advice, they secured a new loan at 8 percent interest, but insisted that Adams come to Holland to sign the obligations so that they could acquire the necessary guilders. In Amsterdam Adams found two thousand bonds awaiting his signature. He sat at a desk for two days, signing his name, he told Abigail, until his "hand could hardly hold the pen." With that task completed, Adams returned to London. Thereafter, Jefferson, Adams informed the Dutch bankers, would conduct the negotiations for any additional American loans.[40]

Early in 1788 the Commissioners of the Treasury in the United States informed Jefferson that Adams's recent loan required renegotiation. Jefferson quickly apprised Adams of this latest financial crisis and asked him to undertake one more negotiation in Holland to tide the country over until it could establish a more effective taxing and credit structure. Adams believed that the sale of the bonds he had signed in the early summer of 1787 should have been sufficient to support American credit. He feared that the Dutch bankers wanted to renegotiate merely to acquire a higher rate of interest. Adams suggested that Jefferson call their bluff. "Depend upon it," he advised Jefferson in February, "the Amsterdamers love Money too well to execute their Threats. They expect to gain too much by American Credit to destroy it." When Jefferson discovered that Adams would shortly return to The Hague to take leave of the Dutch government, he decided to join Adams in Holland to avail himself of Adams's experience. Adams executed bonds for another loan and departed for London and his return to America. Jefferson waited in Amsterdam another 12 days to follow the progress of the new loan.[41]

*****

In July 1787, Jay agreed that Adams should return home where his prospects for additional service to the nation seemed promising enough. "You have, my good friend," wrote Jay, "deserved well of your country; and your services and character will be truly estimated, at least by posterity, for they will know more of you than the people of this day." Adams explained to Jefferson his desire to leave Britain, attributing it more to necessity than to choice. "Congress," he wrote, "cannot consistent with their own honour and Dignity, renew my Commission to this Court—and I assure you, I should hold it so inconsistent with my own honour and Dignity little as that may be, that if it were possible for Congress to forget theirs I would not forget mine, but send their Commission back to them, unless a Minister were sent from his Brittanic Majesty to Congress."[42] To the end, Adams condemned the attitude of the British Court. "In preparing for my departure," he confided to Jay, "I have been personally treated with the same uniform tenor of dry decency and cold civility which appears to have been the premeditated plan from the beginning; and opposition, as well as administration, appear to have adopted the same spirit." On February 20, 1788, Adams had his final audience with the king. After he had assured the king of America's friendship and desire for more liberal commercial relations, the king replied: "Mr. Adams, you may, with great truth, assure the United States that, whenever they shall fulfil the treaty on their part, I, on my part, will fulfil it in all its particulars."[43] What remained for Adams was the unwelcome necessity of taking leave of the queen, the cabinet members, and members of the diplomatic corps.

Across the channel Jefferson also had requested permission to return home; nevertheless, he responded to the news of Adams's desire to return to America with some emotion. "I learn with real pain the resolution you have taken of quitting Europe," he wrote to Adams, "Your presence on this side the Atlantic gave me a confidence that if any difficulties should arise within my department, I should always have one to advise with on whose counsels I could rely. I shall now feel be widowed." At the same time, Jefferson could understand Adams's decision. "I did really expect that that ungracious, rascally court would wear out the patience of Mr. Adams," he wrote to William Smith. "Long habits of doing business together and of doing it easily and smoothly, will render me sincerely sensible to his loss."[44]

The experience of attending Court had scarcely thrilled Jefferson at all. He was too introspective to be impressed with such outward displays of wealth and power. Nor did he hold the diplomats in high esteem. With few exceptions, he later told Gouverneur Morris, they were not worth knowing. Jefferson had little regard for Parisian society or the general extravagance of the rich and aristocratic. He was more at home in French intellectual circles. Regardless of Jefferson's low opinion of the diplomatic corps in Paris, his standing with French officials and other members of the corps remained high. Thomas L. Shippen, the nephew of Arthur Lee, spent several weeks in Paris during January 1788 and accompanied Jefferson to Court. "I observed," Shippen recalled, "that although Mr. Jefferson was the plainest man in the room, and the most destitute of ribbands crosses and other insignia of rank was that he was most courted and most attended to (even by the Courtiers themselves) of the whole Diplomatic corps."[45]

Jefferson had found Vergennes a great minister in European affairs, but with little knowledge of things American. His devotion to despotism rendered him less than sympathetic to the American government, Jefferson admitted, but his fear of England made him generally cooperative. "He is cool, reserved in political conversation, free and familiar on other subjects, and a very attentive, agreeable person to do business with," Jefferson wrote to Madison. "It is impossible to have a clearer, better organised head but age has chilled his heart." Vergennes died in mid-February 1787; the king appointed the Count de Montmorin as his successor. From the beginning, Jefferson thought highly of the new minister. "I am extremely pleased with his modesty, the simplicity of his manners, and his dispositions toward us," Jefferson confided to Lafayette.[46]

Jefferson's crowning diplomatic achievement of his last years in France was the consular convention of 1788 that he negotiated with Montmorin. What made the convention necessary was the danger to American security posed by the extraterritoriality provisions of the convention that Franklin had negotiated with Vergennes in 1784 but which Congress had rejected. Jay, in opposing the convention, argued that Franklin had defied every instruction he received. Now Jay sent Jefferson instructions to negotiate a convention in accordance with Congress's desired changes. Since France wanted consuls in American ports, the United States was willing to have them, but Jefferson informed Montmorin, they could not enjoy immunities, privileges, and powers that did not conform to American laws. The only feature of extraterritoriality that remained was the right of French consuls to try civil cases involving only French subjects—a right which American consuls enjoyed in French ports. Jefferson limited the convention to 12 years. The new convention was an agreement between equals; Jay expressed delight with it.[47]

Jefferson, despite an expressed desire to return home earlier, remained in France until September 1789.

Chapter 4

AMERICAN DIPLOMATS ENGAGE
THE BARBARY PIRATES AND SPAIN

North African corsairs from Algiers, Morocco, and Tripoli—the Barbary pirates—had developed piracy into a national enterprise. They seized merchant ships and held their cargo and crews for ransom. European nations chose to pay tribute to ensure that their ships passed without incident instead of sending their warships into the Mediterranean and forcing the North African sultans to take up another trade. Prior to 1776, American commercial vessels sailed though the pirate-infested sea under British protection; however, afterwards they had to confront the pirates without adequate protection. American diplomats sought to arrange agreements to buy off the troublesome states and suspend this practice—much as had the European nations. With virtually no funds for bribes, little support from Congress, and lacking any political leverage, senior American negotiators became increasingly frustrated. There were only two ways to deal with the pirates, they eventually concluded: the negotiation of peace settlements with the various North African states and Turkey, which involved paying tribute; or to construct a navy sufficient to dissuade the pirates from bothering American ships.

Hostile Spanish officials had never embraced the American rebels. When the peace treaty of 1783 granted a vast trans-Appalachian region to the United States, a boundary dispute arose in the Old Southwest and, potentially more critical, friction over navigation rights on the Mississippi River. The nearly 50,000 American pioneers that crossed the Alleghenies to carve out farms in what would become Tennessee and Kentucky desired to transport their grains and other produce down the Mississippi to ocean-going ships rather than the costly eastward trek over the mountains. To protect their North American possessions from the expanding American frontier, unsympathetic Spaniards who controlled the mouth of the Mississippi declared in 1784 that the river outlet was closed. This action outraged American frontiersmen.

American diplomats—John Adams, minister to London; and Thomas Jefferson, minister to Paris—were instructed by Congress to seek peace treaties with the Barbary states and Secretary for Foreign Affairs John Jay to negotiate with the Spanish envoy Don Diego de Gardoqui regarding these issues.

*****

What initially puzzled Franklin and other American observers was Europe's refusal to combine and destroy the nests of the pirates and free the Mediterranean of such types. Such indulgence gave the United States no apparent choice but to join the other powers in negotiating the necessary tribute to protect its ships. "I think it not improbable," wrote Franklin, "that those Rovers may be privately encouraged by the English to fall upon us, to prevent our Interference in the Carrying Trade; for I have in London heard it as a Maxim among the Merchants, that, *if there were no Algiers, it would be worth England's while to build one.*"[1] Adams was convinced that the Mediterranean trade was worth more than the expense of the tribute required to secure treaties with the pirates; by roaming the seas, the corsairs had raised the insurance rates on all commerce to a level far beyond reason. As he wrote to Jay,

> As long as France, England, Holland, the Emperor, etc., will submit to be tributary to these robbers, and even encourage them, to what purpose should we make war upon them? The resolution might be heroic, but would not be wise. The contest would be unequal. They can injure us very sensibly, but we cannot hurt them in the smallest degree. We have, or shall have, a rich trade at sea exposed to their depredations; they have none at all upon which we can made reprisals.... Unless it were possible, then, to persuade the great maritime powers of Europe to unite in the suppression of these piracies, it would be very imprudent for us to entertain any thoughts of contending with them, and will only lay a foundation, by irritating their passions,

and increasing their insolence and their demands, for long and severe repentance. I hope, therefore, we shall think of nothing but treating with them.[2]

Adams and Jefferson found the task of freeing American commerce from the curse of the Barbary pirates more and more demeaning. Congress had empowered the commissioners to apply whatever money borrowed in Europe, and belonging to the United States, they deemed necessary to negotiate treaties with the Barbary states but not to exceed $80,000. "If we can avoid this humiliating tribute," Adams observed, "I should wish it with all my heart, but am afraid we must sooner or later submit to it."[3] What added to his sense of outrage as well as impotence was the capture of three American ships. During the previous winter, Morocco took the American brig *Betsy*. The Moroccan emperor held the ship and cargo, but he treated the crew with civility, re-clothed them, and delivered them to the Spanish minister who sent them to Cadiz. At the same time, the emperor announced that his country would seize no more American vessels until the United States had an opportunity to negotiate a treaty with Morocco.[4] In their instructions from Congress, Adams and Jefferson were to express American satisfaction over the emperor's willingness to enter into a treaty.

At the same time, Congress authorized the commissioners to appoint an agent to conduct the actual negotiations on their behalf. Because the French Court had promised cooperation in the negotiations, Jay suggested that the commissioners seek the advice and assistance of Vergennes, the French foreign minister. On March 20, before he departed for London, Adams consulted Vergennes who encouraged the Americans to work through the French consuls, but volunteered no information concerning the presents that the king gave to the Barbary rulers. He advised Adams not to invite the emperor of Morocco to send a minister to Paris but rather to dispatch an American negotiator to Morocco.[5]

Shortly after the Moroccan episode, Algeria captured two American brigs, the *Maria* and the *Dauphin*. Algeria held the crewmen captive and demanded a heavy ransom for their release. In August 1785, the American captain, Richard O'Brien, informed Jefferson in Paris of the suffering that the Americans experienced in Algeria and asked him to negotiate for their release. At the news of the captures, Jefferson wrote that his mind was "absolutely suspended between indignation and impotence." The Spanish negotiations with Algeria had disintegrated because the Spanish government refused to pay the required million dollars besides presents. Peace with that country would be expensive. "The immense sum said to have been proposed on the part of Spain to Algeria," Jefferson concluded, "leaves us little hope of satisfying their avarice." It would be wiser policy, he wrote to Monroe, to open the Mediterranean with force. "We ought to begin a naval power, if we mean to carry on our own commerce. Can we begin it on a more honorable occasion, or with a weaker foe? I am of opinion Paul Jones with half a dozen frigates would totally destroy their commerce ... by constant cruising and cutting them to pieces."[6]

Throughout the late summer of 1785, Adams and Jefferson awaited the arrival of Charles Lamb of Connecticut, formerly engaged in the Barbary trade and now appointed by Congress to conduct the negotiations with the North African rulers. To prepare for the forthcoming negotiations, Jefferson in August sent Adams the draft of a treaty for the Barbary states for his approval.[7] When Lamb failed to arrive, the two American ministers decided to dispatch Thomas Barclay, a man of proven capabilities, to negotiate a treaty with Morocco. Early in September, Jefferson prepared a letter to the emperor as well as a set of instructions for Barclay, submitting both to Adams for review. Barclay's best argument for moderate terms, believed Adams, was the fact that the United States had no ships in the Mediterranean and would have none there until it signed treaties with the Barbary states. The North African corsairs, therefore, could capture American vessels only in the Atlantic where they would be exposed to American privateers.[8] When Lamb arrived, at last, in September, he brought with him a commission granting Adams and Jefferson full powers to appoint agents to negotiate with the Barbary states; the two ministers could sign any treaties.[9]

Having appointed Barclay to Morocco, Jefferson suggested Algeria for Lamb. "I have not seen enough of him to judge of his abilities," Jefferson admitted to Adams. "He seems not deficient as far as I can see, and the footing on which he comes must furnish a presumption for what we do not see."[10] Still, finding Lamb less than promising in manner and appearance, Adams and Jefferson appointed John Randall of New York, in whom they had greater confidence, to accompany Lamb. Actually, Congress, after Lamb's departure, had rejected the committee report that recommended Lamb for the North

African negotiation; nothing in his background or experience suggested to members of Congress that he was worthy of the trust. In dispatching Lamb to Algeria, Jefferson said Adams responded to necessity, not to anticipation of success. Adams suggested that Barclay and Lamb seek the support of foreign consuls. Without orders to the contrary, these European officials would have no choice but to aid the negotiations.[11] Adams assumed correctly that no European court would seek to embarrass or obstruct American negotiations with the Barbary states, but he wondered additionally whether even the cooperation of the foreign consuls would help the American negotiations. Only naval power sufficient to threaten Algeria with bombardment or capture, he wrote to Jefferson, would encourage the Dey to sue for peace. Still the United States had no apparent choice but to pursue its diplomacy with the Barbary states under the assumption that it might prove successful. As Monroe reminded Jefferson early in 1786: "These pirates have already made a great impression upon our trade and unless these negotiations prove successful will materially injure it.[12]

With both Barclay and Lamb in Spain en route to North Africa, Adams learned in mid-February 1766 that the roving ambassador from Tripoli was in London and wanted to see him. Adams judged a call necessary and after a tour of other visits stopped at the ambassador's door, intending only to leave his card. The ambassador was announced at home and ready to receive the American minister. Soon the ambassador asked Adams questions about America and its tobacco—better, he believed, than that of Tripoli. By then one of his servants had brought two lighted pipes. Adams placed the bowl of his pipe on the carpet because it was more than two yards in length. Thereafter he matched the ambassador whiff for whiff until the servant brought coffee. "The necessary Civilities being thus completed," Adams reported to Jefferson, "His Excellency...asked many Questions about America: the soil Climate, Heat and Cold, etc. and said it was a very great Country. But 'Tripoli is at War with it.' I was 'Sorry to hear that.' 'America had done no Injury to Tripoli, committed no Hostility; nor had Tripoli done America any Injury or committed any Hostility against her, that I had heard of.' True, said His Excellency 'but there must be a Treaty of Peace. There could be no Peace without a Treaty. The Turks and Africans were the sovereigns of the Mediterranean, and there could be no navigation there nor Peace without Treaties of Peace....America must treat with Tripoli

and then with Constantinople and then with Algiers and Morocco.'"
The ambassador showed Adams his full powers to negotiate what
treaties he pleased. He was ready to hear and propose terms of a
peace with the United States. Adams wanted Jefferson's advice. "The
Relation of my Visit," Adams reported to Jefferson, "is to be sure
very inconsistent with the Dignity of your Character and mine, but
the Ridicule of it was real and the Drollery inevitable. How can We
preserve our Dignity in negotiating with Such Nations?"[13]

Three days later, the Tripolitan ambassador returned the call, arriving at Adams's residence at noon. "He 'called God to Witness,'
that is to say, he swore by his beard," wrote Adams, "that his motive
to this earnestness for peace, although it might be of some benefit to
himself, was the desire of doing good." But time was short and the
sooner peace was made, the better. When Adams asked about terms,
the ambassador suggested that they meet again at his house the following evening. There the ambassador recommended a perpetual
treaty, requiring a sum of 30,000 guineas. This was only half of what
Spain had paid; moreover, he would permit the United States to pay
only 12,500 guineas the first year and 3,000 each year thereafter.
Adams responded that he could not pay such sums until he had special permission from Congress. In his report to Jay, Adams estimated
the total cost of negotiating treaties with the four Barbary states at
about 200,000 pounds sterling, an amount that could be borrowed
only in Holland. A war with the pirates would cost even more. Adams
urged Jefferson to join him in London to pursue the negotiations as
far as conditions would permit.[14]

*****

Jefferson responded quickly to Adams's summons of February
1786, to treat with the ambassador of Tripoli. Early in March, he
set off with his secretary, arriving in London six days later amid
disagreeable weather. He took private lodgings rather than residing with the Adams family. Shortly after Jefferson's arrival, the two
commissioners visited the ambassador of Tripoli. Since the United
States had sent no agents to Tripoli and Tunis, Jefferson explained
to Jay, he and Adams might make an arrangement in London in less
time and at less expense. At their meeting, the ambassador from
Tripoli again advised a perpetual peace to avoid the need of annual
payments. Tripoli, the Americans learned, wanted 50,000 guineas;
Tunis would want a like sum. He could not speak for Morocco or

Algeria, but they would demand more. To arrange a peace with the four Barbary states apparently would cost between 200,000 and 300,000 guineas, many times what Adams and Jefferson had available. The American commissioners asked the ambassador why the Barbary states made such demands on nations that had done them no injury. "The Ambassador," they reported, "answered us that it was founded on the Laws of their Prophet, that it was written in their Koran, that all nations who should not have acknowledged their authority were sinners, that it was their right and duty to make war upon them wherever they could be found, and to make slaves of all they could take as Prisoners, and that every Musselman who should be slain in battle was sure to go to Paradise.... It was the Practice of their Corsairs to bear down upon a ship, for each sailor to take a dagger in each hand and another in his mouth, and leap on board, which so terrified their Enemies that very few stood against them." Congress, Adams and Jefferson agreed, could obtain the necessary funds to make peace with the Barbary states only by seeking another loan in Holland. But Jay had informed them that Congress would appropriate no additional funds and would authorize no new loans in Holland to ransom the captives until it had some prospect of paying the interest on the old loans.[15]

When Jefferson returned to Paris, he learned that Lamb's mission to Algeria had failed totally. Lamb was clearly unsuited for the negotiation. Among other deficiencies, he could speak none of the local languages. Later, Captain O'Brien wrote to William Carmichael, the American charge d'affaires at Madrid, that Lamb "could speak nothing but English; that the French consul and Conde d'Espilly, the Spanish ambassador, would not take the trouble to explain Mr. Lamb's propositions, as the terms of the peace would be advantageous to the Algerines; and that the French and Spaniards advised Mr. Lamb to return to America, that the Algerines would not make peace with the United States of America." Subsequently one Algerine official advised O'Brien that "if the Americans sent an American to Algiers to make the peace, they should send a man who could speak the Spanish or Italian language. He ridiculed much the sending a man that no one could understand what he had to say."[16] In spite of these critical remarks, Jefferson understood the impossible odds that Lamb had faced in Algeria. In August he wrote to Monroe: "I am persuaded that an Angel sent on this business, and so much limited in his terms, could have done nothing. But should Congress propose to try the line of negotiation again, I think they will perceive that Lamb is not a proper agent." Later, when Jefferson suggested to Adams that they might have made a better selection, Adams assured Jefferson that the responsibility for Lamb's failure was not theirs. "We found him ready appointed on our hands," wrote Adams. "I never saw him nor heard of him. He ever was and still is as indifferent to me as a Mohawk Indian. But as he came from Congress with, their Dispatches of such importance, I supposed it was expected We should appoint him."[17] No one sent by Congress, Adams agreed, could have succeeded in Algeria.

From the outset, the negotiations in Morocco were more promising. Barclay reached that country in June 1786; within one month he had concluded a treaty of amity and commerce with the Emperor for 30,000 dollars. This was the first treaty with a Barbary power that did not stipulate tribute or presents. Barclay submitted the treaty to Jefferson who transmitted it to Congress. The treaty was to remain in force for 50 years but, unfortunately, the emperor died soon after the signing. To relieve the burden of renegotiating the treaty with his successor, Congress appropriated $20,000 for presents. Congress finally approved the treaty on July 18, 1787. Except for the treaty with Prussia, the one with Morocco was the only success at treaty-making that Adams and Jefferson achieved, and even that success resulted largely from Spanish support.

As relations with the Barbary powers drifted, Adams and Jefferson agreed that the ultimate American defense of its Mediterranean trade lay in the mutually objectionable alternatives of tribute or war. There would be little American commerce in the Mediterranean until Congress came to terms with the Barbary states, especially Algeria. Adams reminded Jefferson in May 1786 that the Algerines would never make peace with the United States until it had treaties with Turkey, Tunis, Tripoli, and Morocco. The Algerines always resisted negotiations to the last. Vergennes assured Jefferson a week later that a treaty with Constantinople would not protect American ships in the Mediterranean from the Algerian pirates.[18]

Clearly the choices confronting the United States in the Mediterranean were narrow. Adams noted what the United States would pay for not negotiating a peace with the North African states: a heavy insurance on all exports, the loss of much of the trade with Spain and Portugal, and the total loss of the Mediterranean and Levant trade. Those losses, wrote Adams in June 1786, would exceed a half million sterling a year. To fight the pirates would cost an equal amount without protecting the trade. Certainly, concluded Adams, war would cost far more than interest on a loan sufficient to pay the tribute.[19] Adams argued in a letter to Jefferson in early July that the United States lacked the power to punish the Barbary states and therefore had no choice but to bribe them. The United States could not have peace in the Mediterranean unless it paid tribute; that tribute, feared Adams, would increase the longer the delay in negotiating. "From these premises," he wrote, "I conclude it to be the wisest for us to negotiate and pay the necessary sum without loss of time.... The policy of Christendom has made cowards of all their sailors before the standard of Mahomet. It would be heroical and glorious in us to restore courage to ours. I doubt not we could accomplish it, if we should set about it in earnest; but the difficulty of bringing our people to agree upon it, has ever discouraged me."[20]

Jefferson, in his reply, doubted that price of negotiation would necessarily increase with the passage of time; that would depend on the value of any future captures. If the United States would have peace through negotiation, he could see no reason for delay. But Jefferson preferred war. It would, he believed, have the defense of honor, would procure some respect in Europe, and would strengthen the government at home. Jefferson argued additionally that war would cost less than tribute. A peace not enforced with adequate power at sea could be of short duration. No agreement, moreover, would extend beyond the life of the Dey who signed it. Jefferson was equally convinced that the United States, in a war against the pirates, would have the support of Naples and perhaps Portugal. In time, other powers would enter the confederacy to assure the peace of the Mediterranean. Jefferson embodied his preferences for the use of force in a plan for concerted action against the pirates, one that would secure perpetual peace in the Mediterranean without tribute. He proposed a convention that called for cruising along the North African coast by a multi-national naval force directed by a council of ambassadors, perhaps at Versailles. Lafayette found the proposal fascinating, as did some of the smaller European powers. What terminated the project was the financial hopelessness of Congress; this eliminated any decision.

Adams replied graciously in late July that whereas he wanted a navy whether it be applied to the Algerines or not, he still favored negotiation. He believed that Jefferson had underestimated the force required to humble the Algerines. But Adams concluded: "[T]ho I am glad we have exchanged a Letter on the subject, I perceive that neither Force nor Money will be applied. Our States are so backward that they will do nothing for some years.... It is their Concern, and We must submit, for your Plan of fighting will no more be adopted than mine of negotiating. This is more humiliating to me, than giving the Presents would be."[21]

The North African corsairs continued to plague Presidents George Washington and Adams, both of which were forced to purchase settlements with three of these states. When the Pasha of Tripoli declared war on the United States in May 1801, however, Jefferson, now president, resorted to force. He sent warships into the Mediterranean to persuade the Pasha to agree to a favorable treaty; however, the other Barbary states, Algiers and Tunis, were finally brought to terms only after the War of 1812.[22]

*****

Even more serious, in the long view, than the problem of Barbary pirates was that of controlling the great region between the Allegany Mountains and the Mississippi. The peace treaty had assigned spacious boundaries to the United States, but American sovereignty within the boundaries was largely a legal fiction. American settlement beyond the mountains took the form of a narrow wedge with its base stretching from Pittsburgh to the Watauga settlements in eastern Tennessee and its apex at Nashville on the Cumberland River. Within it lay the villages in the Kentucky bluegrass region and at the Falls of the Ohio (Louisville). To these should be added the old French villages on the Wabash and in the Illinois country. All told, there were perhaps 25,000 settlers between the crest of the mountains and the Mississippi. Beyond these limits, to the north, west, and south was the country of unfriendly Indians, and the explorer or trader who penetrated the Indian barrier was likely to find garrisons of British or Spanish troops upon land within the treaty boundaries of the United States. The British army still occupied every strategic point on the Great Lakes, and Spanish soldiers held the Mississippi at Natchez and (a little later) at the sites of the future Vicksburg and Memphis; and both British and Spanish were in alliance or understanding with the Indians for the purpose of preventing the United States from taking possession of the territory assigned to it by the treaty of peace.

There was, furthermore, no assurance that the frontier settlers themselves would be firm in their allegiance to the state governments in the East or to the weak Congress that symbolized their Union. A do-nothing government could not command a vital patriotism. The frontier found its natural outlets through the Mississippi and the St. Lawrence Rivers, and the nations that controlled those watercourses exerted a powerful attraction upon the settlements on their upper waters. Frontier leaders were not always above bartering their allegiance in return for special favors from the British and Spanish governments.

Before the United States could make its actual sovereignty coextensive with its treaty boundaries, it had to accomplish three difficult tasks. It had to make sure of its hold upon the allegiance of the frontiersmen; bring the Indian tribes under its control; and secure from England and Spain, respectively, the execution and the recognition of the terms of the Treaty of Paris. These tasks were interrelated. Only through ousting the British and Spanish from their footholds upon its soil could the United States hope to control the Indians, and only by dealing effectively with both Indians and Europeans could it bind to itself the "men of the western waters." None of these problems proved capable of solution during the period of the Articles of Confederation.

The British held seven fortified posts on United States soil, strung out from the foot of Lake Champlain to Michilimackinac, at the junction of Lakes Huron and Michigan. The British excused this violation of the peace treaty by asserting that the United States had not fulfilled its obligations under the same instrument. In reality, the decision to hold the posts had been taken before the treaty was formally proclaimed, obviously before the nature of the American performance under it could be known. Retention of the posts served to keep a valuable trade in furs in the hands of Canadian traders and enabled the British government to meet its obligations to Indian tribes which had been its allies during the recent war. British authorities did not hesitate to encourage these tribes, living south of the Canadian border, to resist American attempts to purchase and settle their lands. The British also showed an interest in the dissatisfaction of American frontier communities in Vermont and Kentucky, hoping they might be willing to detach themselves from the Confederation.

The Treaty of 1783 between Great Britain and the United States had fixed the southern boundary of the latter, from the

Chattahoochee to the Mississippi, at the 31st parallel, had made the middle of the Mississippi the western boundary, and had declared: "The navigation of the river Mississippi, from its source to the ocean, shall forever remain free and open to the subjects of Great Britain, and the citizens of the United States." In the contemporaneous settlement with Spain, Great Britain had ceded to that nation East and West Florida without defining their boundaries. Louisiana, embracing the region west of the Mississippi and New Orleans east of that river, had been ceded by France to Spain in 1762. After 1783, therefore, Spain hemmed in the United States on both the west and the south.

Spain was not a signatory to the treaty between Great Britain and the United States and refused to consider herself bound by its terms, either as to the southern boundary of the United States or as to the free navigation of the Mississippi. As a result of the successful campaign under Galvez in 1779–1781, Spain claimed a large area in the Southwest by right of conquest and denied the right of Great Britain to cede it to the United States. Holding both banks of the Mississippi from its mouth to far above New Orleans, Spain likewise denied the right of Great Britain to guarantee to citizens of the United States its free navigation. Spanish policy after 1783 included the assertion of title to a region as far north as the Tennessee and Ohio Rivers, the denial to the Americans of the use of the lower Mississippi, except as a privilege granted by Spain, and the cultivation of the friendship and trade of the powerful Indian nations of the Southwest with a view to using them as a barrier against the Americans. In July 1784, Spain took the additional step of closing the river to all but Spanish vessels. James Madison condemned the Spanish decree. It seemed inconceivable to him that Spain could maintain such a narrow policy against the interests of thousands of settlers who required and would demand access to markets. The extreme boundary claims of Spain were apparently set up chiefly for bargaining purposes.[23]

At the same time, King Charles of Spain informed Congress that he had appointed Don Diego De Gardoqui, commissary of the Spanish Royal Armies, as charge d'affaires to reside in the United States for the purpose of facilitating the commerce, negotiating the boundaries, and settling other outstanding issues between Spain and the United States. Gardoqui, who had studied in England and spoke English fluently, reached Philadelphia in May 1785 and soon opened negotiations with John Jay, now the secretary for the Department of

Foreign Affairs. Jay was not unfamiliar with the Spanish diplomatic mentality, having previously spent many bitter months in Madrid in 1781 seeking recognition for the American revolutionaries. Even though Spain had entered the war against Britain as an ally of France, it refused to recognize the United States or even accept Jay as America's official representative. To be sure, the Spanish were willing to supply some secret aid to the revolutionaries, but they wanted no public connection with them or their views on monarchy or the disposition of Spanish colonies in the Mississippi region. Even an offer to waive the American claim of right to navigate the Mississippi River could not persuade Madrid to recognize the young republic. Moreover, by the Treaty of Aranjuez, France and Spain had agreed that neither would make peace until Spain had recovered Gibraltar. Since America had promised not to make peace without France, it could not, if all treaty engagements were observed, make peace until Gibraltar was restored to Spain. At the end, Jay was privately relieved that the Spanish had rejected the offer of Mississippi, regarding Spanish conduct as an insult both to himself and his country.

Like other North American representatives during the Revolutionary War, Jay bore personal testimony to the hard-edged core of 18th-century European diplomacy, which reflected and institutionalized the contemporary practice of power politics, with its relentless, undisguised pursuit of national interest, territorial expansion, and commercial advantage. Jay's firsthand acquaintance of the complexity and intensity of European rivalries while in Paris and Madrid, together with the revolutionaries' original set of values, would mark the diplomacy of his generation: avoiding political entanglements in Europe, a preference for commercial to political treaties, and a belief in legitimacy of territorial expansion.[24]

Gardoqui's plan from the beginning was to separate the Eastern commercial establishment from the country's western inhabitants and their Southern defenders by offering an attractive commercial treaty in lieu of a compromise on the question of Mississippi navigation. Gardoqui was a merchant with strong ties to American commerce. Thus he began his negotiations with Jay, a New Yorker, with high hopes of success. Massachusetts and New York conservatives feared the growth of the West and the diffusion of political power from the coast to the interior, and with it the persistent loss of exploitable labor. Behind Gardoqui's negotiation was always the assumption that the country's commercial and agrarian interests, embodying two approaches to appropriate national policies, were already locked in a struggle to determine the country's future.

Jay understood well that Gardoqui would indeed seek a treaty, but that the Mississippi would be a bone of contention. It also seemed clear that Gardoqui would claim lands east of the Mississippi, extending north of the Natchez settlements.[25] But Gardoqui assured Jay that the way was now prepared for a satisfactory resolution of the issues dividing the two countries.[26] On July 2, Gardoqui presented his credentials to Congress and delivered a brief message to the president of the Congress: "Permit me to assure you, sir, that my best endeavors shall not be wanting to render the continuance of my mission as satisfactory to both countries as this commencement will, I hope, give pleasure to my king, my master, and is agreeable to me." Jay responded formally on July 7 that Congress entertained a similar disposition and would on every occasion join him in the needed effort to reach a settlement satisfactory to both sides. The next day, Gardoqui wrote again assuring Jay that he was "authorized . . . to treat and agree upon the points necessary to be adjusted."[27]

Congress now prepared a commission to Jay, similar in substance and language to that of Gardoqui, to negotiate and sign with the Spanish envoy any treaties or conventions to establish the boundaries and promote the mutual interests of the two countries. Specifically, Jay's commission to negotiate with Gardoqui included the cardinal provision that he "enter into no treaty, compact or convention whatever, with said representative of Spain, which did not stipulate our right to the navigation of the Mississippi, and the boundaries as established in our treaty with Great Britain." Equally significant, the commission's instructions bound Jay "previous to his making his propositions to Don Diego de Gardoqui, or agreeing with him on any article, compact, or convention to communicate to Congress the propositions to be made or received relative to such article, compact, or convention.[28] Jay soon asked for modification of his instructions, declaring he could not negotiate adequately with Gardoqui if he complied with the requirement that he communicate to Congress every proposition that he believed expedient to make in the course of negotiations. Jay's request for modification of his instructions resulted in revised instructions from Congress, on August 25, 1785, withdrawing its demand to see each proposal made during his discussions with Gardoqui. This would hopefully free up the discussion between the two men so that some resolution of their issues might be achieved. The secretary for foreign affairs was informed, however, that Congress still held firm to "the right of the United States to their territorial Bounds, and the free Navigation of the Mississippi from the Source to the Ocean, as established in their Treaties with Great Britain." Moreover, Jay was told that he could "neither conclude or sign any Treaty, Compact or Convention" with Spain "until he hath previously communicated it to Congress, and received their Approbation."[29]

Although negotiations had scarcely begun, Jay was not sanguine over the outcome. Gardoqui, in adhering to the demands of the Spanish court, was simply not prepared to compromise on the Mississippi question; and Jay doubted that he could remove the obstacles to an agreement. He only hoped that the predictable failure of the negotiations would create no permanent irritation on either side since Congress had to approve any agreement on territorial boundaries and Mississippi navigation. Meanwhile Gardoqui complained to Congress in September that citizens of Georgia had appeared at Natchez, seeking to settle in the vicinity of the Spanish port. The Spanish commandant at the post granted lands to the settlers, but Gardoqui asked Congress to avoid complicating the situation that existed in those territories since the end of the war. Congress replied in October that although the United States claimed all the territory to the Mississippi assigned by the definitive Treaty of Peace, it would do everything in its power to prevent emigrants from disturbing the existing tranquility between the two countries.[30] For his part, Jay confronted Gardoqui with the complaints of other American citizens who faced arrest and incarceration because of their presence in the Natchez district. Some reported that Natchez officials had stopped boats moving down the river. Jay informed Congress that Spain's determination to exclude all nations from that part of the Mississippi that ran through the territories gave the United States the stark choice of settling the controversy by arms or treaty. The New Yorker concluded that the time had not arrived for using force and that the treaty negotiations must not be rendered more difficult by taking up the cause of American citizens who faced Spanish resistance on the river.

After months of stalemate in the negotiations, Gardoqui urged Jay to bring the matter of Mississippi navigation before Congress. He hoped that Jay understood that the Spanish king would not permit any nation to navigate the Mississippi through the territories of East and West Florida held by Spanish forces at the end of the war. The Peace Treaty of 1782 could not fix the limits of territories that did not belong to England. Gardoqui then reminded Jay that Spain had maintained cordial relations with the United States, aided the United States in its dealings with Morocco, and delayed in requesting payments of interest and principal on the wartime debts contracted in Spain. Unless the United States recognized promptly Spain's rights to the Mississippi, it ran the risk of losing its markets in Spain where America received gold and silver rather than merchandise for its products. Gardoqui informed Jay that the king would grant the United States a commercial treaty with most favored nation status, guaranteeing America its favorable trade, if it complied with Spain's demands regarding the Mississippi question. Upon receiving Gardoqui's communication, Jay asked Congress to appoint a committee "with power to instruct and direct/him/on every point and subject relative to the proposed treaty with Spain." The committee, Jay hoped, would be kept secret and refrain from any conversations on the subject of the treaty except in designated meetings of Congress.[31]

Again in June 1786, Gardoqui complained that citizens of Georgia continued to invade territories along the Mississippi claimed by Spain. These settlers deprived the Indians of their lands and forced them to seek the protection of Spanish officials. And again Gardoqui asked Congress to request the state of Georgia to stop these violations of Spanish territories and prevent surveyors from entering that territory. Congress had no choice but to come to terms over boundaries as quickly as possible. Congress, on July 12, resolved to inform the state of Georgia of the violations of its citizens of rights claimed by Spain. Congress, while determined to assert U.S. claims to territory awarded by the Treaty of Peace, desired also to maintain cordial relations with the government of Spain. It was the responsibility of Georgia to prevent the excesses of its citizens who were creating trouble with the Spanish authorities.[32] Early in August 1786, Jay sent a lengthy report to Congress discussing the various issues with Spain and, especially, the delicate state of his negotiations with Gardoqui. Jay asserted that he was persuaded that a proper commercial treaty with Spain was more essential than one with any other country. France, bound by its family compact with Spain, would remain neutral should a conflict occur between the United States and Spain. France, moreover, had no interest in defending American claims to the navigation of the Mississippi. Only cordial relations with Spain, believed Jay, gave the United States any influence in the French court. Britain, feared Jay, would rejoice over a Spanish-American conflict, especially since the British regarded the United States as its principal rival for Spanish trade. Among the Barbary states of North Africa, the Spaniards enjoyed an influence that the United States could not match. Finally, commercial relations with Spain were of special importance because almost every American product could be exchanged in the ports of Spain for gold and silver. Still, these advantages required the defense of a treaty.

In Jay's considered estimation, the fundamental interests of the United States in peace and commerce depended on good relations with Madrid. The treaty offered by Spain included commercial arrangements based on the principle of reciprocity, granting American merchants all the commercial privileges enjoyed by Spanish merchants in the Spanish kingdom, including the Canaries and adjacent islands. Through the Canaries, U.S. products could enter the markets of Spanish America. All American products and manufactures, with the exception of tobacco, could be carried freely into Spain on either Spanish or American vessels. All duties and imposts would be regulated on the basis of perfect reciprocity. The Spanish government even agreed to purchase its masts and timber in the United States in exchange for specie. Such provisions, declared Jay, gave the United States many commercial advantages at no cost.

What barred such a beneficial treaty was the persistent question of navigation and boundaries of the lower Mississippi. Gardoqui insisted that the United States relinquish its claims to the region; no American argument had produced a compromise. Not even the warning that nothing could prevent the continued flow of American citizens into the contested territories and their insistence on using the Mississippi to transport their goods to market would persuade Gardoqui that it was in the Spanish interest to concede its claim to the lower Mississippi. Gardoqui acknowledged the danger; he argued only that it lay too far into the future to influence an immediate settlement in favor of the Spanish claims. Jay, insisting that he adhered completely to the American position, suggested a temporary compromise that would keep the Mississippi closed to American shipping for 25 years. During that period, western settlers would need to accept the commercial limitation placed on them. The alternative, Jay warned, was war: a war for which the United

States was not prepared, as well as the loss of a highly desirable commercial treaty. A treaty excluding American commerce on the Mississippi for 25 years would reduce the value of western lands, but Spain's refusal to permit the trade would have the same effect. It seemed preferable to embody the restrictions in a treaty than to suffer the indignities that accompanied the seizure of American goods by Spanish officials. Gardoqui, Jay hoped, would accept the 25-year compromise. Jay expressed regret that events had forced the Mississippi question on the country at such an early date, but he assured Congress that no better treaty was available than the one he outlined in his carefully prepared statement to Congress. To reject the treaty would scarcely serve America's reputation in the courts of Europe.[33] Until the United States had a vigorous national government with the power to tax, Congress could expect no more of its negotiations.

The same day Jay's extensive report was presented, Gardoqui sent a statement to Congress concerning trade between the nations that was read to the members. It cleverly emphasized the substantial commercial benefits of a Spanish-American pact and stressed Britain's efforts to prevent it. "England," he declared, "exerts the utmost to prevent that the American States should come to friendly good understanding with Spain." Gardoqui obviously hoped that the benefits of the commercial treaty with Madrid would prompt Congress to consider compromising on the boundary dispute and navigation of the Mississippi.[34] Congress responded by asking Jay to determine the views of France regarding American claims to the Mississippi, as well as the question of territorial claims of Spain in the southwest. Jay reported that Spain claimed the two Floridas, with West Florida extending up the Mississippi, beyond the line marked by the Treaty of Peace, but Gardoqui had never delineated the boundaries north and east of the treaty line that Spain claimed in the negotiations. Certainly they fell well short of those claimed by Count Aranda in 1782.[35] Jay's review of the French diplomatic correspondence during the treaty negotiations of 1783 convinced him that France had indeed accepted the provisions of the Treaty of Peace with Britain.

On August 29, Congress repealed its instructions to Jay that he establish by treaty the boundaries and navigational rights to the Mississippi conveyed by the treaty with Britain.[36] Jay then informed Gardoqui that he was now prepared to renew the negotiations.

Unfortunately, Jay's subsequent negotiations with the Spanish envoy produced no agreement on navigation or boundaries. Gardoqui, in his continued refusal to compromise, even rejected Jay's 25-year proposal. In instructing their diplomat, Madrid complained that the Americans had shown little gratitude for their assistance in dealing with Morocco and that there had been no demand for repayment of earlier loans. Spanish authorities supported Gardoqui's refusal to accept any agreement that failed to mention the Mississippi for the basic reason that the Americans "would think themselves authorized by our very silence to do whatever they want." Moreover, while officials in Madrid view their situation realistically, they could only hope to "postpone for a time the events that eventually appear inevitable: that the Americans will take possession of all those countries up to the Mississippi and the Ocean, no excepting the Floridas, objectives which we cannot doubt that they have in mind."[37] Unable to establish the elusive line that Spain would accept, Jay suggested that Spain agree to a settlement though commissioners.

Restless settlers in western Virginia had become alarmed that Congress was unable to secure their right to move goods down the Mississippi without Spanish interference. Dissatisfied with Jay's continuing unsuccessful negotiations with Gardoqui, Virginia's House of Delegates vote unanimously to instruct is congressional delegation "to oppose any attempt that may be made in Congress to barter or surrender use of the river Mississippi." The Virginians contended that "a sacrifice of the rights of any one part [of the Confederacy] to the supposed or real interests of another part, would be a flagrant violation of Justice, a direct contravention of the end for which the federal Government was instituted, and an alarming Innovation of the System of the Union." The instructions to the Virginia delegation emphasized that "our Western brethren" are much concerned that their "essential Rights and Interests" might be "sacrificed and sold" in an unjust manner. Writing to Jay at the end of January 1787, Jefferson weighed in with his concern that "the right of navigation of the Mississippi may be abandoned to Spain." He continued: "I never had any interest Westward of the Alleghaney; & I never will have any[,] but I hve had great opportunities of knowing the character of the people who inhabit the country[,] and I will venture to say that the act which abandons the navigation of the Missisipi is an act of separation between the Eastern & Western country. [I]t is a relinquishment of five parts out of eight of the territory of the United states...." He predicted that the westerners would take matters into their own hands if a satisfactory agreement was not reached.[38]

"The Spanish project sleeps," Madison wrote Jefferson on March 19. The matter rests "wholly with Mr. Jay how far he will communicate with Congress as well as how far he will negociate with Guardoqui," he continued. "But although it appears that this intended sacrifice of the Mississippi will not be made, the consequences of the intention and the attempts are likely to be very serious." Patrick Henry had announced he would not attend the Philadelphia Convention to keep "himself free to combat or espouse the result of it according to the result of the Mississippi business among other circumstances." An irritated, thinly represented Congress instructed Jay on April 4 to provide it with information regarding his negotiations with Gardoqui.[39] On April 11, 1787, Jay reported to Congress that his repeated conversations with Gardoqui regarding the navigation of the Mississippi and its limits had "produced nothing but debate, and in the course of which we did not advance one single step nearer to each other. He [Gardoqui] continued and still continues deciding in refusing to admit us to navigate the river below our limits on any terms or conditions, nor will he consent to any article declaring our right in express terms, and stipulating to forebear the use of it for a given time."[40] For all to see, the negotiations had proved "dilatory, unpleasant and unpromising."

Hardening his position, Jay contended that the United States had fundamental, navigation rights on the Mississippi, and that unless Spain compromised its claims, the United States, to preserve its dignity, should assert the rights of its citizens to navigate the Mississippi and, if it faced refusal, should declare war on Spain. Until Spain accepted some accommodation, the United States faced the simple choice either of capitulation or war. It was high time, argued Jay, for Congress to declare its acceptance of the proposed treaty with Spain or, if demanded more, select another member to conduct negotiations. At the same time, the conduct of Americans along the banks of the Mississippi caused Jay deep embarrassment. He advised Congress to make a decision: "If war is in expectation, then their ardor should not be discouraged, nor their indignation diminished, but if a treaty is wished and contemplated, then those people should be so advised and restrained...." Issues of such magnitude would either greatly advance or retard the nation's prosperity. He also wisely reminded Congress that a treaty unacceptable to half of the country would be subject to violation, and a war opposed by the other half would have no success, especially under a government as unpopular as that of the United States.[41]

Against the background of continuing western plots to attack the Spanish in the lower Mississippi and growing concern that Congress was about to surrender the country's claims to the navigation of the river, Jay's subsequent negotiations with Gardoqui hit a dead end. In one of its final actions, in September 1788, the Continental Congress determined to put an end to negotiations with Spain, while declaring that the free navigation of the Mississippi was a clear and essential right of the American people. On October 17, 1788, Jay duly informed Gardoqui that Congress deemed it expedient that all negotiations be terminated until March 1789, when the new federal government would assemble.[42] With no possibility of any immediate agreement on the Mississippi question, Gardoqui informed President George Washington in July 1789 that he had received permission to return to Spain to settle his domestic affairs.[43] The Treaty of San Lorenzo (Pinckney's Treaty) that followed in 1795, under a new government, ultimately recognized the principal territorial claims of the United States while opening the free navigation of the Mississippi River to the sea. But that is another story.

Chapter 5

THE CRISIS OF 1786: CALL FOR CONSTITUTIONAL REVISION

Historians concerned with the questions of democratic governance that dominated the Constitutional Convention of 1787 generally find the convention's ties to the past in the early republic's intellectual, political, and economic environment, almost to the exclusion of the country's experiences in the external world. This seems strange. James Madison called the crucial Annapolis Convention of September 11, 1786, to address the troublesome issue of American commerce. With only five state delegations in attendance, the convention dispensed with commercial matters, but adopted Alexander Hamilton's resolution asserting that unspecified defects in the Articles of Confederation had created a situation "calling for an exertion of the united Virtues and Wisdom of all the Members of the Confederacy." The long debates at Philadelphia sought to define the nature and powers of Congress, the executive, and judiciary, and to establish a balance among the three branches of government as well as between the large and small states. The decisions designed to strengthen the country's foreign relations scarcely solicited debate because the universal experience of independence had demonstrated the powerlessness of Congress to sustain the country's external interests and responsibilities.

Three deficiencies in the Articles of Confederation were especially compelling in the call for a constitutional convention. The Articles granted Congress the power to enter treaties of commerce, but they extended it no authority to control the country's foreign commerce and thus protect it against Europe's unfair trade practices. Congress under the Articles received no taxing power, only the right to seek contributions from the states. It lacked, therefore, the means to create an army or navy, to cover its expenses, or to redeem its foreign obligations. Finally, the Articles provided Congress no power to enforce treaties. Following independence, Congress quickly discovered that it could compel neither the states nor the London government to fulfill the provisions of the peace treaty. In defiance of Article VII, the British did not evacuate New York until November 1783. Also, in defiance of the treaty, they exported hundreds of Negroes that had, by invitation, taken refuge behind the British lines. Meanwhile, British continued to occupy the frontier posts along the shores of the St. Lawrence and the Great Lakes. At the same time, the American states defied the peace treaty by passing laws that deprived English creditors and Loyalists of their treaty rights under Articles IV and VI.

U.S. diplomats in Europe, conscious of the London government's deep sense of obligation to the Tories, repeatedly admonished the American people to fulfill the treaty in good faith. James Madison commented that the European powers would not forever tolerate state violations of American treaties. "As yet," he admitted in April 1787, "foreign powers have not been rigorous in animadverting on us. This moderation however cannot be mistaken for a permanent partiality to our faults...."[1]

*****

By 1786 the growing conflict over treaty enforcement had emerged as the central issue in U.S.-British relations. The British in 1789 continued to hold the posts scattered along the northern frontier of the United States, especially at Niagara and Detroit. The London government, in response to John Adams's queries, had stated Britain would continue to hold the posts until Congress compelled the states to rescind their laws that prevented British creditors from collecting their debts from Americans in accordance with Article VI of the peace treaty. The treaty with Britain determined the obligations of the United States to British creditors, not subsequent notions of what the states regarded as acceptable policy. Unmoved by Britain's power and determination to hold the posts, the states refused to remove their impositions.

Additionally, British officials also were concerned with the ill treatment being accorded Loyalists—in violation of treaty terms—that had supported the king during the Revolutionary War. The mounting controversies over Articles IV, VI, and VII reflected the impossibility

of burying the wartime hatreds toward Britain and British Loyalists (Tories) in a treaty of peace. Charles Thomson, president of
Congress, reminded Jay as early as January 1784 that the peace treaty
would in no way erase the wartime passions of the American people.
"[C]onsidering what many have suffered…, and considering that
our newly established governments have not attained their full tone
and vigour," he wrote, "it can hardly be expected that people will in
a moment forget what is past and suddenly return to an interchange
of friendly officies with those whom for years past they have considered as their most bitter enemies."[2]

Despite the bitterness many Americans displayed toward the
British, Adams on various occasions acknowledged the validity of
London's position. In May 1786, he urged Jay to put the matter
before Congress and suggested "that every Law of every State,
which concerns either Debts or Royalists, which can be impartially
construed as contrary to the Spirit of the Treaty of Peace, be immediately repealed." "Your ideas and mine," Jay replied to Adams,
on the matter of frontier posts "very nearly correspond.…The result of my inquiries into the conduct of States relative to the treaty,
is, that there has not been a single day since it [the peace treaty]
took effect, on which it has not been violated in America, by one or
other of the States."[3] Yet few were optimistic that the states would
respond favorably. "If you tell the Legislatures they have violated
the Treaty of Peace, & invaded the prerogatives of the confederacy," George Washington complained on August 1, "they will laugh
in your face."[4]

Jay responded to Adams's appeal for congressional action by preparing a detailed report on the violations of the peace treaty that he
sent to Congress on October 12, 1786. The secretary dwelt master-
fully on the infractions on both sides, but emphasized the justice of
the British charges by citing a long catalogue of state acts that alleg-
edly violated the terms of the treaty. However one might view the
deviations from the treaty before ratification, he said, the American
deviations preceded those of Great Britain. Therefore American
violations, rather than being justified by British acts, afforded the
British an excuse for their infractions. Jay explained further:

As to the detention of our posts, your secretary thinks that
Britain was not bound to surrender them until we had ratified
the treaty. Congress ratified it 14th January 1786, and Britain

on the 9th April following. From that time to this, the fourth and sixth articles of the treaty have been constantly violated on our part by legislative acts then and still existing and operating. Under such circumstances, it is not a matter of surprise to your secretary that the posts are detained; nor in his opinion would Britain be to blame in continuing to hold them until America shall cease to impede her enjoying every essential right secured to her, and her people and adherents, by the treaty.

Jay proposed that Congress declare the treaties to be "part of the law of the land" and urged the states to repeal all laws "repugnant to the treaty of peace." No state, Jay added, had the right to pass any act for interpreting or construing any clause of a treaty or impede or retard its operation and execution.[5]

Jay followed his October 12 report with an even stronger statement a day later, asserting congressional sovereignty in foreign affairs. In it he reminded Congress that Article IX of the Articles of Confederation expressly conveyed to it the sole and exclusive power of determining peace and war, and of entering treaties and alliances. Therefore, any treaty made, ratified, and published by Congress was binding on the states and their citizens. The state legislatures possessed no authority to pass judgment on the construction or meaning of such treaties; only parties to a treaty had the power to alter, correct, or explain it. "A contrary doctrine," Jay explained, "would not only mitigate against the common and received principles and ideas to this subject, but would prove as ridiculous in practice as it appears irrational in theory; for in that case, the same article of the same treaty may, by law, mean one thing in New Hampshire, another in New York, and neither one nor the other in Georgia." Congress, in March 1787, adopted Jay's report unanimously, resolving that all laws "as may be now existing in any of the States, repugnant to the Treaty of peace, ought to be forthwith repealed." Jay drafted a letter to the states that Congress approved on April 13, in which he repeated his earlier appeal to the states.[6]

The secretary then informed London that Congress acknowledged the violations of the fourth and sixth articles of the peace treaty and had taken measures that it hoped would be effective. In its ratification proclamation, Congress urged the states to comply with the treaty. In Virginia, Patrick Henry disapproved of Jay's circular letter and objected to federal enforcement of treaties. Still in November 1787, the Virginia legislature rescinded its laws against British creditors.[7] Other states did likewise.

*****

What assured the country's continued nonperformance in external affairs was Congress's inability to fulfill its foreign financial obligations. The United States entered and sustained its war for independence on borrowed money, with the obligation to repay its debts with interest at the war's end. But the demands of war always exceeded what Franklin, Adams, and Jay could borrow in Europe. All three diplomats, negotiating in France, Holland, and Spain, respectively, complained of the humiliation of running from court to court in search of funds. Franklin managed to contract two large French loans, the first in July 1782, the second in February 1783. Thereafter Adams negotiated loans with Holland, but persistently complained of the increasing difficulty of borrowing through Dutch bankers. Adams reported to Franklin from The Hague on January 24, 1784: "I find I am here only to be a witness that American credit in this Republic is dead never to rise again, at least until the United States shall all agree upon some plan of revenue, and make it certain that interest and principal will be paid."[8] In all, American diplomats were able to obtain something over ten million dollars in loans from France, Spain and Holland by 1788. Yet powerless to impose taxes on individuals or the states, Congress frequently paid neither principal nor interest on its foreign obligations. Indeed, Adams's later negotiations with Dutch bankers for loans was to obtain funds to pay the interest due on earlier ones.

French officials in the United States pleaded with Congress to take steps that would enable it to meet its financial commitments some time in the future. Louis Guillaume Otto, French charge d'affaires in New York, reminded Congress in November 1785 that the arrears were driving up the country's indebtedness. Month after month, French officials confronted Jay with embarrassing demands that the United States fulfill its financial obligations to both the French government and French citizens who had invested heavily in the American cause. "The Department of Finances," Otto reported to Vergennes, "has never been so destitute as it is at this moment, and one of the Commissioners has assured me that it has nothing more with which to meet current expenses."[9]

The inability of Congress to directly collect taxes caused problems at home as well. The threatened non-payment of soldiers in Philadelphia set off a mutiny in June 1783 that forced Congress to retreat to Princeton, New Jersey, in quest of greater security. In July, Congress, still meeting in Princeton, voted to reduce federal expenditures by discharging all soldiers who enlisted for the duration of the war, with the discharges acting as furloughs until the ratification of the final peace treaty. Daniel Shay's rebellion in Massachusetts captured the country's attention in the late months of 1786. Jay informed Jefferson of the affair on October 27: "A spirit of licentiousness has infected Massachusetts, which appears more formidable than some at first apprehended....A reluctance to taxes, an impatience of Government, a rage for property, and little regard to the means of acquiring it, together with a desire of equality in all things, seem to actuate the mass of those, who are uneasy in their circumstances." The uprising merely reaffirmed the conclusion that the governmental structures of the United States were inadequate. Just as he had earlier forecast, a British consul general reported to London, the necessary funds "for the support of Government & to pay the interest only of [the] public debt" was proving "too great and weighty for these people to bear....Mobs, Tumults, & bodies of men in arms, are now on tiptoe in various parts of this Country! all tending to the Dissolution of, not only what is called the Supreme power (Congress) but to bring into Contempt & disregard, the Legislatures & Governments of several States."[10] Not a few in Europe had been anticipating or desiring the dissolution of the union.

The lack of public funds that sparked the rebellion merely reflected the country's excessive financial obligations at home and abroad. Already in a crisis mood over the failure of the United States in foreign affairs, the country found in the insurrection of Daniel Shays in Massachusetts during the late months of 1786, in Madison's words, a "ripening incident." That state, in an effort to settle its public debt, laid on taxes that exceeded what the public would accept. Shays led the attack on what appeared to be the impositions of the coastal wealthy. The problems of backcountry citizenry, as historian Richard B. Morris explained, "were the fiscal policies of the state, which seemed to discriminate against the yeoman farmer and favor the Eastern businessman." Then, too, there was the matter of freely printed paper money that quickly depreciated. When the state of Massachusetts in 1781 rejected its own currency as legal tender and demanded specie that was in short supply, the western communities were convinced that "the tax burden was being disproportionately shifted upon their shoulders by the commercial interests." And the tax rolls proved it. Several other states, especially Rhode Island, had sought to escape their financial burdens by issuing paper money, thereby threatening the country with inflation and a further loss of credit. As states sought to enforce the collection debts and taxes in specie, they also found themselves confronting similarly outraged debtor farmers.[11]

On the eastern coast, merchants, investors, and almost all other conservative citizens supported the call for a federal government that would stop the states printing of virtually worthless paper money, prevent the erection of intrastate commercial barriers, and create the leverage that would bring about favorable trading conditions abroad.

*****

No less than Adams and Jefferson, members of Continental Congress chafed at the hindrances to American trade embodied in European commercial practices. Not even commercial treaties were a guarantee of equal advantage. Compelled by the mercantilist practices of the age to retreat from the idea of free trade, Americans adopted the principle of the most favored nation. They discovered quickly enough that the most-favored-nation principle assured no privileges in the exchange of goods. Nations in the late 18th century generally treated all nations as equals; most-favored-nation policy, therefore, did not grant favored treatment but merely the right to trade under the same restrictions imposed on others, and all nations protected their own productions with heavy duties on trade. Americans hoped to avoid such unequal practices by insisting on complete reciprocity in all commercial relations. Indeed, all American commercial treaties embodied the principle of reciprocity, but the United States had no power to force the European nations to adopt arrangements that would open all ports to American commerce or relieve the trade of restrictive duties.

"[T]his favoured Nation System," Elbridge Gerry complained to Jefferson in February 1785, "appears to me a System of Cobwebs to catch Flies. [A]ttend to it as it respects Restrictions, prohibitions, and the Carrying Trade, and it is equally distant from a Rule of Reciprocity, which is the only equable and beneficial Rule for

forming Commercial Treaties." Gerry observed accurately that the
United States could protect itself from unequal trade practices only
if Congress had the power to deny other nations the advantages
they enjoyed in American ports. "To obtain reciprocal advantages,"
Monroe agreed, "cannot possibly be the object with other powers
in treating with us, for more than this they now possess." Monroe
wondered whether the United States might negotiate treaties with
one or more European states whereby, in exchange for certain commercial advantages in those countries, it would agree to impose
higher duties on competitors in the American trade. This would
scarcely substitute for reciprocal trade arrangements, but it would
enable the United States to respond effectively to some offending
nations.[12]

What troubled members of Congress even more than the failure
of reciprocity was the loss of the British West Indian trade, the only
pre-Revolutionary trade that yielded a favorable balance. Parliament
had decreed, moreover, that American vessels could not carry rice;
tobacco; pitch; tar; turpentine; oil; and other articles, formerly another major source of remittances, to British ports. British ships
carried off full cargoes from all the Northern ports while American
ships rotted at anchor. Parliament's prohibitive duty on whale oil, designed to reserve the industry for British ships and sailors, was ruin-
ing the New England whaling villages. Merchants excluded from the
British trade resented those who managed to profit from it. Through
two years of independence, the United States failed to develop any
new commercial channels to compensate for that loss. Thus British
vessels so filled the harbor of Charleston, concluded one South
Carolina pamphleteer, that the British enjoyed as much control of
the state's economy as they had before the Revolution. "What makes
the British Monopoly the more mortifying," wrote Madison, "is the
abuse they make of it.... In every point of view indeed the trade of
this Country is in a deplorable Condition."[13]

The American addiction to British goods not only sustained the
adverse commercial relationship but also encouraged Americans to
consume to the limits of their credit. It was this refusal of Americans
to curtail their consumption of British goods, observed Charles Pettit
of Pennsylvania, which invited the treatment they received. "[T]hey
[the British] severally shut the Door of commercial Hospitality
against us," he complained, "while ours being open they enter and
partake with us at their pleasure." London's capacity to legislate

the Republic's commercial relations with Europe was, for some Americans, an unacceptable assault on the nation's sovereignty. The time had come, believed Madison, when the United States had either to meet the British challenge or renounce its claims to a fair profit. "The policy of G.B. (to say nothing of other nations)," he wrote in August, 1785, "has shut against us the channels without which our trade with her must be a losing one; and she has consequently the triumph, as we have the chagrin, of seeing accomplished her prophetic threats, that our independence, should forfeit commercial advantages for which it would not recompence us with any new channels of trade."[14]

In search of some effective power to coerce European powers, James Madison had suggested as early as April 10, 1784, that the states needed to vest Congress for a limited time with the power to ban imports and exports to and from nations not having a treaty of commerce with the United States. Acting on this suggestion, Congress had passed a resolution on April 30, 1784, requesting the states to grant it, "for the term of fifteen years with the power to prohibit any goods[,] wares or merchandize from being imported into or exported from any of the states in vessels belonging to, or navigated by the subjects of any power with whom these states shall not have formed treaties of Commerce."[15]

A congressional committee, appointed to determine the resolution status, reported on October 23, 1786, that Delaware had passed an act in full compliance with the recommendation. Massachusetts, Rhode Island, New York, New Jersey, Virginia, and George had also adopted measures in conformity with the resolution, but restrained their operation until the other states had granted such powers to Congress. Connecticut, Pennsylvania, and Maryland had responded to the resolution, but had fixed a time when Congress could exercise its new powers. South Carolina, New Hampshire, and North Carolina had passed laws that granted Congress the needed authority, but with phraseology that departed from the congressional resolution. It was the failure of these states to comply with the recommendation, the committee complained, that perpetuated the ruinous restrictions on American commerce. In its resolution, the committee recommended that the legislatures of New Hampshire, North Carolina, South Carolina, Connecticut, Pennsylvania, and Maryland, at their next sessions, pass acts that conformed to the April 30, 1784, congressional resolution.[16]

Centralized government with the power to retaliate with commercial restrictions alone seemed capable of terminating Britain's unilateral impositions. Writing from New York in January 1785, Pierse Long argued for nothing less than the congressional control of commerce: "And when it is done I hope it will effectually put a stop to the daring Conduct as Great Britain is pursuing. It is amazing to see the quantity of Vessels in this City from all parts of England now in this Harbour carrying our goods to market, and a delay has so long been made to draw an equitable line of proceeding, I hope very soon there will be an end put to so diabolical a trade."[17] For Madison, Congress alone could exercise effective power over commerce. "If it be necessary to regulate trade at all," he wrote to Monroe, "it surely is necessary to lodge the power, where trade can be regulated with effect, and experience has confirmed what reason foresaw, that it can never be so regulated by the States acting in their separate capacities. They can no more exercise this power separately, than they could separately carry on war, or separately form treaties of alliance or Commerce." Virginian John Landon of Portsmouth observed to Jefferson on December 7, 1785: "We have no body to blame, but ourselves, that our trade is in its present situation; vesting Congress with full powers, and exerting ourselves with a little spirit, would soon remove the embarrassements we now labour under."[18] Rufus King of Massachusetts believed that Britain's impositions on American commerce would in time arouse a spirit of resistance and "not only direct but drive America into a system more advantageous than treaties and alliances with all the world—a system which shall cause her to rely on her own ships and her own marines, and to exclude those of all other nations." James Sullivan speculated to John Adams that additional calamities might compel the United States into the necessity of behaving as one nation.[19]

Throughout 1785, Monroe and other members of Congress continued their earlier efforts to invest that body with the power to regulate the commerce of the United States. Delegates generally favored some obstruction to British shipping, but many still opposed any surrender of state sovereignty to the federal government. British mercantile policy produced its most direct distress in Boston, New York, and Philadelphia: where shippers especially called for the augmentation of congressional power to bring them relief. Many Southerners, however, feared that effective restraints on British shipping would grant New England carriers a virtual monopoly of American ocean-borne commerce. The tobacco states produced a valuable export commodity but purchased their manufactured goods elsewhere. Under the assumption that competition for the American market would assure the highest price for Southern exports and the lowest price for industrial imports, the South favored the opening of American ports to the world. The Northern states, some Southerners feared, would seek a high price for manufactured articles through policies of exclusion. Richard Henry Lee of Virginia believed that the South, through a careful and limited restraint of trade, could avoid major injury to itself. "But it seems to me clearly beyond doubt," he wrote to Madison, "that the giving Congress a power to legislate over the trade of the Union would be dangerous in the extreme to the five Southern or Staple States, whose want of ships & Seamen would expose their freightage & their produce to a most pernicious and destructive Monopoly.... In truth it demands most careful circumspection that the Remedy be not worse than the disease, bad as the last may be."[20] Similarly, Lee reported to Jay in September 1785 that he had little confidence in New England carriers who "might fix a ruinous Monopoly upon the trade & productions of the Staple States." Madison observed to Jefferson in January 1786 that the adversaries of centralized restrictions on British trade "were bitter and illiberal against Congress & the Northern States, beyond example." Some argued that the South might better encourage the British marine.[21]

In spite of Adams's failure to obtain a commercial treaty with Britain, all foreign endeavors under the Confederation were not an unrelieved disaster. In addition to favorable relations with France and the Netherlands, there were commercial treaties with Prussia, Sweden, and Morocco. Morocco in particular had made a special, if unsuccessful effort, to help free American sailors held captive in Algiers. Denmark, Portugal, and Sardinia had expressed interest in a commercial agreement with the United States. And even Russia, as John Paul Jones repeatedly noted, was more supportive of the United States than it had been during the American Revolution. In France, friends of America such as Lafayette were tireless in their efforts to advance American commerce, not only for America's sake but to move the United States out of the British economic orbit and into a mutually advantageous economic partnership with France. There was some limited progress toward this goal as Jefferson attempted to break the monopoly of France's Farmers General in tobacco imports and to open ports in France and the West Indies to American ships.

*****

Yet despite modest advances in relations with Europe, by 1786 the impotence of Congress to protect the general interests of the American people abroad—especially obtaining a commercial treaty with Britain—drove the nation's conservative leadership toward the demand for a new frame of government. The perceived failure of the Confederation to maintain internal order, to meet its financial obligations, to defend its frontiers, and to control interstate commerce contributed to the unrest of American leaders. Granting the urgency of domestic problems, those leaders responsible for the conduct of foreign relations, primarily Jay in New York as secretary for foreign relations and the two principal envoys in Europe—John Adams in the Hague and London, and Thomas Jefferson in Paris— were even more upset with state of America's relations with Europe. "The federal government seems to be as near a crisis as it is possible for it to be," Adams heard from a friend back home in November 1786. "The State governments are weak and selfish enough, and they will of course annihilate the first. Their stubborn dignity will never permit a federal government to exist."[22]

"To be respectable abroad," Jay wrote in July, "it is necessary to be so at home; and that will not be the Case until our public Faith acquires more Confidence and our Government more Strength."[23] No longer for Jay did the answer lie in commercial regulation. Washington agreed that commercial regulation alone would never establish the United States as an equal among nations. "Experience has taught us," he wrote to Jay in August, "that men will not adopt and carry into execution measures best calculated for their own good, without the intervention of a coercive power. I do not conceive that we can exist long as a nation without having lodged somewhere a power, which will pervade the whole Union in as energetic a manner as the authority of the State governments extends over the several States." In November Washington commented to Madison:

No morn ever dawned more favourable than ours did and no day was ever more clouded than the present! Wisdom, & good examples are necessary at this time to rescue the political machine from the impending storm.... Without some alteration in our political creed, the superstructure we have been seven years raising at the expence of much blood and treasure, must fall. We are fast verging to anarchy & confusion!...Thirteen sovereignties pulling against each other, and all tugging at the federal head will soon bring ruin on the whole; whereas a liberal, and energetic Constitution, well guarded, & closely watched, to prevent incroachments, might restore us to that degree of respectability & consequence, to which we had a fair claim, & the brightest prospect of attaining.[24]

Madison had little faith in conventions. He continued to seek whatever revision of the Articles would enable Congress to regulate trade, despite the discouraging knowledge that any revision would require unanimous approval of the states. As late as January 1786, he hoped that some miraculous development would bring the two most reluctant states, Rhode Island and Georgia, into some agreement that would save the Union from perishing from insolvency and commercial strangulation.

Madison reacted favorably to the proposed meeting of commercial commissioners from all the states, scheduled for Annapolis in early September 1786. "I am far from entertaining sanguine expectations for it, and am sensible that it may be viewed in one objectionable light," he admitted to Monroe. "Yet on the whole I cannot disapprove of the experiment, Something it is agreed is necessary to be done, towards the commerce at least of the U.S., and if anything can be done, it seem[s] as likely to result from the proposed meeting, and more likely to result f[rom] the present crisis, than from any other mode or time." Madison was concerned that the states would not send sufficient numbers of delegates, that the delegates who attended would not agree on proposals, or that the states would not ratify the proposals with the required unanimity. "I admit despair of success," he wrote to Jefferson. "It is necessary however that something should be tried & if this be not the best possible expedient, it is the best that could possibly be carried thro' the legislature here. And if the present crisis cannot effect unanimity, from what future concurrences...is it to be expected?"[25]

*****

Although there had been several earlier proposals for a convention to strengthen the Confederation, none of them met with success until the Virginia legislature in January 1786 authorized a panel of delegates to meet with other states to examine common issues, especially commerce. The states would meet "for the purpose of forming such regulations of trade as may be judged necessary to promote the general interest." Virginia's governor, Edmund Randolph, invited the states to send delegates to a convention being held in Annapolis, Maryland, scheduled to meet on the first Monday of September 1786. Jay failed to see how the proposed convention could meet the nation's needs; however, he saw the country experiencing an important, if largely imperceptible, change. Earlier, he had assured Adams privately that his revelations regarding the country's ineffectiveness were disseminating and enforcing the critical conviction that the federal government was incompetent. In his October 1785 letter, he argued that it was the duty of the country's leaders "co-operate in Measures for enlarging and invigorating it."[26]

Now in late January 1786, Jay recommended that Congress communicate Adams's letters to all state executives with an accompanying message "urging the necessity of ordering all the general concerns of the Union, by a stable, well digested system; and to that end of delegating such powers as may be adequate to the great objects of...protecting the Union and of drawing forth and directing its resources, both of wealth and power, as exigencies may require."[27] Next, Jay turned to Washington in March with his concerns. "Experience," he wrote, "has pointed out errors in our national government which call for correction, and which threaten to blast the fruit we expected from our tree of liberty." How to effect the change remained unclear. The Articles of Confederation empowered Congress to make alterations, but only with the approval of the states. Jay placed little faith in Congress and the states; the forthcoming Annapolis Convention seemed too narrowly focused on the federal control of commerce. To him, the country required a general convention to revise the Articles of Confederation.[28]

Some New Englanders were suspicious of the motives behind the proposed Annapolis meeting because it was not called by those who desired the creation of a federal commercial system. In all, nine states elected delegates, of which four chose not to attend—Massachusetts, New Hampshire, Rhode Island, and North Carolina. Thus, only representatives from Virginia, Delaware, Pennsylvania, New Jersey, and New York reached Annapolis. The delegates who attended included Alexander Hamilton and Egbert Benson of New York; Abraham

Clark, William C. Houston, and James Schureman of New Jersey; Tench Coxe from Pennsylvania; George Read, John Dickinson, and Richard Bassett from Delaware; and Edmund Randolph, James Madison, and St. George Tucker from Virginia.

The meeting was brief and concise. The delegates met on September 11, chose John Dickinson chairman, agreed upon a report and adjourned on the 14th. The report, however, was not without significance. In the report of the convention, Hamilton, who had long been an ardent nationalist, acknowledged that several of the commissioners had come to Annapolis with the power to consider a uniform system of commercial relations that might serve the common interests of the states. Those present at Annapolis, more importantly, agreed there were the defects in the government of the United States. In the Address of the Annapolis Convention, Hamilton emphasized "the embarrassments which characterize the present State of our national affairs—foreign and domestic...merited a deliberate and candid discussion, in some mode, which will unite the Sentiments and Councils of all the States."[29] The mode that the meeting adopted was the calling of a convention of delegates from all the states to investigate a plan for correcting the defects of the Articles of Confederation that it might discover. The commissioners, if the states concurred, were to meet at Philadelphia on the second Monday in May 1787, "to devise such further provisions as shall appear to them necessary to render the constitution of the Federal Government adequate to the exigencies of the Union."[30] Copies of the report were dispatched to the legislature of the five states attending the Annapolis meeting as well as to the governors of the other states. Additionally and importantly, a copy was sent to Congress.

Jefferson expressed disappointment over the failure of the Annapolis Convention to produce substantial results because of poor representation. But if the convention produced a full meeting at Philadelphia in May, it could still succeed. "To make us one nation as to foreign concerns, & to keep us distinct in Domestic ones," he instructed Madison, "gives the outline of the proper division of powers between the general & particular governments."[31] For Adams the essential task of the forthcoming Philadelphia Convention was that of restoring an equilibrium in the nation's governmental structure. His political philosophy, he stated simply: "[P]ower is always abused when unlimited and unbalanced." Unchecked government would always become despotic whether the ruling power lay in a monarch, an aristocracy, or the people. Any of these, unless limited by countering power, would become intolerant, oppressive, and tyrannical. Sound and durable government required a distribution of authority that would enable the ambition and power of some to offset the ambition and power of others. Adams wrote:

> The great art of lawgiving consists in balancing the poor against the rich in the legislature, and in constituting the legislative a perfect balance against the executive power, at the same time that no individual or party can become its rival. The essence of a free government consists in an effectual control of rivalries. The executive and the legislative powers are natural rivals; and if each has not an effectual control over the other, the weaker will be the lamb in the paws of the wolf. The nation which will not adopt an equilibrium of power must adopt a despotism. There is no other alternative.[32]

It was the consensus of those at Annapolis that in order for the proposed Constitutional Convention to gain legal or constitutional recognition, it must be endorsed by Congress. Opponents to the proposed conference believed that its supporters wanted to go beyond mere revision of the Articles of Confederation: to cast aside the federal system and replace it with another. Although there was doubt as to what Congress's response would be, its support of the Annapolis report was understood to be crucial. A positive congressional response, however, was by no means assured. The Annapolis delegates, Henry Lee wrote to St. George Tucker, a former delegate, on October 20, 1786, "their conviction of the inadequacy of the present federal government render them particularly zealous to amend and strengthen it. But different opinions prevail as to the mode; some think with the Annapolis meeting, others consider Congress not only the constitutional but the most eligible body to originate and propose necessary amendments to the confederation, and others prefer State conventions for the express purpose, and a congress of deputys, appointed by these conventions with plenipotentiary powers."[33]

Understandably, Congress showed little interest in the Annapolis's proposal to bypass that body and initially tried to bury it in committee on October 11, 1786. There it languished until examples of disaffected yeomen taking matters in their own hands in Massachusetts, Virginia, and other states stirred the conservatives. However, if Shay's rebellion became an issue in the calling of the Constitutional Convention, it was not because of its significance, but because it lent an air of urgency to a projected revision of the Articles of Confederation long under consideration. Shay's rebellion did not greatly affect the long-term behavior of Massachusetts; that state's position on public issues remained well within the norm during the months that led up to the meeting at Philadelphia. Adding to that air of urgency were frontiersmen outraged by stories of Spanish seizures of goods moving down the Mississippi River. Congress belatedly endorsed the calling of the Philadelphia Convention in February 21, 1787, defining it as a convention *"for the sole and express purpose of revising the Articles of Confederation* and reporting to Congress and the several legislatures such alterations and provisions therein."[34] Thereafter the selection of delegates gained momentum.

For Jefferson and Adams, no less than for their associates in America, the Philadelphia Convention loomed as a critical test for the new Republic. Franklin believed the convention's success essential simply because the price of failure would be unacceptable. "Indeed," he wrote to Jefferson in April 1787, "if it does not do Good it must do Harm, as it will show that we have not Wisdom enough among us to govern ourselves; and will strengthen the Opinion of some Political Writers, that popular Governments cannot long support themselves." Monroe expressed his anxieties to Jefferson in July: "The affairs of the federal government are, I believe, in the utmost confusion; the convention is an expedient that will produce a decisive effect. It will either recover us from our present embarrassments or complete our ruin...."[35]

"But whatever may be our situation, whether firmly united under one national government, or split into a number of confederacies, certain it is, that foreign nations will know and view it exactly as it is; and they will act towards us accordingly. If they see that our national government is efficient and well administered, our trade prudently regulated, our militia properly organized and disciplined, our resources and finances discreetly managed, our credit re-established...they will be much more disposed to cultivate our friendship than provide our resentment." It is fitting that these sentiments appeared in Federalist Number 4, among the earliest of the Federalist Papers.[36]

It reflects the all-consuming preoccupation of the American establishment—especially John Jay, the author of this paper—with
the mortal weaknesses of the Articles of Confederation and the
vital need for the new Constitution. Their perceived failure of the
Confederation to maintain internal order, to meet its financial obligations, to defend its frontiers, to control interstate commerce,
and to obtain satisfactory commercial treaties abroad had led to the
Annapolis Convention. Granting the urgency of domestic problems,
those leaders responsible for the conduct of foreign relations—
primarily, Jay in New York as secretary of foreign affairs and the two
principal envoys in Europe: Adams at The Hague and London, and
Jefferson at Paris—were even more upset with the state of America's
relations with Europe.

Chapter 6

EXTERNAL RELATIONS AND THE CONSTITUTION, 1787

Delegates to the Constitutional Convention, who gathered slowly in Philadelphia during May 1787, shared a common concern. The country, they feared, with little exaggeration, was drifting rapidly toward chaos, its external affairs even more disordered than its domestic. In some measure, this widespread perception of national failure reflected the derangement of powers within the state government, permitting unchecked legislatures to pursue policies detrimental to the welfare of their own citizens and to the nation itself. Overwhelmingly, however, the convention delegates attributed the country's weakness at home and disregard abroad to Congress's lack of power in the areas of taxation, commerce, and treaties.

The want of authority to regulate commerce, the delegates were aware, had enabled foreign countries, especially Great Britain, to adopt monopolizing policies injurious to American trade and destructive of American navigation. The same absence of general authority over commerce encouraged states to exercise this power separately, thereby engendering rivalries and retaliatory regulations. This anarchy in the nation's commercial policies, together with the continuing unfavorable trade balances that it assured, drained the country of its metals and furnished pretexts for the substitution of paper money and the postponement of taxes. It also failed to provide for repayment of foreign debts. The delegates were reminded that Congress, because of powerlessness to compel state to comply with the law of nations, could not prevent war. Referring to various state violations of the 1783 treaty of peace, the British consul in New York reflected little respect for the current government. "I am of opinion that the respective States who have violated the treaty," will not follow Congress's recommendation to bring themselves into compliance, he wrote, "which will shew to the world that Congress is not a power competent for Sovereigns to transact business with."[1]

*****

For Jefferson and Adams, no less than for their associates in America, the Philadelphia Convention loomed as a critical test for the new Republic. Benjamin Franklin believed the convention's success essential simply because the price of failure would be unacceptable. "Indeed," he wrote to Jefferson in April 1787, "if it does not do Good it must do Harm, as it will show that we have not Wisdom enough among us to govern ourselves; and will strengthen the Opinion of some Political Writers, that popular Governments cannot long support themselves." Monroe also expressed his anxieties to Jefferson: "The affairs of the federal government are, I believe, in the utmost confusion; the convention is an expedient that will produce a decisive effect. It will either recover us from our present embarrassments or complete our ruin.[2] What mattered in the crisis was the quality of those individuals who would decide the country's future. Adams hoped that the forthcoming convention would "consist of members of such ability, weight, and experience that the result must be beneficial to the United States."[3] Franklin reported to Jefferson that the delegates were men of prudence and of high character.

The delegates gathering in Philadelphia indeed comprised an outstanding body. "If all the Delegates named for this Philadelphia Convention attend," the French chargé d'affaires in New York noted, "there will never have been seen, even in Europe, an Assembly more respectable for the talents, knowledge, disinterest and patriotism of those who compose it." While in Paris, Jefferson deplored the delegates' decision to keep their deliberations secret; he nonetheless regarded them highly. "It is really an assembly of demigods." From London, Adams responded with equal enthusiasm as he saw the convention comprised "heroes, sages and demigods to be sure." More significantly, the delegates were experienced political leaders. Among them were 3 former members of the Stamp Act Congress, 7 who served in the First Continental Congress, 8 who had signed the Declaration of Independence, and 2 who signed the Articles of Confederation. Also present were 2 future presidents,

1 vice president, 2 chief justices of the Supreme Court, 16 who had or would hold state governorships, and 42 who had served in the Continental Congresses.[4]

However talented they were, these delegates and the ones to ratifying conventions were not sufficiently of one mind for their "intent" to be easily discerned by subsequent constitutional scholars or judges. Even the influential James Madison later declared on the floor of Congress in 1796: "Whatever veneration might be entertained for the body of men who formed our Constitution, the sense of that body could never be regarded as the oracular guide in expounding the Constitution."[5] Many troublesome issues in American constitutional law, consequently, received no mention in the Constitution or in the records of the Philadelphia Convention. Treaty-making carries no such burden of inattention.

The founders addressed questions of international affairs with a profound understanding of the European state system and the brilliant 17th- and 18th-century writings that described that system and defined the rules that governed it. For that reason, the principles embodied in the institutions for managing the country's foreign relations had a uniquely timeless quality. Whatever the relative authority that the makers intended for the president and the Senate, they divided responsibility for the nation's external relations to assure decisions that reflected fully the young Republic's rich experience and sound learning.

Two external issues were especially compelling in the call for the Constitutional Convention. Widespread perceptions of national failure reflected the powerlessness of Congress in the areas of commerce and treaties. What further undermined the country's prestige and effectiveness abroad was the determination of the states to violate not only the Treaty of Peace with Britain, but the treaties with France and Holland as well. "Examine...your treaties with foreign powers; those solemn national compacts, whose stipulations each member of the Union was bound to comply with," Charles Pinckney of South Carolina implored the delegates on May 28. "Is there a treaty which some of the States have not infringed?" As a consequence of such conditions, wrote Madison, "the Fedl. authy had ceased to be respected abroad, and dispositions shewn there, particularly in G.B. to take advantage of its imbecility, and to speculate on its approaching downfall."[6] Madison wondered how long other countries would tolerate the treaty violations of the states or how long the weakness of the general government would permit the states so to endanger the peace of the United States.[7]

*****

During the weeks before the Philadelphia Convention opened, the Virginia delegates had perfected a plan of government, known as the Virginia Plan. On May 29, Governor Edmund Randolph presented that plan to the convention. In his introductory statement, he advocated the creation of a government with the power to defend the United States from invasion and control the nation's commerce. To terminate the gross violations of treaties and thereby prevent the states from provoking war, Randolph declared that the national government required the power to punish infractions of treaties or the law of nations. The Virginia resolutions themselves focused only on the two fundamental issues before the convention: the question of national versus state power and the establishment of three separate branches of government.

Historian Merrill Jensen defined the first issue concisely: "The men who wrote the Articles of Confederation created a federal government wherein the state governments retained sovereign power and the central government was their creature." Thus the Articles had enumerated carefully the powers to be exercised by Congress, but the Virginia Plan advocated only that the national legislature "ought to be empowered to enjoy the Legislative Rights vested in Congress by the Confederation & moreover to legislate in all cases to which the separate States are incompetent, or in which the harmony of the United States may be interrupted by the exercise of individual Legislation."[8] The convention quickly agreed without debate that the national legislature would indeed act in all cases where the states were incompetent, but Madison acknowledged his preference for an enumeration of the specific powers to be exercised by the national legislature. It was left for Roger Sherman of Connecticut, on June 6, to suggest what some of those powers should be: defense against foreign danger and internal disputes resulting in force, treaties with foreign countries, regulation of foreign commerce, and the collection of revenue from it.[9]

Meanwhile the convention faced the more exacting task of distributing powers among three branches of government. Under the Articles, all powers of government—legislative, executive, and judicial—were centered in the Congress. The executive committees of Congress in no way established an executive branch; all powers remained in the hands of Congress. Long before the Constitutional Convention met, John Jay, the secretary for foreign affairs, advocated a reorganization of the government that would separate the executive from the legislative functions, assigning to each department those it would be best constituted to perform. Jay wrote to Thomas Jefferson on August 18, 1786: "To vest legislative, judicial, and executive powers in one and the same body of men, and that, too, in a body daily changing its members, can never be wise. In my opinion, these three great departments of sovereignty should be forever separated, and so distributed as to serve as checks on each other." The Virginia Plan, having proposed a government of three branches, asked in its seventh provision for the creation of a national executive, to be chosen by the national legislature, with authority to execute the national laws and "to enjoy the Executive rights vested in Congress by the Confederation."[10] When the convention, on June 1, turned to the seventh provision, it readily accepted the notion of a national executive but rejected the prescription that the United States, in the British tradition, would consign all powers over foreign affairs, formerly embodied in Congress, to the national executive unless the convention were prepared to limit those powers by a strict definition.

Several leading delegates to the convention now addressed the question of executive leadership in external affairs. Charles Pinckney opened the discussion by advocating a vigorous executive but feared that "the Executive powers of (the existing) Congress might extend to peace & war &c which would render the Executive a Monarchy, of the worst kind, to wit an elective one."[11] John Rutledge, also from South Carolina, added that he favored a single executive, "tho' he was not for giving him the power of war and peace." James Wilson of Pennsylvania argued that a single executive alone could give the office the necessary despatch and responsibility. He did not, however, "consider the Prerogatives of the British Monarch as a proper guide in defining the Executive powers. Some of these prerogatives were of a Legislative nature. Among others that of war & peace &c. The only powers he conceived strictly Executive were those of executing the laws, and appointing officers, not (appertaining to and) appointed by the Legislature." William Pierce of Georgia, in his notes of the convention, recorded another of Wilson's observations: "Making peace and war are generally determined by Writers on the Law of Nations to be legislative powers."[12]

When Randolph retorted that a single executive would lead to monarchy, Madison observed that the issue of a single or plural executive was less important than determining the extent of the executive authority. In remarks recorded by Rufus King of Massachusetts, Madison agreed with Wilson that executive powers "do not include the Rights of war & peace &c, but the powers shd. be confined and defined—if large we shall have the Evils of elective Monarchies." Madison then moved to strike out the clause in the seventh provision relating to executive powers and to substitute the words "that a national Executive ought to be instituted with power to carry into effect, the national laws, to appoint to offices in cases not otherwise provided for, and to execute such other powers as may from time to time be delegated by the national Legislature." Pinckney offered an amendment to exclude legislative or judiciary powers from those that the national legislature might delegate to the executive. Even then, Pinckney believed that Madison's motion gave the executive too much authority; he declared that the national executive should have only the power "to carry into effect the national laws." The convention accepted Pinckney's argument that the legislature might delegate improper powers to the executive. Thus the convention amended the resolution proposed by the Virginia Plan to limit the executive power to that of executing the national laws and appointing "to offices in cases not otherwise provided for."[13]

Alexander Hamilton's plan of June 18 was the first presented to the Constitutional Convention that addressed explicitly the question of allocating power between the executive and legislative branches on the issue of negotiating treaties. For Hamilton, peace and war were not executive prerogatives. To the Senate he would give the sole power "of declaring war, the power of advising and approving all Treaties, the power of approving or rejecting all appointments of officers except the heads or chiefs of the departments of Finance War and foreign affairs." To the supreme executive Hamilton would extend the power to execute all laws passed by the legislature, "to have with the advice and approbation of the Senate the power of making all treaties; to have the sole appointment of the heads or chief officers of the departments of Finance, War and Foreign Affairs; to have the nomination of all other officers (Ambassadors to foreign Nations included) subject to the approbation or rejection of the Senate."[14] Hamilton offered no resolution for a vote. Throughout the following month, no delegate made any effort to alter the limited definition of executive power that the convention had adopted on June 1. By late July, the convention had hammered out compromises on many critical issues; the broad outlines of the new federal system were already clear. Still the convention had made no decisions about the conduct of foreign affairs.

On July 23 the Constitutional Convention assigned to a Committee of Detail, consisting of five members, the task of "reporting a Constitution conformably to the Proceedings" of the convention. Three days later, the convention adjourned to permit the committee to complete its assignment. On August 6 the Committee of Detail submitted its report to the convention. During the final six weeks of debate, the convention reconsidered and modified certain clauses in the report but found the distribution of powers over external affairs generally satisfactory. For the Committee of Detail, the treaty-making power was neither wholly legislative nor wholly executive. For that reason, it refused to add the authority to make treaties to the list of powers granted to the legislative branch. It regarded such power, like the authority to make war, as essentially a legislative power, but one not to be given to Congress as a whole. The treaty-making power, believed the committee, belonged properly to the Senate because of its smaller size, its greater ability to maintain secrecy, and its presumed invulnerability to hysteria and the demands of special interests. The Articles of Confederation had assigned the authority both to appoint ambassadors to foreign countries and to receive ambassadors from abroad to Congress. The Committee of Detail divided these two powers. Because envoys sent abroad spoke for the nation, the committee vested the important power to appoint ambassadors to the Senate; to the executive it assigned the ceremonial function of receiving ambassadors from foreign countries.[15]

Thus the article in the draft constitution detailing the powers of the Senate began: "The Senate of the United States shall have the power to make treaties, and to appoint Ambassadors, and Judges of the supreme Court." The president did not share these powers. The committee did include in its draft the following sentence: "The Executive Power of the United States shall be vested in a single person," designated the president. But the executive authority did not include the important powers to make war, make treaties, or appoint ambassadors; these powers the committee assigned specifically to legislative bodies.[16] Clearly the Committee of Detail was no more convinced than the convention itself that national leaders would always display wisdom in the conduct of the country's external relations; it sought, therefore, to maximize the constraints on the exercise of the treaty-making as well as the war-making powers.

Delegates soon questioned the decision of the Committee of Detail to grant the treaty-making and appointment powers exclusively to the Senate by a simple majority vote. As early as June 26, James Wilson had argued that the upper house of the national legislature would probably be the depository of the powers relating to treaties and predicted that the Senate, because of its stability, would be especially "respectable in the eyes of foreign nations" and thus would create the confidence necessary for successful negotiations."[17] With that prospect, the Committee of Detail agreed. But the great compromise of July 16 that terminated the debate over representation had granted each state equal voting power in the Senate, while the representation in the House of Representatives would be proportional to population. This arrangement satisfied the small states, which wanted all representation by states, as well as the larger states, led by Virginia, which favored representation in both houses by population. In cases that required the concurrence of both houses, the balance between the large and small states seemed assured. With that compromise, however, Senate control of the treaty-making power seemed to assign disproportionate authority to the smaller states. There were many issues touching the economic interests of the states, especially matters of commerce, which would be involved in treaty negotiations. On August 15, George Mason of Virginia warned that the Senate, through its treaty-making power, might, without legislative sanction, concede territories in the West that belonged to Virginia. He denounced the Senate's monopoly of the critical power to make treaties. The Senate, he declared, could sell the whole country by means of treaties. In an appeal to the South, he added: "If Spain should possess herself of Georgia therefore the Senate might by treaty dismember the Union."[18] Elbridge Gerry of Massachusetts, determined to protect New England's fishing interests from Senate action, declared on September 7: "In Treaties of peace the dearest interests will be at stake, as the fisheries, territories &c." Sharing that fear of the Senate, Wilson proposed an amendment to the treaty clause that would add after the word "Senate" the words "and House of Representatives."[19]

Meanwhile the disagreement over Senate control of treaty-making raised the question of the two-thirds rule for the approval of treaties. This question did not pit the large states against the small, but the eastern states, with their maritime and commercial interests, against the southern states with their plantation and western interests. Only the provision in the Articles of Confederation that treaties required the approval of nine states in Congress had enabled the five southern states to eliminate the proposed treaty with Spain that would have denied the free navigation of the Mississippi River for 25 years. To southern delegates, it seemed clear that the protection of their regional interests required a two-thirds vote for the approval of treaties. Without that provision, Mason warned, the South could not protect itself from injury by commercial treaties.[20] Whereas the Committee of Detail, by favoring the approval of treaties by majority vote, had offered no special guarantees to the South on the matter of treaties, it had done so on three other sectional issues. It had proposed an absolute ban on federal interference in the slave trade, an absolute prohibition of export duties, and a requirement that navigation acts receive a two-thirds vote in each house. On August 21, the convention voted to ban export taxes, but so bitter was the sectional debate on the other two issues that the convention ultimately sent them to a special committee.

*****

For some convention delegates, then, a possible answer to the sectional conflict of interest lay in compelling the Senate to share the treaty-making power with the executive. As early as August 15, John Francis Mercer of Maryland argued that the Senate should have no power over treaties at all. "This power," he said, "belonged to the Executive department; adding that Treaties would not be final so as to alter the laws of the land, till ratified by legislative authority. This was the case of Treaties in Great Britain; particularly the late Treaty of Commerce with France."[21] Mercer's claim for executive authority over treaty-making received no endorsement from other members of the convention. During the debates of August 23 on treaty-making, Edmund Randolph observed that no one liked the committee's decision to assign the power over treaties to a Senate majority. At the same time it was apparent to the convention that treaty-making entailed some purely executive functions. Madison, in his own words, "observed that the Senate represented the States alone, and that for this as well as other obvious reasons it was proper that the President should be an agent in Treaties." Later that day Madison favored an arrangement that would allow "the President &

Senate to make Treaties eventual and of Alliance for limited terms—and requiring the concurrence of the whole Legislature in other Treaties."[22] In large measure, Madison returned to the relationship between Congress and the secretary for foreign affairs under the Articles of Confederation. Gouverneur Morris of Pennsylvania followed by questioning the Senate's exclusive role in treaty-making. He offered an amendment that read: "The Senate shall have the power to treat with foreign nations, but no Treaty shall be binding on the United States which is not ratified by a law."[23] This proposal would necessarily make the House of Representatives a partner in the approval of any treaty.

On August 31, the convention referred the burgeoning sectional questions, including that of treaty-making, to the so-called "grand" committee formed to deal with "such parts of the Constitution as have been postponed, and such parts of Reports as have not been acted on."[24] The southern states, with some northern support, had sustained the principle that navigation acts should require a two-thirds vote in both houses. At the same time, abolitionist delegates from the North insisted on the total abolition of the slave trade. As part of a sectional compromise that eliminated the two-thirds vote from navigation laws, the convention voted to permit the importation of slaves until 1808.[25] When on August 29 the convention dropped the recommendation of the Committee of Detail for a two-thirds vote on navigation acts, thus breaking the South's veto power over United States commercial policy, southern delegates argued that they deserved further compensation elsewhere. The new Committee on Postponed Parts responded by adopting a two-thirds rule on treaty-making. The committee's draft, presented on September 4, read as follows:

> The President by and with the advice and Consent of the Senate, shall have power to make Treaties; and he shall nominate and by and with the advice and consent of the Senate shall appoint ambassadors and other public Ministers, Judges of the Supreme Court, and all other Officers of the U[nited] S[tates], whose appointments are not otherwise herein provided for. But no Treaty shall be made without the consent of two thirds of the members present.[26]

This provision excluded the House of Representatives from the treaty-making process, but it introduced four additions or alterations of major importance. It assigned a role to the president, added the phrase "advice and consent of the Senate," provided a common procedure for all appointments, and granted the president the sole power to nominate ambassadors and other public ministers. The new phraseology limited the Senate's role to the approval or rejection of the executive's nominees.

Nowhere did the treaty clause give the president any exclusive right to propose a course of action in foreign affairs. Moreover, the convention called for the advice and consent of the Senate as an organized body, not for the advice of its individual members. The American tradition as it had developed under the Articles of Confederation had assumed that the legislature possessed the authority to determine the objectives in any treaty negotiation. Policy matters, at the beginning no less than at the end, were to reflect the collaboration of the legislature with the executive officers charged by Congress to conduct the actual negotiation. Madison, as a member of the Committee on Postponed Parts, was probably responsible for the inclusion of the phrase "advice and consent." Hamilton had sent Madison a plan of government in which he dealt with the role of the president in the following terms:

> All treaties, conventions and agreements with foreign nations shall be made by him, by and with the advice and consent of the Senate. He shall have ... the nomination; and by and with the Consent of the Senate, the appointment of all other officers to be appointed under the authority of the United States, except such for whom different provision is made by this Constitution.

Whether or not Hamilton's plan reached Madison before the deliberations of the Committee on Postponed Parts, Madison had available Hamilton's remarks of June 18 in which he declared that the executive shall "have with the advice and approbation of the Senate the power of making all treaties."[27]

During the final debate over the treaty power, Madison moved to exempt treaties of peace from the two-thirds rule, arguing that such treaties should face less obstruction than other treaties. The convention accepted Madison's motion temporarily. Madison then moved, as he recorded in his own words, "to authorize a concurrence of two thirds of the Senate to make treaties of peace, without the concurrence of the President."[28] The president, Madison feared, would necessarily derive so much power and importance from a state of war that he might be tempted, if so authorized, to forestall a treaty of peace. Pierce Butler of South Carolina seconded Madison's motion "as a necessary security against ambitious & corrupt Presidents." Nathaniel Gorham of Massachusetts believed this restriction on presidential authority unnecessary inasmuch as the means for carrying on a war would be in the hands of the legislature, not the president. Congress, with the power of the purse, could always terminate an unwanted or unneeded war. Accepting that argument, Gouverneur Morris now advocated the exception of treaties of peace from the two-thirds rule. If a majority of the Senate favored peace, it would terminate any war merely by refusing to vote supplies. Morris believed, moreover, that any peace treaty should have the concurrence of the president.[29] The convention voted down Madison's motion, eight to three, as an unnecessary infringement on the principle of joint executive-senatorial control of the treaty-making process. The convention now reconsidered Madison's motion to exempt peace treaties from the two-thirds rule, adopted earlier by a unanimous vote. After a last-minute flurry of proposals to modify the treaty power, the convention, on September 8, struck down Madison's motion on peace treaties. Again the decision of the Committee on Postponed Parts emerged triumphant.

If the advise-and-consent clause of the Constitution reflected a deep distrust of executive power, the convention failed to establish any procedure whereby the president would seek or receive the advice and consent of the Senate. The debates in the ratifying conventions, which began in late 1787 and continued through 1788, quickly demonstrated the infeasibility of any such procedure. Those who defended the Constitution stressed the primacy of the executive in treaty negotiations. In Britain no less than other European countries, the king had sole authority to make treaties. When Parliament discussed the provisions of a treaty, it did so not to confirm but to make alterations in the system that the treaty affected. Foreign powers regarded an English treaty binding without the approval of Parliament unless the treaty itself called for parliamentary action.[30] To perform effectively in the international arena, the United States likewise required a chief executive with the authority to conduct the nation's diplomacy. William R. Davis explained to the North Carolina Convention that treaty-making, as an executive function, "has not only been grounded on the necessity and reason arising from that degree of secrecy, design, and despatch, which is always necessary in negotiations between nations, but to prevent their being impeded, or carried into effect, by the violence, animosity, and heat of parties, which too often infect numerous bodies."[31] Successful negotiations, declared John Pringle of South Carolina, "must be conducted with despatch and secrecy not to be expected in larger assemblies." For Charles Cotesworth Pinckney of South Carolina, the president, as the ostensible head of the Union, of necessity possessed the authority to propose treaties.[32]

Still, even those who recognized the essential role of the executive in treaty-making emphasized the importance of safeguards against excessive executive authority. Charles Pinckney assured the South Carolina Convention that the president could neither appoint to office nor enter into any treaty without the concurrence of the Senate. So great was the fear of executive power, asserted William Davie, that the Philadelphia Convention was compelled to grant approval authority over treaties to the Senate. Pierce Butler reminded a British relative that the U.S. Constitution, in placing restraints on the president's treaty-making authority, had pointedly departed from British precedent.[33] Charles Cotesworth Pinckney found little comfort in even those restraints. The British king, concerned with his country's welfare and unable to leave it, would always negotiate wisely. "But the situation of a President," he warned, "would be very different from that of a king: he might withdraw himself from the United States, so that the states could receive no advantage from his responsibility...; and he might receive a bribe which would enable him to live in greater splendor in another country than his own; and when out of office, he was no more interested in the prosperity of his country than any other patriotic citizen."[34] Hamilton clarified his continuing distrust of executive power in similar terms:

> However proper or safe it may be in governments where the executive magistrate is an hereditary monarch, to commit to him the entire power of making treaties, it would be utterly unsafe and improper to entrust that power to an elective magistrate of four years duration,... The history of human conduct does not warrant that exalted opinion of human virtue which would make it wise in a nation to commit interests of so delicate and momentous a kind as those which concern its intercourse with the rest of the world to the sole disposal of a magistrate,

created and circumstanced, as would be a president of the United States.[35]

*****

If those who defended the Constitution found the Senate's role in treaty-making indispensable, opponents denounced the power that the Constitution conveyed to the Senate. For them it appeared dangerous, even incongruous, to place the power over treaties in 10 men, two-thirds of a Senate quorum. What made that power especially unacceptable was the constitutional provision that "all treaties made, or which shall be made, under the authority of the United States, shall be the supreme law of the land." To its critics, the Constitution had simply granted too much authority to the Senate. "Is there not," asked Richard Henry Lee of Virginia, "a most formidable combination of power thus created in a few?"[36] "How unsafe we are," warned one North Carolina critic, "when we have no power of bringing [the Senate] to an account....Our lives and property are in the hands of eight or nine men." A New York Convention delegate added, "The Senate, as they are now constituted, have little or no check on them. Indeed, sir, too much is put into their hands."[37] Even Charles Pinckney feared that the treaty-making procedure "destroyed that responsibility which the Constitution should have been careful to establish."[38]

At least, Governor Thomas Johnston assured the North Carolina Convention, the Senate could not make a treaty without the concurrence of the president. For opponents of the Constitution, this was no guarantee at all. In responding to Governor Johnston, Samuel Spencer denied that the president could prevail against the Senate in an argument over treaties; the powers of appointment and impeachment alone would give the Senate an overbearing and uncontrollable influence over the president, one incompatible with the safety of the country.[39] What troubled Judge Pendleton of South Carolina was the country's inability to hold the president responsible for a bad treaty that he had negotiated under the advice of the Senate. Through their power over treaties, warned George Mason, the president and the Senate together possessed the power to repeal state laws and endanger the rights and liberties of the people. Elbridge Gerry doubted that the treaty-making power offered the country any security against either the president or the Senate.[40]

Patrick Henry of Virginia shared such fears. With their paramount power, he declared, the president and the Senate could make any treaty they chose. Certainly the House of Representatives had no authority to block them. "You prostrate your rights to the President and Senate," declared Henry.[41] For Mason, Henry, and other critics, the country's only defense against a bad treaty lay in an amendment that would place treaties under a majority of both houses of Congress.[42]

For the defenders of the Constitution, the legislative capacity of the House of Representatives as well as the authority of the president adequately checked the power of the Senate. James Wilson, who dominated the Pennsylvania Convention, asked his fellow Pennsylvanians to entrust the treaty-making process to limitations embodied in the Constitution. "I am not a blind admirer of this system," Wilson acknowledged. "Some of the power of the senators are not with me the favorite parts of it, but as they stand connected with other parts, there is still security against the efforts of that body." What appeared improper were the special powers the Senate received in trying impeachments and, with the concurrence of the president, over treaties and appointments. But Wilson reminded the Pennsylvania Convention that "in the exercise of every one of them, the Senate stands controlled; if it is that monster which it [is] said to be, it can only show its teeth, it is unable to bite or devour.... The Senate can make no treaties; they can approve of none unless the President of the United States lay it before them."[43] George Nicholas of Virginia asserted that the president indeed offered security against a bad treaty. "Will he not injure himself," Nicholas asked, "if he injures the states, by concurring in an injurious treaty?" In no way, he declared, could the president and Senate make treaties repugnant to the spirit of the Constitution or inconsistent with their delegated powers. Edmund Randolph added that under no circumstances would the president and the Senate ignore the nation's interests or adverse public opinion. The president and the Senate, after all, were responsible to their constituents. If they abused their trust, declared John Rutledge of South Carolina, the people would soon find ways to punish them.[44]

Everywhere, proponents of the Constitution argued that treaties of the United States, no less than those of other powers, must be the supreme law of the land. They noted that Blackstone, in his *Commentaries*, not only acknowledged the king's prerogatives in making treaties but also insisted that a treaty, once made, was binding on the whole community. "Whatever contracts, therefore, he engages in," wrote Blackstone, "no other power in the kingdom can legally delay, resist, or annul."[45] Proponents noted as well that Emmerich de Vattel, the famed author of *Law of Nations,* agreed. "There would be no more security, no longer any commerce between mankind," wrote Vattel, "did they not believe themselves obliged to preserve their faith, and to keep their word. Nations, and their conductors, ought, then, to keep their promises and their treaties inviolable." Burlamaqui, another renowned writer on international affairs, declared that "two sovereigns, who enter into a treaty, impose, by such treaty, an obligation on their subjects to conform to it, and in no manner to contravene it."[46]

In acknowledging the supremacy of treaties the Constitutional Convention did not break with the past; even under the Articles of Confederation, treaties were presumed to be the law of the land whether Congress had the power to enforce them or not. Because Congress had failed to enforce the Treaty of Peace, observed William Davie, the British had "refused to deliver up several important posts within the territories of the United States, and still held them, to our shame and disgrace." Only the adoption of the Constitution, George Nicholas told the Virginia Convention, would give the United States any chance of gaining those posts.[47]

Without the enforcement of treaties, said the Constitution's defenders, the United States would never establish its rightful prestige among the nations of the world. "Shall we not," asked Charles Cotesworth Pinckney, "be stigmatized as a faithless, unworthy people, if each member of the Union may, with impunity, violate the engagements entered into by the federal government? Who will confide in us? Who will treat with us if our practice should be conformable to this doctrine?" No government would negotiate a treaty with another that refused to acknowledge the superiority of treaties to local law. "Establish once such a doctrine," warned David Ramsey of South Carolina, "and where will you find ambassadors? If gentlemen had been in the situation of receiving similar information with himself, they would have heard letters read from our ambassadors abroad, in which loud complaints were made that America had become faithless and dishonest."[48] Proponents of the Constitution warned the critics that non-enforcement of treaties, if continued, could endanger the country's peace no less than its diplomacy and its reputation. To counteract a treaty with a local law, said Madison, "would bring on the Union the just charge of national perfidy, and involve us in war." Only by making treaties the supreme law of the land, observed Pinckney, would the United States "avoid the disputes, the tumults, the frequent wars, we must inevitably be engaged in, if we violate treaties." Francis Corbin of Virginia pointed to the resulting danger "if a small part of the community could drag the whole confederacy into war." William Davie added that the "due observance of treaties makes nations more friendly to each other, and is the only means of rendering less frequent those mutual hostilities which tend to depopulate and ruin contending nations.[49]

*****

In defending the work of the Philadelphia Convention, delegates to the state conventions admitted readily that the treaty-making provisions of the Constitution were a compromise; they agreed only that it was the best available. Charles Cotesworth Pinckney summarized the consensus of the majorities. The power to make treaties, he said, "must necessarily be lodged somewhere: political caution and republican jealousy rendered it improper for us to vest it in the President alone; the nature of negotiation, and the frequent recess of the House of Representatives, render that body an improper depository of this prerogative. The President and Senate joined were, therefore, after much deliberation, deemed the most eligible corps in whom we could with safety vest the diplomatic authority of the Union."[50] Hamilton believed the balance between the executive and legislative branches so complex and so skillfully contrived that it was scarcely possible that "an impolitic or wicked measure should pass the scrutiny with success." Francis Corbin reminded the Virginia Convention that the entire system of treaty-making steered "with admirable dexterity between the two extremes, neither leaving it to the executive, as in most other governments, nor to the legislative, which would too much retard such negotiation."[51] For proponents of the Constitution, the treaty-making power had been well placed in the president and the Senate.

Treaties required the concurrence of other countries. They were made, at least in theory, between equal parties, each side making half the bargain. It was because they demanded compromise and accommodation that they required the utmost secrecy as well. "Treaties," explained James Wilson, "...are truly contracts, or compacts, between the different states, nations, or princes, who find it convenient or necessary to enter into them." Treaty negotiations could not be placed in a public body, especially in time of war, because it would be improper to reveal such negotiations to many people. "For my part," added Wilson, "I am not an advocate for secrecy in transactions relating to the public; not generally even in forming treaties, because I think that the history of the diplomatic corps will evince, even in that great department of politics, the truth of an old adage, that 'honesty is the best policy,' and this is the conduct of the most able negotiators; yet sometimes secrecy may be necessary, and therefore it becomes an argument against committing the knowledge of these transactions to too many persons."[52] Madison agreed that negotiations, to be successful, had also to be confidential. "The policy of not divulging the most important transactions, and negotiations of nations, such as those which relate to war-like arrangements and treaties," said Madison, "is universally admitted."

If negotiations required secrecy, they required full information as well. For that reason, warned James Iredell, the future success of United States treaty-making would rest in large measure in the accuracy and completeness of the president's communications with the Senate. It was unacceptable, he declared, for a president not to give the Senate full information or to conceal "important intelligence which he ought to have communicated, and by that means induced them to enter into measures injurious to their country, and which they would not have consented to had the true state of things been disclosed to them."[53]

Throughout the debates on the Constitution, its defenders argued that the existence of any power presented the possibilities for its abuse. John Marshall reminded doubters in the Virginia Convention that the Constitution could not provide good men to fill all positions of authority in the U.S. government. It was equally true, he added, that the people could not exercise the powers of government themselves. Therefore, he continued, "You must trust to agents. If so, will you dispute giving them the power of acting for you, from an existing possibility that they may abuse it? As long as it is impossible for you to transact your business in person, if you repose no confidence in delegates, because there is a possibility of their abusing it, you can have no government; for the power of doing good is inseparable from that of doing some evil."[54] If the Constitution itself could not protect the country against poor leaders, erroneous ideas, inadequate information, or other evils, then the ultimate responsibility for the performance of government lay with the people. They alone were responsible for the quality of the nation's leaders. If states were negligent in their selection of senators, the fault would be theirs, not that of the Constitution. Thus the treaty-making power would serve the interests of the United States only in accordance with the circumspection of the nation's citizens.[55]

*****

The Philadelphia Constitutional Convention spent almost four months in drafting the United States' new Constitution; it spent scarcely three days on the provisions controlling foreign affairs. Still it managed to embody in the document the accumulated experience of the young Republic. Article I answered the perennial pleas of those who advocated the centralized control of the nation's commerce. In granting Congress the power to regulate foreign commerce, it declared that no state, without the consent of Congress, could lay any imposts or duties on imports or exports; nor could it lay tonnage dues on foreign ships. At the same time, the new frame of government provided Congress with the necessary powers to retaliate against nations that might impose on the United States the power to lay and collect taxes, to establish and maintain an army and navy, and to provide for the common defense. Second, the Constitution defended the nation against state laws that might embarrass its external relations. Article VI declared: "This Constitution and the laws of the United States which shall be made in pursuance thereof and all treaties made, or which shall be made, under the authority of the United States, shall be the supreme law of the land...." The Constitution declared, additionally, that no state could keep troops or ships of war in time of peace, or enter into any agreement or compact with a foreign power. Finally, Article II sustained the traditional executive authority over the country's external relations. It declared the President commander in chief of the army and navy with the added authority to make treaties with the advice and consent of the Senate, provided that two-thirds of the members present concurred. It also assigned the president the responsibility to appoint and receive ambassadors and other public ministers and with it exclusive control of the recognition of foreign governments.

Ultimately, however, sound policy-making would reflect qualities of mind, not structure or procedure. Nothing in the Constitution could assure performance in the country's external relations that embodied the highest wisdom of the American people. Even the early Republic opinions were scarcely uniform, and the most astute perceptions of international trends and national interests did not necessarily lodge in any single individual, group, or branch of government. National leaders faced little intellectual challenge from their followers, and they would, in general, be unreceptive to the views of others. The relationship between national policy and democratic procedures would remain elusive. In distributing the power to manage the country's treaty-making between the president and the Senate, the Constitutional Convention sought to compel the sharing of intelligence as well as power. Whether through time the Senate could sustain any measure of influence over executive formulation of foreign policy was always doubtful. Yet any procedure that ignored the Senate would deny the executive the full range of that body's learning and diminish national support for policy in like measure. Such avoidance of the clear intent of the framers, therefore, would hardly serve the country's interests; for the Constitution, as a frame of government and nothing more, could guarantee no national performance in treaty-making more successful than the wisdom of those in power would permit.

Chapter 7

THE RATIFICATION DEBATE: HOW IMPORTANT IS FOREIGN POLICY?

On September 17, 1787, the Constitutional Convention convened for the last time in Independence Hall, Philadelphia. Of the initial 55 members, 38 were present; the others had left to either resume other tasks or to exhibit their displeasure with the emerging document. As Secretary William Jackson read the engrossed document for the last time, few, if any, were totally pleased with the frame of government they were about to propose to the American people. It was basically a bundle of compromises preconceived by no one. For the moment, they could suppress their misgivings because they alone knew what difficulties they had surmounted to produce the concededly imperfect design of government. The reading completed, Benjamin Franklin addressed the signers to urge unanimous agreement. As George Washington acknowledged, the Constitution could not satisfy the concerns of all, but he concluded that the document was "liable to as few exceptions as could reasonably have been expected." Still, three refused to sign—Elbridge Gerry of Massachusetts, Edmund Randolph and George Mason of Virginia. After fixing the procedure for ratification, Washington noted in his diary that members of the Convention "adjourned to the City Tavern, dined together, and took a cordial leave of each other."[1]

It had been decided that the proposed Constitution would be submitted to Congress with the recommendation that state conventions, made up of delegates elected by the people, would ratify the document. As soon as nine states voted affirmatively, ratification would be complete, and new government would be elected. On September 28, Congress voted unanimously to submit the Constitution to the states for action. "This apparent unanimity," George Washington informed James Madison, "will have its effect."[2] The ratification struggle moved on to the states.

*****

Essentially the debates on ratification of the U.S. Constitution turned on two competing conceptions of the external world and the presumed requirements for successful coexistence with it. Was the international environment so dangerous and the country's interests so extended that only the powers that the Constitution conveyed to the general government would enable the Republic to guarantee its security and well-being from foreign encroachment? Federalists contended no less. For them, the United States would survive, if at all, by reentering the game of world politics with a strong hand. The record of external failure under the Articles of Confederation had clarified the need for a new frame of government. That government, complained one critic, "exposed us to ruin and distress at home and disgrace abroad. At the peace...America held a most elevated rank among the powers of the earth; but how [have] the mighty fallen! disgraced have we rendered ourselves abroad and ruined at home."[3] Another commentator admonished his readers in the *Pennsylvania Gazette* (Philadelphia): "Listen to the insults that are offered to the American name and character in every court in Europe." Daniel Clymer asserted before the Pennsylvania Assembly that the Articles of Confederation had brought on the country "the contempt of every surrounding tribe and the reproach and obloquy of every nation." One disillusioned observer beheld the American name "insulted and despised by all the world!"[4]

For Federalists, then, the evidences of national decline were universal. Everywhere, they complained, other nations took advantage of America's imbecility. The fur trade had gone to Canada. British garrisons continued to hold the forts along the northern frontier, largely because Congress still failed to obtain the full compliance of the states with the Treaty of Peace. Charles Cotesworth Pinckney complained of such weakness in the South Carolina ratifying convention: "Inquire of our delegates to Congress if all the despatches from your public ministers are not filled with lamentations of the imbecility of Congress; and whether foreign nations do not declare they can have no confidence in our government, because it has not power to enforce obedience to treaties."[5] Public and private finances were in extreme disorder. Congress's perennial failure to requisition adequate funding from the states had driven it to the expedient of negotiating new loans in Europe both to pay interest on the foreign debt and to support the civil government at home. Unpaid debts had almost demolished the country's credit in Europe. Alexander Hamilton believed it strange that anyone could deny the defects in the Articles of Confederation and the need for a more efficient govermnent.[6]

Far more dramatic perhaps were the descriptions of the distress that prevailed in the cities. Shipyards were quiet while foreign flags flew triumphantly on the masts of the ships that crowded the nation's harbors. "Look at the melancholy countenances of our mechanics...without employment," cried one Pennsylvania Federalist. "See our ships rotting in our harbors, or excluded from nearly all of the ports of the world."[7] In New York, reported the *Newport Herald* in October 1787, "there are now sixty ships, of which fifty-five are British."[8] Industrial productions continued to decrease in value. Instead of transporting American goods, carriers flooded the market with the gewgaws of Europe. Without some change, warned the *Newport Herald*, "the Northern States will soon be depopulated and dwindle into poverty, while the Southern ones will become silk worms to toil and labor for Europe."[9] Clearly, the problem lay in the powerlessness of American shippers to penetrate foreign markets. "Is there an English, or a French, or a Spanish island or port in the West Indies," John Jay complained, "to which an American vessel can carry a cargo of flour for sale? Not one. The Algerines exclude us from the Mediterranean, and adjacent countries; and we are neither able to purchase, nor to command the free use of those seas." Another observer, writing in the *New Haven Gazette*, invited his readers to view "that indigent and begging situation to which our commerce is reduced in every part of the globe. Where is the port worth visiting, from whence we are not utterly excluded, or loaded with duties and customs sufficient to absorb the whole?"[10]

For Federalist leaders, such obvious weakness in external affairs necessarily exposed the Republic to more and more violent assaults on its political and territorial integrity. The *Boston Independent Chronicle* observed flatly that the United States, without a national government, "would soon become a prey to the nations of the earth." Unfortunately the European powers, all unfriendly to the United States, had noted the country's divisions. "If we continue so," Oliver

Ellsworth warned the Connecticut ratifying convention, "how easy it is for them to canton us out among them, as they did the Kingdom of Poland.[11] Hostile nations, he said, could easily sweep off a number of separate states, one by one. Hugh Williamson, the North Carolina Federalist, noted the country's lack of defenses and the dangers it posed. The United States, he observed in *The State Gazette of North Carolina,* had some five hundred troops scattered along the Ohio River to protect frontier inhabitants, but these were poorly paid and about to be disbanded. "You are not in a condition to resist the most contemptuous enemy," he continued. "What is there to prevent an Algerine pirate from landing on your coast, and carrying your citizens into slavery? You have not a single sloop of war."[12] Spain, with its extensive possessions in the Southwest, was immediately threatening, but it was Great Britain—powerful, warlike, and vindictive—that remained the country's major antagonist. One day, Federalists predicted, that country might seek to revenge its loss and retrieve its laurels buried in America. Unless the United States could underwrite its European engagements with greater force, added North Carolina's William R. Davie, it would be perpetually involved in destructive wars. To Federalists the American ship of state was eminently unfit to encounter its enemies.[13]

In state conventions and legislatures, Federalists continued a blistering assault on the Confederation's inability to protect the nation's interests. Edward Rutledge of South Carolina could see no defense of American security in the old Confederation. It was so weak, so inadequate to meet the needs of the nation, he feared that unless it was radically altered, the country would soon lose it independence. Since the government could not raise money, it could not meet its fiscal obligations, and its credit had evaporated. If under such domestic and foreign conditions the government could not discharge its debts, what would it do in time of danger? "Without a ship, without a soldier, without a shilling in the federal treasury, and without a...government to obtain one, we hold the property that we now enjoy at the courtesy of other powers." Edmond Randolph of Virginia complained: "The Confederation, sir, on which we are told we ought to trust our safety, is totally void of coercive power and energy. Of this the people of America have been long convinced; and this conviction has been sufficiently manifested to the world.... [I]f we trust to it, we shall be defenceless."[14]

James Wilson reminded the Pennsylvania Convention that without a government that would assure domestic vigor and stability, the United States would never achieve its proper respect among the world's powers. With peace had come, not the establishment of the United States as a nation among nations, but disgrace and distress. "Devoid of *national power*," he declared, "we could not prohibit the extravagance of our importations, nor could we derive a revenue from their excess. Devoid of national *importance*, we could not procure, for our exports, a tolerable sale in foreign markets. Devoid of national *credit*, we saw our public securities melt in the hands of the holders, like snow before the sun. Devoid of national *dignity*, we could not, in some instances, perform our treaties, on our part; and, in other instances, we could neither obtain nor compel the performance of them, on the part of others. Devoid of national *energy*, we could not carry into execution our own resolutions, decisions, or laws." He denied that the government under the Articles could act on a national scale. "Can we do any thing to procure us dignity, or to preserve peace and tranquility? Can we relieve the distress of our citizens?...If we offer to treat with a nation, we receive his humiliating answer: 'You cannot, in propriety of language, make a treaty, because you have no power to execute it.'"[15]

Alexander Hamilton told the New York Convention that he thought it strange that citizens who acknowledged the need of changes in the structure and power of government proceeded to deny that the defects in the Articles of Confederation were no cause for the calamities that the nation had experienced. "I will not agree with gentlemen who trifle with the weakness of our country, and suppose that they are enumerated to answer a party purpose....No. I believe these weaknesses to be real, and pregnant with destruction." More specifically, Oliver Ellsworth wondered: "Will our weakness induce Spain to relinquish the exclusive navigation of the Mississippi, or the territory which she claims on the east side of that river? Will our weakness induce the British to give up the northern posts?"[16]

The United States existed in a world where power governed politics, Robert R. Livingston reminded the New York Convention, and each nation had the responsibility to define and protect its interests. "Disputes will not be referred to a common umpire, unless that umpire has [the] power to enforce his decrees; and how can it be expected that princes, jealous of power, will consent to sacrifice any portion of it to the happiness of those people, who are of little account in their estimation? Differences among them, therefore, will continue to be decided by the sword, and the blood of thousand will be shed before the most trifling controversy can be determined."[17] In such a world, wars are natural. John Marshall brought the same concern before the Virginia Convention. "There must be men and money to protect us." There must be money to maintain an army. While some say that America is not in danger of war, he point to experiences from the past. "Look at history....Look at the great volume of human nature." History warns us that a defenseless country cannot remain secure; "the passions of men stimulate them to avail themselves of the weakness of others. The powers of Europe are jealous of us. It is our interest to watch their conduct, and guard against them."[18] If war erupted, force would be required to protect American neutrality.

Federalist concern about the prospect of a European war was not without substance. French objections to Prussia's interference in Dutch political affairs prompted the possibility of war in 1788 with Prussia and Britain. Given the tension rising on the continent, George Washington warned that the United States needed to prepare itself to avoid being pulled into a European war. Should a general war come to Europe, he wrote to Jefferson, "we shall feel more than ever the want of an efficient general Government to regulate our Commercial concerns, to give us a national respectability and to connect the political views and interests of the several States under one head in such a manner as will effectually prevent them from forming separate, improper, or indeed any connection, with the European powers which can involve them in their political disputes." To Washington it would be "extremely imprudent for us to take a part in their quarrels; and whenever a contest happens among them, if we wisely & properly improve the advantages which nature has give us, we may be benifitted by their folly—provided we conduct ourselves with circumspection."[19] Similarly he wrote Henry Knox on January 10, 1788: "Whether war or Peace will be the Issue of the present dispute between France and England seems yet undecided. [I]f the former we shall certainly get involved unless there is energy enough in the Government to keep our people within proper bounds...and that this is not the case at present I believe none will deny."[20]

Federalists continually pressed the theme that a strong central government was required to avoid becoming entangled with foreign combatants. "I hope the United States will be able to keep disengaged from the labyrinth of European politics and war," Washington wrote to Sir Edward Newenham on July 20, 1788, "and that before long they will, by the adoption of a good national government, have become respectable in the eyes of the world, so that none of the maritime Power, especially none of those who hold possessions in the New World or the West Indies shall presume to treat them with insult or contempt. It should be the policy of United America to administer to their wants, without being engaged in their quarrels." Should Britain and France go to war Madison similarly favored the United States adopting a position of neutrality. America "is remote from Europe," he noted, "and ought not to engage in her politics or wars." A neutral nation must be respected, or it would be attacked; thus the United States required the power to maintain its neutrality in time of war. If weak, America would be insulted in its own ports, and its vessels would be seized. But if the United States has a respectable navy, it can enjoy neutral trade without being drawn into war. In any case, none would want to add America to its list of enemies.[21]

Fortunately for the nation, the Constitution before it offered salvation from all the country's domestic and foreign ills. Under the new plan of government, the United States would quickly regain its commercial prosperity. "Commerce, Arts and every species of industry," predicted one ardent Federalist, "will rapidly increase..., and the fullest wishes of every true American will in a short time be realized. Our government once established what a harvest would an European war be for our country—in a state of peace, with a warring world, our vessels would become the carriers to all Europe."[22] Shipbuilding would revive. American sails would whiten the Atlantic as the nations of Europe sought the nation's friendship. Far more important, under the new Constitution, the United States would achieve its proper rank among the nations of the earth. Andrew Allen, a Loyalist writing from London, observed that the American people would then have it within their power to retrieve their lost national character. An energetic government, chimed the *Newburyport Essex Journal*, "would raise us from the lowest degree of contempt, into which we are now plunged, to an honorable, and consequently equal station among the nations."[23] James Wilson declared, simply, that the new system of government would make the United States a nation, commanding the respect of others. To George Washington, the adoption of a national government would render the United

States sufficiently respectable that no nation would thereafter dare to treat it with contempt. William Samuel Johnson of Connecticut issued a final warning: "If we reject a plan of government, which with such favourable circumstances is offered for our acceptance, I fear our national existence must come to a final end."[24]

*****

For Antifederalists, the Federalist assault on the nation's mind and emotions was formidable indeed. Undaunted by the Federalist appeal to American nationalism, opponents of the Constitution accepted the challenge of countering the Federalist effort to anchor the ratification program to an exaggeration of the nation's insecurity. Patrick Henry, Virginia's famed patriot—turned—Antifederalist, accused the Constitution's leading proponents of attempting to hang dangers over the citizens of Virginia to induce them to abandon the Articles of Confederation. "Unless there be great and awful dangers," he declared before the Virginia convention, "the charge is dangerous, and the experiment ought not to be made. In estimating the magnitude of these dangers, we are obliged to take a most serious view of them—to see them, to handle them, and to be familiar with them. It is not sufficient to feign mere imaginary dangers; there must be a dreadful reality. The great question between us is, Does that reality exist?"[25] For Henry, it was essential that the Constitution be debated on its merits and not forced on the American people with descriptions of danger that did not exist. That plea, repeated by countless others, inaugurated a pervading American sense of isolationism, a view of the world based principally on the assumption of an international environment of sufficient security to eliminate the need for extensive and costly defenses; international alliances; or demanding, tension-producing foreign policies.

Antifederalists denied that the American experience under the Articles of Confederation had been disastrous. For them, the country's past and present achievements were astonishing, in need of no reinforcement from a powerful, centralized government. Melancthon Smith, a member of the New York state convention, challenged the Federalist effort to paint the country's condition in hideous and frightful colors. "From this high-wrought picture," Smith concluded, "one would suppose that we were in a condition the most deplorable of any people upon earth. But suffer me, my countrymen, to call your attention to a serious and sober estimate of the situation in which you are placed.... What is your condition? Does not everyman sit under his own vine and under his own fig tree, having none to make him afraid? Does not every one follow his calling without impediments and receive the reward of his well-earned industry?"[26] James Winthrop of Massachusetts, in his "Letters of Agrippa" published in the *Massachusetts Gazette* (Boston), offered an equally reassuring portrait of the country. Everything revealed improvement: "Agriculture has been improved, manufactures multiplied, and trade prodigiously enlarged."[27] Never, he added, had the country presented a better appearance of industry, progress, and tranquility; never had there been greater production of all things in the nation, demonstrating a general prosperity. The courts in every state had executed the laws fairly and punctually. Some of the states were discharging their debts, especially New York and Pennsylvania. The anticipated sale of western lands promised to reduce, if not eliminate, debts of the U.S. government. How many Americans, concluded George Mason, would care to change places with the people of France or Russia, Europe's two leading powers? The people of the United States, whatever their woes, were as independent, as prosperous, and as respectable as any people on earth.[28]

What actual embarrassments the country suffered, ran the Antifederalist judgment, resulted from special circumstances, not the defects of government. The recent war had diminished the fortunes of countless citizens, preventing the payment of debts. Other adverse circumstances the American people had imposed on themselves. What had damaged American commerce and shipbuilding, Antifederalists repeated endlessly, was less the absence of adequate governmental power than the decline of frugality as Americans engaged in a profuse consumption of foreign commodities. The nation's citizens had acted imprudently when they exported their gold and silver to pay for non-essential luxuries. "Orators may declaim on the badness of the times as long as they please," wrote one Pennsylvanian, "but I must tell them that the want of *public virtue, and the want of money,* are two of the principal sources of our present grievances; and if we are under the pressure of these wants, it ought to teach us *frugality.*"[29] No constitution, added John Williams before the New York Convention, could defend the American people from their extravagance, from wearing the manufactures of England, or from deluging the country in debt.[30] The answer to the problem of American commerce lay in greater industry and economy, limiting expenditures to income.

"The truth is," declared Melancthon Smith, "the country buys more than it sells. . . . There are too many merchants in proportion to the farmers and manufacturers. Until these defects are remedied, no government can relieve us. Common sense dictates, that if a man buys more than he sells, he will remain in debt; the same is true for the country."[31]

Persuaded that the nation's problems were largely homegrown, Antifederalists accused the Federalists of overpromising in their vision of national growth and progress under the new plan of government. Richard Henry Lee reminded Americans that men in public life often stated facts, not as they were, but as they wished them to be. "When we want a man to change his condition," wrote Lee, "we describe it as miserable, wretched, and despised; and draw a pleasing picture of that which we would have him assume. And when we wish the contrary, we reverse our descriptions."[32] With considerable logic, critics especially challenged the notion that the new Constitution would produce a flourishing economy, capable of erasing all public and private debts. One widely read Antifederalist, writing in the *Philadelphia Freeman's Journal,* rebuked the friends of the Constitution for duping the American people into believing that a new government would revolutionize the nation's commerce. Perhaps the power to regulate trade and lay imposts would bring some relief to the cities, but it would not, predicted Melancthon Smith, bring the promised benefits. Another noted Antifederalist termed imaginary the prospect of improved commerce under a new government. What would produce a flourishing trade, he wrote, was less the power of government than the freedom and energy of the people. Commerce was the handmaid of liberty. Any government with the power to create monopolies, and thereby encourage avarice, would damage rather than expand the nation's trade.[33]

Antifederalists predicted as well that America's troubles with Europe would find no solutions in any new frame of government. To them the nation's standing in the world was no reflection of its form of government. The foreign observer Louis Guillaume Otto proclaimed that it was wrong to describe the United States as the laughing stock of Europe. The United States, he said, held a position in world affairs precisely commensurate with its youth and the means that it possessed. The country was neither rich enough, nor sufficiently populated and established to appear with more luster. Thus the new plan of government would not alter the country's standing abroad. Perhaps the Federalists could be reproached, he admitted, "for the impatience of anticipating their future grandeur."[34]

Whatever the British view of the new U.S. Constitution, its mere adoption would change little in British-American relations. The British maintained their possession of the frontier posts in large measure because it was in their interest to do so. To declare war for the recovery of the posts was unthinkable under any form of government simply because the American interest in the posts lay far below the threshold of a policy of force. Time, patience, and diplomacy alone would remove the British. As early as June 1787, Luther Martin, Maryland's noted lawyer, advised the Constitutional Convention that the state of the country's relations with Europe could not be attributed to the weakness of Congress. Countries, he said, pursued their own interests, and the recent dismemberment of the British Empire, exceedingly offensive to the British people, scarcely encouraged any tolerance in British diplomacy. For that reason, Martin concluded:

> The Court of St. James, affects to treat us with contempt & avoids a treaty, & France our great & good Ally resents the Conduct of our Ministers in the course of the negotiations for a peace, & immediate Interest unites all the powers of Europe, in a combination to exclude from their West-India Islands, if not all our Vessels at least those of considerable burthen & enumerated Articles, comprising nearly every particular, which we can export to those Markets.... The variety of situations under which the Colonies were situated when they became States, the disproportioned Magnitude of the several independent Sovereignties, & that a very great proportion of the Inhabitants secretly wish destruction to the Polity under which they live, & we must confess, that our Patriotism must in some measure be put to the Test, under any Form of Government that may be introduced.[35]

Similarly, William Gordon, writing from London, characterized as outright deceitful the Federalist argument that the failure of the United States to gain a commercial treaty with England reflected a deficiency in the power of Congress. Britain, he noted, was disinclined to negotiate such a treaty, and the new Constitution would not produce it.[36]

Antifederalists accepted Patrick Henry's supposition that the United States faced no immediate dangers from abroad. Europe was engaged; the Republic was tranquil. No country menaced it with war, and the United States itself embraced no external causes of sufficient importance to merit a resort to arms. So negligible were the external dangers, Antifederalists argued, that the states alone were capable of protecting the peace and meeting any foreseeable exigencies. "The apprehension of danger," observed Melancthon Smith, "is one of the most powerful incentives to human action, and is therefore generally exerted on political questions: But still, a prudent man, though he foreseeth the evil and avoideth it, yet he will not be terrified by imaginary dangers."[37] Sensitive to the power of such appeals, Antifederalists chided those in the constitutional debate who sought to gain advantage by aggravating and exploiting the nation's insecurities. Richard Henry Lee complained that too many of the nation's leaders were seeking to hasten the adoption of the Constitution by inventing a crisis. What concerned the Constitution's supporters, added James Winthrop, was not the presence of danger but the fear that the country's security simply denied the need for a centralized government.[38]

Cognizant of the vicissitudes of international life, Antifederalists agreed that human wisdom could never anticipate all the circumstances that might endanger a nation's peace or security. Whatever the degree of warning, there were times when a country's power, exerted with utmost vigor, could not repel an attacking force, much less fend off an unexpected attack. Every country of necessity formed a rational judgment of what power it would require to defend itself against a probable enemy. In response to extraordinary challenges, the United States, no less than other countries, would rely on the good order and patriotism that the people derived from a wise and prudent administration. But geographic isolation, observed the Antifederalists, permitted the American people to make a far more accurate estimate of their dangers than could other peoples of the world. The vast ocean that separated the United States from Europe vastly extended the country's margin for error. One widely read Antifederalist essayist, writing as "Brutus," analyzed in detail the security which derived from the country's geographical isolation:

We have no powerful nation in our neighbourhood; if we are to go to war, it must either be with the Aboriginal natives, or with European nations. The first are so unequal to a contest with this whole continent, that they are rather to be dreaded for the depredations they may make on our frontiers, than for any impression they will ever be able to make on the body of the country. Some of the European nations, it is true, have provinces bordering upon us, but from these, unsupported by their European forces, we have nothing to apprehend; if any of them should attack us, they will have to transport their armies across the Atlantic, an immense expence, while we should defend ourselves in our own country, which abounds with every necessary of life. For defence against any assault, which there is any probability will be made upon us, we may easily form an estimate.[39]

To fight the United States on the ground from either European or hemispheric bases would be a formidable task. Enemy vessels, hovering off the coasts, could scarcely touch the country at all. The advantages of size and distance from Europe rendered the country remarkably strong. The United States, concluded Patrick Henry, had nothing to fear from Europe and little to fear from its neighbors.[40]

America's ultimate defense against European encroachment lay in the European balance of power. John Adams and Thomas Jefferson observed repeatedly from London and Paris that as long as England and France, occupying the two poles of the European equilibrium, remained strong and antagonistic toward one another, the United States was safe. During the ratification debates, it was left for John Tyler of Virginia to attribute the absence of any European threat specifically to the European equilibrium. "Will the French go to war with you," he asked the delegates to the Virginia Convention, "if you do not pay them what you owe them? Will they thereby destroy that balance, to preserve which they have taken such immense trouble? But Great Britain will go to war with you, unless you comply with the treaty. Great Britain, which, to my sorrow, has monopolized our trade, is to go to war with us unless the treaties be binding. Is this reasonable? It is not the interest of Britain to quarrel with us. She will not hazard any measure which may tend to take our trade out of her hands. It is not the interest of Holland to see us destroyed or oppressed. *It is the interest of every nation in Europe to keep the balance of power, and therefore they will not suffer any nation to attack us, without immediately interfering.*"[41]

Some Antifederalists even suggested that the United States, with its remarkable wealth, its geographical advantages, and its pervading security, concentrate on internal matters and disregard the politics and interests of distant lands. They recognized the limits of American

power in managing the affairs of Europe as well as the dangers of over
involvement in affairs abroad that lay outside the nation's interests and
control. If the world was competitive, the United States had no compelling reason to enter the competition. Why should the Republic, asked
James Winthrop, dissipate its resources in foreign quarrels merely for
the sake of acting like other nations? Indeed, "Brutus" recommended
that the American people let the European monarchs share the glory
of war while the United States furnished the world "an example of a
great people, who in their civil institutions hold chiefly in view, the at-
tainment of virtue, and happiness among ourselves."[42] With its superb
climate and vast expanses of land, the country seemed capable of producing all the necessities of life in abundance. It scarcely needed the
goods of Europe or the centralized authority to underwrite needless
and dangerous entanglements in the European world of power politics. At the same time, the political system and the internal concerns
of the United States could be no business of Europeans as long as the
country paid its debts, fulfilled its treaty obligations, and avoided open
infringements on the interests of others.[43]

*****

Congress's incapacity for protecting the country's foreign trade was
so evident that few questioned the decision of the Constitutional
Convention to grant the power over commerce to the general government. It mattered little to some that American diplomacy had
gained no commercial treaties with Europe's leading states; the formal arrangements with France, Holland, and Prussia demonstrated
the rule that treaties in themselves would not extend commerce.
Regulation, not some elusive treaty in which the British had no interest, would break that country' s monopoly of America's external
commerce. Boston's James Bowdoin expressed the country's overwhelming sentiment when he declared, "The manner in which the
states have suffered, for the want of a general regulation of trade,
is so notorious, that little need be said upon the subject."[44] Once
the American people were dependent only on Great Britain; now,
complained Oliver Ellsworth, they were dependent "on every petty
state in the world and every custom house officer in foreign ports."
The power to regulate commerce, always a national matter, would at
last enable the country to challenge the commercial policies of self-
interested powers.[45] If the mere absence of commercial regulation
was indeed responsible for the country's economic ills, Federalists

could proclaim the Constitution's commercial provisions a sure guarantee of its future salvation.

For Antifederalists, though, the Constitution's commerce clause raised questions of propriety and limits. Regulation would enable the United States to retaliate against British commercial policy, perhaps to good effect, but critics doubted that the times called for sweeping controls. James Winthrop noted that the commerce of Massachusetts was expanding without benefit of national regulation. Congress, he feared, might exercise its power over commerce to enhance the trade of one commercial center at the expense of another. "When commerce is left to take its own course," he declared, "the advantage of every class will be nearly equal. But when exclusive privileges are given any class, it will operate to the weakening of some other class connected with them."[46]

Southern Antifederalists were untroubled by the federal control of commerce, but they distrusted the decision of the Philadelphia Convention to place that power in the hands of a bare congressional majority. George Mason, who had declined to sign the Constitution over that very issue, feared that the full power assigned to Congress gave that body the authority to extend special commercial privileges. The further assumption that the seven or eight non-Southern states would have a majority in Congress merely reinforced the Southern dread of the commerce power.[47] For that matter, any navigation act that excluded foreign vessels from the American carrying trade would grant a monopoly to the shipping interests of the Eastern states and permit them to raise freight charges on Southern products. To protect the South against a possible Eastern commercial monopoly, Mason prepared an amendment to the Constitution that declared: "No Navigation Law, or Law for regulating Commerce shall be passed without the Consent of two thirds of the Members present in both Houses." In late June 1788, Patrick Henry submitted that proposal to the Virginia Convention.[48]

Federalists condemned Mason's amendment as irrelevant and misguided. James Iredell of North Carolina reminded his Southern opponents that Congress, under the new plan of government, could grant no monopolies in trade and commerce. The Constitution declared specifically that "no preference shall be given to the ports of one State over those of another." Citizens of each state, moreover, were entitled under the Constitution "to all privileges and immunities of citizens in the several States."[49] Federalists wondered why

Southerners would fear the commercial control of Congress. Tench Coxe, writing in Philadelphia's *Independent Gazetteer,* reminded Mason and his Southern associates that Delaware and New Jersey were no less agricultural than the South's five planting states, giving the non-commercial states a clear majority in both houses of Congress. Despite Philadelphia's primary interest in commerce, moreover, the bulk of Pennsylvania's delegates in Congress represented agricultural, not commercial districts. Similarly, in New York and Massachusetts, commercial interests did not control the state delegations. Connecticut, Rhode Island, and New Hampshire were overwhelmingly rural. And in the North, agriculture, not commerce, was the predominant economic interest. Coxe concluded that even in the commercial quarter of the country, the shipping, manufacturing, and fishing interests included no more than one-eighth the property and people devoted to agriculture. "In short," Coxe concluded, "agriculture appears to be the spring of our commerce, and the parent of our manufactures."[50]

Federalists, North and South, wondered why Southern Antifederalists harbored such animosity and fear toward the Eastern shipping interests. Ellsworth accused Mason and his supporters of preferring the British to Americans who happened to reside in New England. He complained that such Virginians wanted the government to protect all of Virginia's advantages, whatever the disadvantages to other states.[51] Federalists argued that the commerce clause in the Constitution protected Southern interests no less than those of the carrying states. Edward Carrington of New York acknowledged that any navigation act that benefited American shipping would indeed serve Eastern interests. But the carrying states, he reminded Thomas Jefferson, expected no less from the Revolution than the expansion of their commerce. For the South, there was more security in employing the vessels of New England and the middle states than those of strangers.[52] Any unreasonable increase in the price of freight would merely promote ship-building in the South and offer additional employment to the coastal population. Any law that expanded American shipping would concomitantly promote the country's maritime power, much to the South's advantage. In the event of foreign invasion, Virginia would of necessity look to the seafaring North for its defense.[53]

*****

If Antifederalists accepted in principle the federal control of commerce, they rejected totally the extended powers of the general government over taxation and national defense. Indeed, these twin issues carried the burden of the Antifederalist assault on the work of the Philadelphia convention. Without the power to levy taxes on the people, ran the Federalist conviction, a government was useless, an expense without advantage. Congress under the Articles had the authority to make requisitions on the states. Some states paid nothing, producing a limited, uneven, and badly distributed congressional income to satisfy the country's internal and external demands.[54] Those "pompous petitions for public charity," as New York's Robert Livingston termed the requisitions, had not permitted the United States to settle its foreign and domestic debts or establish an adequate military establishment. The taxing power as embodied in the new plan of government would at last permit Congress to create a uniform, enforceable revenue system.[55]

In defending the taxing power, Federalists acknowledged reassuringly that the states, in granting such power, in no measure denied themselves a co-equal right to tax, except in the area of import duties. They merely assigned a portion of their taxing authority to permit collective action where the states could not perform. It was essential only that the states have no authority to limit the ability of the federal government to obtain whatever it required to fulfill its obligations to the nation.[56] Hamilton reminded the New York Convention that since a frame of government could not set bounds to a nation's need, it dare not set limits to its resources. The Constitution granted Congress the power of the purse, added Madison, because "the means ought to be commensurate to the end. The end is general protection."[57] Federalists doubted that external taxes, or import duties, would meet the country's financial requirements; already the demands on the government were too extensive for that. Hamilton observed in The Federalist No. 30 that "*in the usual progress of things, the necessities of a nation in every stage of its existence will be found at least equal to its resources.*"[58]

What especially troubled Antifederalists was the provision that Congress alone possessed the authority to determine the needs of the United States. This presumably set no limits on the power of Congress to tax. Richard Henry Lee declared that internal taxes, whether poll or land taxes; excises; or duties on written instruments, would be aimed at every person or species of property and carried to extreme lengths. John Tyler termed such taxing power "too dangerous to be vested in any set of men whatsoever."[59] Earlier efforts to increase Congress's taxing authority had limited such power to definite objects. When the United States was pressed on every side by British forces, the American people had recognized no need for such extensive taxing power. James Monroe complained as late as the Virginia Convention that the country still faced no problems that necessitated such dangerous governmental powers; nor would it in the future. "It is a great maxim," echoed Melancthon Smith, "that all governments find a use for as much money as they can raise. Indeed, they have commonly demands for more. Hence it is that all...are in debt. I take this to be settled truth, that they...will at least live up to their income. Congress will ever exercise their powers to levy as much as the people can pay."[60] For Hamilton, the needs of government would establish the level of taxes; for Smith, the available taxes would determine the needs of government.

Throughout the ratification debates, the question of taxation remained inseparable from that of a standing army. Federalists who argued that the country was seriously endangered viewed internal taxes as the essential means for maintaining an adequate national defense. For Hamilton, the possibility of invasions or long, costly wars required a government with the power to fully enlist the country's financial resources. "The contingencies of society," he told the New York Convention, "are not reducible to calculations. They cannot be fixed or bounded, even in imagination. Will you limit the means of your defence, when you cannot ascertain the force or extent of the invasion?" Madison assured the Virginia Convention that except for the presence of external dangers, he would not advocate the principle of direct taxation at all. Yet Congress, Madison argued, must have both the power of the purse and the power to raise the armed forces. Both powers resided in all governments because security against foreign danger was always a fundamental object of civil society.[61]

Perhaps the United States, because of its relatively isolated position, would not require the burdensome defenses of the European powers. But if the dangers were remote, James Iredell advised, no one should preclude that there were no dangers at all. Others who defended the principle of a standing army believed the dangers more acute. One Massachusetts Federalist declared in convention that the United States was "circumscribed with enemies from Maine to Georgia."[62] Such perceptions transformed the absence of an adequate defense into an invitation to aggression. This explained why most countries, James Wilson reminded his fellow Pennsylvanians, found it necessary to maintain an appearance of strength even in times of profound tranquility. By assuring enemies that the country was prepared to resist attack, a standing army might eliminate the necessity of larger forces to meet an actual invasion. For Wilson, it was essential that the country never be compelled to declare war when it was not prepared to fight.[63] Congress would determine what defenses were necessary and proper. It alone could declare war and provide military supplies, with no appropriation to extend longer than two years. But Congress represented the people. Ultimately, Federalists assured the country, any military program would rest on public consent. It remained for Congress alone to strike off a balance between the dangers and the necessities of a standing army. "On any scale," wrote Madison, "it is an object of laudable circumspection and precaution. A wise nation will combine all these considerations; and whilst it does not rashly preclude itself from any resources which may become essential to its safety, will exert all its prudence in diminishing both the necessity and the danger of resorting to one which may be inauspicious to its liberties."[64]

Antifederalists agreed that the general government required the power to raise an army in time of war; a peacetime army they rejected as a needless drain on the country's resources and a threat to its liberties. Even a small, disciplined force could control a large population. One delegate warned the Virginia convention against the establishment of an army "whose only occupation would be idleness; whose only effort the introduction of vice and dissipation; and who would, at some future day, deprive us of our liberties." Benjamin Harrison confessed to Washington his fear that a standing army "must sooner or later, establish a tyranny, not inferiour to the triumvirate...of Rome."[65] Congress, declared Patrick Henry, could, under the pretence of danger, sustain large armies as long as a majority believed it necessary; it could extend two-year appropriations to the end of time.[66] Antifederalists denied that the country faced dangers that required such costs and risks. Why should the United States, they asked, sacrifice its peace and its established government to prepare for war against enemies that no one could define?[67] To defend the nation against such wasteful and dangerous decisions, Nathaniel Wythe proposed to the Virginia Convention an amendment that any congressional effort to create an army would require the consent of two-thirds of the states. "Brutus" in the *New York Journal* called for a two-thirds majority in both houses of Congress to authorize an army.

Richard Henry Lee, in his "Letters of a Federal Farmer," advocated a two-thirds or three-fourths vote in Congress on all matters of national defense.[68]

For Antifederalists the state militia appeared adequate for the country's needs. They objected only to the extensive powers over the militia that the Constitution assigned to Congress. Not only did the new plan of government establish congressional controls over arms and discipline, leaving to the states the actual training of the militia and the selection of officers, but also, in time of crisis, placed the militia under the direct control of Congress and the president. For George Mason, Patrick Henry, and the entire array of Antifederalist writers, such federal authority transcended what was necessary and reasonable. Henry could discover no constitutional guarantees to protect the people against the power of Congress to declare a national emergency and call the militia. In time, such congressional power would become irretrievable. "It is easier to supply deficencies in power," he warned, "than to take back excess of power."[69] Critics objected equally to Congress's authority to employ the militia in accordance with its own judgment of danger. To call the Georgia militia to suppress a disturbance in New Hampshire, declared Mason, would create such harassment that people might actually prefer a standing army. Mason agreed that the general government should have ultimate power over the militia, but only with the approval of the states. In real emergencies, the states, concerned with the nation's safety, would never withhold their consent. But in no case, he declared, could militia be marched beyond the limits of an adjoining state without the approval of the state legislature. Maryland's Convention offered an amendment to permit the federal movement of militia, only if selected, by lot or voluntarily enlisted, beyond an adjacent state.[70] Federalists retorted that such restraints on the calling of the militia would render it useless in defending the country against invasion or insurrection.

Ultimately the long, impassioned debate over ratification turned on the presumed conflict between liberty and security. For Antifederalists, the dangers besetting the American people did not lie in European ambitions, but in the proffered constitutional system itself. What troubled them especially was the unbounded quality of the power that the projected plan of government assigned to the legislative branch. The first article granted Congress "power to lay and collect taxes, duties, imposts, and excises, to pay the debts and provide for the common defense and the general welfare of the United States."

The sixth article, no less threatening, ordained that "this constitution and the laws of the United States which shall be made in pursuance thereof, and all treaties made, or which shall be made under the authority of the United States, shall be the supreme law of the land."[71] Such extravagant and arbitrary authority, Robert Whitehill warned the Pennsylvania convention, would enable the federal government to absorb every subordinate jurisdiction. Indeed, such powers seemed sufficient to melt down the country into one consolidated empire, annihilating the independence and sovereignty of the states. Any process that destroyed the states would destroy the nation's liberties as well. "The vast Continent of America," one Antifederalist predicted gloomily, "cannot be long subject to Democracy, if consolidated into one government—you might as well attempt to rule Hell by Prayer.[72]

Antifederalists accepted readily the need to grant Congress limited revenue and a limited authority to regulate foreign commerce, but they could detect no dangers, at home or abroad, that dictated such pervading infringements on the states and, potentially, on the liberties of the people. For them the choice before the nation was not, as the Federalists contended, between adoption of the new plan of government and absolute ruin. There were no dangers, proclaimed Richard Henry Lee, that compelled the American people to hurry into a decision so momentous and potentially disastrous. Everywhere, Antifederalists accused their opponents of alarming the public with non-existent dangers. George Mason decried the Federalist program of raising phantoms "to show a singular skill in exorcisms, to terrify and compel us to take the new government with all its sins and dangers."[73] Samuel Bryan of Philadelphia, writing in the *Independent Gazetteer,* simply denied that the country was in a crisis. "The present distracted state of Europe," he concluded, "secures us from injury in that quarter, and as to domestic dissensions, we have not so much to fear from them, as to precipitate us into this form of government."[74] Critics wondered why the American people, when under no compulsion, would willingly give up their confederated Republic and assign such apparently limitless and dangerous powers to a central authority.[75]

*****

The division between Federalists and Antifederalists reflected the broad geographical and occupational lines that separated American society. This contributed to their views toward the importance that foreign affairs played in the Constitutional debates. The overall rhetorical opposition of the Antifederalists was perhaps more strident than that of the Federalists because they found themselves on the defensive. Federalists tended to be men of affairs, often eastern or coastal and involved in commercial enterprises, who viewed the problems posed by other nations and the Confederations' inadequate responses. The Antifederalists, by contrast, were often rural and more isolated. Western areas, too, had long opposed dictation from the eastern seats of power and naturally opposed any greater concentration of the authority they resented. If many planters rejected the new system, commercial interests generally saw the new Constitution protecting their interests. Economic status apparently did not play a major role. "These two parties [the poor and wealthy]," Richard Henry Lee acknowledged, "are really insignificant compared with the solid, free, and independent part of the community." To what extent did ideas, not economic status, determine views toward the Constitution? Those who resided along trade routes tended to favor the new government, but it is conceivable that their Federalist leanings, if not determined by economic interests, reflected a greater access to the information and argumentation emanating from the coastal regions.

The country in 1787–1788, thus, was divided by many of the factors that long antedated the debates on the Constitution. Many fledgling Antifederalists suspected that conservatives predominated at the Philadelphia Convention, and they would ignore their interests. Hence they expected a government format they were predisposed to reject. Not persuaded that their well-being required a new, stronger government, they viewed the well-organized Federalist crusade as a conspiracy driven by economic interests. These dissidents, neither stubborn nor ignorant, led by men equally renowned and accomplished as those who led those determined to set aside the Articles of Confederation, resisted Federalist descriptions of the country's disabilities and failures. The Antifederalists' singular concern for state sovereignty and individual rights presented a strong case, one that had wide appeal.[76] If economic interests and geographical and sectional factors influenced public attitudes toward a new government, they also foretold popular divisions that would ultimately find their way into the Federalist and (Jeffersonian) Republican political parties.

Consequently, the nationwide ratification debates, in newspapers and conventions, were perhaps the finest example of democracy in action in the history of mankind. There were exaggerations, seldom totally false. Both Federalists and Antifederalists orators and publicists argued acutely, intelligently, and fairly, with an amazing display of historical knowledge, political philosophy, and common sense. They attracted the nation's best minds in a determined, successful, free, and honest effort to set the country on what appeared the best course available. As Francis Hopkinson wrote to Jefferson in Paris on July 17, 1788: "I believe no Question has ever been more repeatedly and strictly scrutinized or more fairly and freely argued, than this proposed Constitution."[77]

*****

In their defense of the Constitution, the Federalists had the final word, arguing effectively that the new frame of government would enhance the nation's security without endangering the states or the people's liberty. They denied that the new assignment of power to Congress would consolidate the government or annihilate the states. The Constitution conveyed no such authority. Nor would Congress harbor such intentions. Congressional interests were inseparable from the interests of the people; that union of interests would continue.[78] In many important processes, the federal government rested on state action. To prevent licentiousness, the Constitution gave adequate powers to the government; to prevent tyranny, it distributed such powers judiciously among three branches of government.[79] Federalists acknowledged readily that the Constitution would deprive the states of some powers, but in operation, they predicted, it would enhance the power of the states as well.

Federalists argued essentially, in conventions and in the press, that the Constitution assigned to Congress only those powers absolutely necessary to perform the functions of good government, none that the states could exercise more effectively.[80] James Wilson, who dominated the Pennsylvania Convention, observed repeatedly that Article I contained only what was required to render effective the specific powers granted. To deny Congress the power to do mischief, added fellow Philadelphian Thomas McKean, would deny it the authority to do any good.

Above all, ran the Federalist argument, the United States required the power to conduct the country's external relations justly and effectively.[81] In the real world of competition and conflict, security required a government empowered to tax, to muster human and material resources, to build armies and navies, and to deter the aggressiveness of others. On the eve of the final adoption of the Constitution in February 1788, Adams assured Jay "that, as soon as there shall be one [national government], the British Court will vouchsafe to treat with it."[82]

Whatever the wisdom of Federalist assumptions, James Wilson admitted at the end that the Constitution was not perfect, that some parts he preferably would have altered. "But," he concluded, "when I reflect how widely men differ in their opinions, and that every man...had an equal pretention to assert his own, I am satisfied that that anything nearer to perfection could not have been accomplished."[83] With that judgment, the Federalists—who controlled the ratification process, and ultimately the nation—agreed.

EPILOGUE

The signing of the new constitution and the formation of a new government promised a truly united America, yet ratification did not immediately resolve the nation's long-festering disputes with foreign powers. That would take nearly three decades. The early 1790s found the Washington administration confronting chaotic times—the outbreak of the French Revolution with its later muscular ambitions, Indian forays on the Ohio frontier, and the Spanish challenges to American settlers along the Southern frontier. Not all was bleak, however, as London dispatched its first full-fledged diplomatic representative, George Hammond, to represent its interest to the new U.S. government, while the Secretary of the Treasury Alexander Hamilton revived America's credit and undertook to service its foreign debts. The French Revolution's wars brought to the fore America's commitments under the Franco-American pact of 1778 that resulted in President George Washington's controversial decision on U.S. neutrality. His leadership postponed hostilities with Britain for a decade and a half as America consolidated its domestic strength to successfully ward off disaster.

John Jay meanwhile returned from London in 1794 with a treaty that again divided the nation and launched America's initial political parties—the Federalists and (Jeffersonian) Republicans. Although the Republicans denounced Jay's Treaty, it did result in the British withdrawal from posts along the Great Lakes ceded to the United

States in the 1783 peace treaty and in a relatively generous commercial treaty. The following year, Thomas Pinckney secured a treaty
with Madrid that assured free navigation of the Mississippi River and
the right of deposit for American products at New Orleans to facilitate their transshipment. The Pinckney Treaty did not end the
controversy regarding the Southern borders until John Adams's son,
John Quincy, finally acquired the Floridas in the Adams-Onis pact
of 1819. A few years earlier, President Thomas Jefferson employed a
navy largely inspired by President John Adams and some bribery to
bring the Barbary states to terms.

   Throughout this political turmoil, the new government and suc-
cessive ones struggled to deal with the fundamental issue of which—
the president or Congress—was ordained by the Constitution to take
the lead in foreign affairs.

*****

Contending views of the roles of the executive and legislature in
foreign relations emerged early. While it has been argued that the
constitutional division of authority over foreign affairs invited the
two branches to struggle for supremacy, this is not necessarily so.
"The Constitution," Professor Jack N. Rakove suggests, "does not so
much invite struggle as permit it to flourish once it has arisen for
other reasons—reasons that are almost invariably rooted in different views of national interest rather than principled notions of how
foreign policy should be made in the abstract.... If we could always
agree where our true interest lie, the untidiness inherent in the
Constitution would matter little. But for most of our history, consensus about foreign policy has proven far more elusive than most
Americans, with their chronically stunted recall of the past, realize."[1]

   Yet among the Founding Fathers, few questioned the projected
predominance of Congress in foreign affairs. For James Madison,
John Adams, Alexander Hamilton, and other predominant members
of the Constitutional Convention, peace and war were not executive
prerogatives. Nowhere did the treaty clause give the president any
exclusive right to propose a course of action in external affairs. In
treaty-making, the Constitution called for the advice and consent
of the Senate as an organized body, not of individual members. Even
those who recognized the essential role of the executive in treaty-
making emphasized the importance of safeguards against excessive executive authority. It may be recalled that Charles Cotesworth

Pinckney of South Carolina argued that a king might negotiate wisely, but an elected president was not worthy of such trust.[2] Hamilton expressed this distrust of executive power in similar terms:

> However proper or safe it may be in governments where the executive magistrate is an hereditary monarch, to commit to him the entire power of making treaties, it would be utterly unsafe and improper to entrust that power to an elective magistrate of four years duration....The history of human conduct does not warrant that exalted opinion of human virtue which would make it wise in a nation to commit interests of so delicate and momentous a kind as those which concern its intercourse with the rest of the world to the sole disposal of a magistrate, created and circumstanced, as would be a president of the United States.[3]

Such views of congressional authority dominated the war powers debate in the Constitutional Convention.

Nowhere did the Constitution define the process whereby the president would seek and obtain the advice and consent of the Senate in the matter of treaty-making. The process required some definition. On May 25, 1789, President George Washington submitted several negotiated Indian treaties to the Senate for its approval.[4] Two weeks later, the president submitted a French consular convention, signed in November 1788, to the Senate. On the advice of John Jay, the acting secretary of state, the Senate approved both the Indian treaties and the consular convention unanimously, for all documents had already been negotiated.[5] During its deliberations, the Senate debated the method of giving its advice and consent and agreed to a voting procedure.[6]

Some members of the Senate questioned the procedure. On August 3, 1789, the Senate appointed a committee to discuss the matter with the president. A week later, he and the Senate committee agreed that the president would meet the Senate in the Senate chamber and that all questions would be posed by the president of the Senate. The senators would indicate their assent or dissent by a voice vote.[7] Washington put the new procedure to the test when, on the same day, his secretary informed the Senate clerk that the president would come to the chamber on the following day to seek Senate advice and consent on a treaty to be negotiated with the Southern Indians.

When the Senate convened, the doorkeeper announced the president's arrival. After Washington, supported by General Henry Knox, the Secretary of War, had explained the issues in conflict with the Indians, he asked the Senate for its advice. He met with dead silence. Finally, William Maclay, the Senate diarist, requested additional information, explaining that the Senate had no opportunity to inform itself on the subject. It had become equally apparent to Maclay that there could be no free discussion "while the President of the United States sat there, with his Secretary of War, to support his opinions, and overawe the timid and neutral part of the Senate..."[8] One senator moved that the papers be referred to a committee of five, whereupon Washington declared that the proposal defeated his purpose in coming. He had, he complained, brought Secretary Knox with him to answer their questions. Several days later, Washington appeared at the Senate chamber, but never again returned to discuss another treaty.

Years later William Crawford recalled Washington's reaction to this encounter with the Senate over the projected Indian treaty. "They debated it and proposed alterations," wrote Crawford, "so that when Washington left the Senate Chamber he said would be damned if he ever went there again. And ever since that time treaties have been negotiated by the Executive before submitting them to the consideration of the Senate."[9] Maclay judged Washington's behavior from the viewpoint of the Senate: "The President wishes to tread on the necks of the Senate.... He wishes us to see with the eyes and hear with the ears of his Secretary only. The Secretary to advance the premises, the President to draw the conclusions, and to bear down our deliberations with his personal authority and presence. Form only will be left to us."[10]

Several days later, Washington again appeared in the Senate. He, with General Knox, discussed with members of the Senate the propositions that he had introduced earlier. The Senate accepted some and rejected others. The experience illustrated again the reluctance of senators to argue treaty matters in the presence of the president. Washington thereafter never sought the advice and consent of the Senate when negotiating treaties, nor did he again appear in the Senate chamber to discuss a treaty.[11] He submitted his subsequent treaty with the Western Indians in a message carried to the Senate by his secretary.

Jay's Treaty, signed with Great Britain in November 1794, established the Senate's role in treaty-making in something approaching final form. Alexander Hamilton and his Federalist allies, in firm control of the executive and the Senate, had determined to bind U.S. policy toward Britain with a treaty. Taking their advice, Washington, in April 1794, nominated John Jay, now Chief Justice of the United States, for the London mission. A bitterly divided Senate confirmed Jay's appointment, 18–8. Jay had discovered in London that the British were not in a compromising mood. He would boast of his achievement in London, but the treaty Jay negotiated was so vulnerable to criticism that Washington hesitated to submit it to the Senate. Finally, on June 17, 1795, the Senate received a resolution favoring ratification. It suspended a portion of Article III and asked the president to reopen negotiations with Britain on the question of the West Indian trade. Eventually the resolution passed the Senate in the original form, 21 to 10. The final exchange of ratifications of the Jay Treaty, in 1796, established a procedure for treaty-making that changed little thereafter."[12] That procedure, with the president placing a negotiated treaty before the Senate for its approval, rested less on the Constitution than on the power of the president to command the necessary two-thirds majority in the Senate.

*****

For the Founding Fathers, treaty-making was essential as the United States sought to establish itself as a nation among nations. But as the country increasingly gained recognition, the vast bulk of its foreign relations was not concerned with treaties. Nor was such diplomatic activity covered by the Constitution. This explains, in part, why the country's foreign relations became a free-for-all. There were no guidelines, no center of authority. The control of external policy did not differ from the normal executive-congressional war waged over other public issues, domestic or foreign. In such struggles the president required the support of the House as well as the Senate. The House had control of the purse, the greatest of all governmental powers. For the Founders placed the ultimate power of government under democratic control—if a House majority chose to exercise it. At issue always was the nature and location of political power. Generally those who possessed public support would control the policy.

Over the years, what gave the president his essential advantage over his detractors, in Congress and out, was the broad assumption that the executive branch, because of its extensive foreign affairs and later intelligence establishment, possessed knowledge superior to that available elsewhere in the country. In times of crisis, whether real or contrived, the president often behaved as if that assumption was correct and, through arguments and assertions that played on national insecurities, went to extreme lengths to overcome congressional and public opposition. Because opinion was the essence of executive power, a president could scarcely claim constitutional privileges when public or congressional sentiment turned against him. As a last resort, however, the president could seek an escape from the limitations of law or adverse opinion by resorting to deception and evasion, operating secretly through White House operatives, employing funds from previous appropriations. Such behavior underscored the limited control that the American constitutional system exerted over the conduct of foreign policy. During the ratification debates both friends and foes of the new Constitution warned that the president, as commander in chief of the armed forces, possessed the power to ruin the country.

In external matters, the president could dominate both Congress and the public most readily when the nation was in a crisis mood, when external conditions appeared to demand strong national leadership. James Madison warned the country that the gravest dangers to its liberties would lie in "provisions against danger, real or pretended, from abroad." He reminded delegates to the Constitutional Convention that governments in time of insecurity gave immense discretionary powers to the executive. "Constant apprehension of War," he continued, "has the...tendency to render the head too large for the body. A standing military force, with an overgrown Executive will not long be safe companions to liberty. The means of defense agst. Foreign danger, have been always the instruments of tyranny at home."[13]

*****

In its distribution of the powers of war and peace, the Constitutional Convention overwhelmingly favored the Congress. The Constitution, in Article I, assigned to Congress the power to declare war, to raise and maintain the land and naval forces to execute the laws of the United States, suppress insurrections, and repel invasions. In

Article II, it designated the president as "Commander in Chief of the Army and Navy of the United States and of the militia of the several states when called into the actual service of the United States...." This distribution of powers reflected the Convention's well-founded fear of presidential authority.

Nothing in the Constitution prohibited a president from acting directly and decisively as commander in chief or as head of the federal bureaucracy. Nor did the Constitution limit the authority of the president to place the armed forces of the United States wherever he chose. However, a president's essential power to advance his foreign policy agenda rested, not on any exclusive constitutional mandate, but on his capacity and determination to build and sustain the necessary base of congressional and popular support. The Constitution always permitted the executive to do whatever the public would approve. When assured of strong public support in his clash with congressional critics, a president faced almost no limits to his control of external policy. In placing the country's armed forces where he believed they would best protect the interest and security of the American people, a president could create a war situation that left Congress only the choice but to recognize it, if not with a declaration of war, at least with military appropriations.

Throughout U.S. history, wars enhanced executive power, as the Founding Fathers predicted. But the repeated American wartime executive-congressional struggle for power was never endemic. It resulted from questionable executive decisions, reflecting the reality that the nation's wisdom on external matters was never an executive monopoly. What passed for majority opinion too often reflected the preferences of small but commanding, minorities who, with media support, created and fostered the decisions that led the country astray. This was true for the comparative few who sponsored the long and pointless non-recognition of China as well as the prosecution of the Vietnam and Iraqi wars—both of which became profoundly unwinnable and divisive, with consequences that challenged their alleged necessities as well as the assured cost-free triumphs that underwrote them.

History suggests that under the American constitutional system, the executive-congressional struggle to command external policy is as endless as the challenges of an ever-changing world. But aside from certain formal arrangements, such as the Senate's authority to approve treaties, the Constitution cannot govern the exertion of influence by either the executive or Congress. The division of power is permeable, with each contestant choosing the interpretation that suits its policy preferences. The critical issue in the perennial struggle between the president and Congress for control of external policy ultimately is the quality of the policies that the government pursues and the merit of the arguments designed to sustain them. It could not be otherwise.

NOTES

PREFACE

1. CBS News, June 26, 2007.

2. Thomas F. Madden, *Empires of Trust: How Rome Built—and America Is Building—a New World* (New York: Dutton/Penguin, 2008). Also see Nigel Hamilton, *American Caesars: Lives of the Presidents from Franklin D. Roosevelt to George W. Bush* (New Haven: Yale University Press, 2010) as well as a revealing interview with Admiral Mike Mullen, "War: The World Tour," *The Weekend Australian Magazine,* September 4–5, 2010.

3. Testimony of Rebecca Rimel (president and CEO, The Pew Charitable Trusts), "The Founding Fathers Papers: Ensuring Public Access to our National Treasurers," Judiciary Committee of the United States, February 7, 2008.

PROLOGUE

1. See Norman A. Graebner, "An American Tradition In Foreign Affairs," *Virginia Quarterly Review* (Autumn 1989): 600–18.

2. In Wharton, Francis, ed., *The Revolutionary Diplomatic Correspondence of the United States,* 6 vols. (Washington: Government Printing Office, 1889), II: 667–68.

3. Friedrich von Gentz quoted in Moorhead Wright, ed., *Theory and Practice of the Balance of Power, 1486–1914* (London: Dent, 1975), 94.

4. The classic account of 17th-century diplomatic method is Monsieur de Cahières, *On the Manner of Negotiating with Princes,* trans. A. F. Whyte (Notre Dame: University of Indiana Press, 1963).

5. Carl von Clausewitz noted that Poland had been a bone of contention among the European powers; the powers divided it to prevent it from becoming a province of Russia. See Clausewitz in Wright, *Theory and Practice of the Balance of Power,* 107.

6. Fénelon, "Two Essays on the Balance of Europe," in Wright, *Theory and Practice of the Balance of Power,* 41.

7. On this theme, *see* Carl von Clausewitz, *On War,* ed. and trans. Michael Howard and Peter Paret (Princeton: Princeton University Press, 1976), 75–76, 87–88.

8. For superb studies on the European state system, see Edward V. Gulick, *Europe's Classical Balance of Power* (Ithaca: Cornell University Press, 1955) and Alfred Vagts, "The Balance of Power: Growth of an Idea," *World Politics* I (October 1948): 82–101.

9. On the theme of Britain's insular position, see Felix Gilbert, *To The Farewell Address: Ideas of Early American Foreign Policy* (Princeton: Princeton University Press, 1961), 19–43.

10. Adams to Calkoen, October 16, 1780, John Adams, *The Works of John Adams,* 10 vols. (Boston: Little, Brown, 1851–1865), VIII:285.

11. For Adams's acceptance, and that of American leaders, generally, of the system of power politics, see James H. Hutson, "Intellectual Foundations of Early American Diplomacy," *Diplomatic History* 1 (Winter 1977): 1–19.

12. John Adams to James Warren, March 20, 1783, in *Warren-Adams Letters: Being Chiefly a Correspondence Among John Adams, Samuel Adams, and James Warren* 2 vols. (Boston: Massachusetts Historical Society, 1925), II:192.

13. Adams to Robert Livingston, May 24, 1783, in *The Works of John Adams,* VIII:60.

14. William M. Van der Weyde, ed., *The Life and Works of Thomas Paine,* 10 vols. (New Rochelle: Thomas Paine National Historical Association, 1925), II:93–182.

15. Hamilton quoted in N.A. Graebner, *Ideas and Diplomacy: Readings in the Intellectual Tradition of American Foreign Policy* (New York: Oxford University Press, 1964), 49.

16. Alexander Hamilton, John Jay, and James Madison, *The Federalist: A Commentary on the Constitution of the United States,* ed. by Edward Mead Earle (New York: National Home Library Foundation, 1937), 27–33.

17. Henry Cabot Lodge, ed., *The Works of Alexander Hamilton* (New York: 1885), IV: 157–71, 175, 178–80, 183; also see Norman A. Graebner, *Ideas and Diplomacy: Readings in the Intellectual Tradition of American Foreign Policy* (New York: Oxford University Press, 1964), 58–76.

18. Quote in Graebner, "An American Tradition in Foreign Affairs," 600–14.

CHAPTER 1

1. Max Savelle, *The Origins of American Diplomacy: The International History of Angloamerica, 1492–1763* (New York: Macmillan, 1967), 182–83.

2. For a brief but excellent account of American efforts to squeeze the French out of North America, see Richard W. Van Alstyne, *Empire and Independence: The International History of the American Revolution* (New York: Wiley, 1965), 2–11.

3. "The Interest of Great Britain Considered With Regard to Her Colonies," in Albert Henry Smyth, ed., *Writings of Benjamin Franklin,* 10 vols. (New York: Macmillan, 1905–1907), IV:40–81. For background, see Fred Andersen, *Crucible of War: The Seven Years' War and the Fate of the British Empire in British North America, 1754–1766* (New York: Alfred A. Knopf, 2000).

4. Franklin to Lord Kames, January 3, 1760, in Leonard W. Labaree, ed., *The Papers of Benjamin Franklin,* 39 vols. (New Haven: Yale University Press, 1966), IX:6–7.

5. For the postwar problems confronting Britain, see Van Alstyne, *Empire and Independence,* 24–25.

6. Ibid., 21, 25–26. Also see Colin G. Galloway, *The Scratch of a Pen: 1763 and the Transformation of America* (New York, Oxford University Press, 2006).

7. Thomas Hutchinson quoted in Bernard Bailyn, *The Ideological Origins of the American Revolution* (Cambridge, MA: Harvard University Press, 1967), 220.

8. Lord North quoted in Van Alstyne, *Empire and Independence,* 36; Edmund Burke quoted in Barbara W. Tuchman, *The March of Folly: From Troy to Vietnam* (New York: Ballantine Books, 1984), 200.

9. Lord Mansfield quoted in Van Alstyne, *Empire and Independence,* 60.

10. In this resolution, Lord North proposed that if any colony agreed to make a grant for the common defense, Parliament would not assess any other tax for that purpose on the colony. For Americans, the resolution changed the form of the tax without lightening the burden. In the Virginia Resolutions on Lord North's Conciliatory Proposal of June 10, 1775, Thomas Jefferson explained why Virginia rejected the resolution: "*Because* to render perpetual our exemption from an unjust taxation, we must saddle ourselves with a perpetual tax adequate to the expectations and subject to the disposal of Parliament alone." For the Virginia resolutions, see Julian P. Boyd, ed., *The Papers of Thomas Jefferson,* 33 vols. (Princeton, NJ: Princeton University Press, 1950), I:171.

11. "The Farmer Refuted," February 23, 1775, in Harold C. Syrett and Jacob E. Cooke, eds., *The Papers of Alexander Hamilton,* 27 vols. (New York: Columbia University Press, 1961–1987), I:160.

12. Lee to Landon Carter, April 1, 1776, in James Curtis Ballagh, ed., *The Letters of Richard Henry Lee,* 2 vols. (New York: Macmillan, 1911), I:173.

The British were equally confident that they could resolve the American problem with force.

13. Hartley quoted in Van Alstyne, *Empire and Independence,* 65. Hamilton also predicted French and Spanish involvement in his "The Farmer Refuted," in Syrett and Cooke, *Papers of Hamilton,* I:159.

14. For the French interest in America, see Robert Rhodes Crout, "In Search of a 'Just and Lasting Peace': The Treaty of 1783, Louis XVI, Vergennes, and the Regeneration of the Realm," *International History Review* 5 (August 1983): 372–75.

15. Lyman H. Butterfield, ed., *Diary and Autobiography of John Adams,* 4 vols. (Cambridge, MA: Harvard University Press, 1961–1966), III:328–39.

16. Lee to Landon Carter, June 2, 1776, in Ballagh, *Letters of Richard Henry Lee,* I:198 (emphasis added).

17. Gerry quoted in James H. Hutson, *John Adams and the Diplomacy of the American Revolution* (Lexington: University Press of Kentucky, 1980), 9.

18. Samuel Adams to Samuel Cooper, February 4, 1777, in Harry A. Cushing, ed., *Writings of Samuel Adams,* 4 vols. (New York: G. P. Putnam's Sons, 1904–1908), III:354.

19. Worthing Chauncy Ford and Gaillard Hunt, eds., *Journals of the Continental Congress, 1774–1789,* 34 vols. (Washington, DC: Government Printing Office, 1904–1937), VI:1057; Franklin to Aranda, April 7, 1777, in Francis Wharton, ed., *The Revolutionary Diplomatic Correspondence of the United States,* 6 vols. (Washington: Government Printing Office, 1889), II:304.

20. Paul Chrisler Phillips, *The West in the Diplomacy of the American Revolution,* Illinois Studies in the Social Sciences, 11:1–2 (Urbana: University of Illinois, 1913), 50–53.

21. John Adams to Samuel Adams, July 28, 1778, in Wharton, ed., *The Revolutionary Diplomatic Correspondence,* II:668. For the role of the French Navy, see Jonathan R. Dull, *The French Navy and American Independence: A Study of Arms and Diplomacy, 1774–1787* (Princeton, NJ: Princeton University Press, 1975); Adams to James Warren, August 4, 1778, in *Warren-Adams Letters: Being Chiefly a Correspondence Among John Adams, Samuel Adams, and James Warren* (Boston: Massachusetts Historical Society, 1925), II:40; Butterfield, *Diary and Autobiography of John Adams,* IV:38–39; Adams to Warren, August 4, 1778, in *Warren-Adams Letters,* II:40.

22. Proceedings of Congress as to Conditions of Pacification and particularly as to the Mississippi and Fisheries, February 23, 1779, March 19, 1779; and Proceedings of March 22, 1779, Wharton, *The Revolutionary Diplomatic Correspondence,* III:59–60, 89, 95–96.

23. Washington to Henry Laurens, November 14, 1778, in John C. Fitzpatrick, ed., *The Writings of George Washington,* 37 vols. (Washington, DC: Government Printing Office, 1931–1940), XIII:256.

24. Adams to Edmond Charles Genêt, May 17, 1780, in *The Works of John Adams,* 10 vols. (Boston: Little, Brown, 1853), VII:172–75.

25. Whipple to Josiah Bartless, July 27, 1779, in Edmund C. Burnett, ed., *Letters of Members of the Continental Congress,* 8 vols. (Washington, DC: Carnegie Institution, 1928), IV:346.

26. Jenifer to George Weedon, June 5, 1781, Ibid., VI:112.

27. Thomas Rodney to Caesar Rodney, June 15, 1781, Ibid., 121–22.

28. Vergennes to Gerard de Rayneval, October 26, 1778, in John J. Meng, ed., *Dispatches and Instructions of Conrad Alexander Gerard, 1778–1780* (Baltimore, MD: Johns Hopkins Press, 1939), 356.

29. Proceedings of Congress, March–September 1779, in Wharton, *Revolutionary Diplomatic correspondence,* III:95–96, 294, 301, 311, 324–26; Spanish capture of Mobile in the spring of 1780 caused the Madrid government to become even more demanding; see Henry P. Johnston, ed., *Correspondence and Public Papers of John Jay,* 4 vols. (New York: G. P. Putnam's Sons, 1890–1893), I:386.

30. A list of foreign loans may be found in Rafael A. Bayley, *The National Loans of the United States, from July 4, 1776 to June 30, 1880,* 2nd ed. (Washington, DC: Government Printing Office, 1882), 5–28; also see Merrill Jensen, *The New Nation: A History of the United States during the Confederation, 1781–1789* (New York: Vintage Books, 1950), 39.

31. Jay to Robert R. Livingston (secretary of foreign affairs), November 17, 1782, in Wharton, *Revolutionary Diplomatic Correspondence,* VI:22–23.

32. Jay quoted in Richard B. Morris, *The Peacemakers: The Great Powers and American Independence* (Boston: Northeastern University Press, 1983), 306.

33. Jay quoted in Ibid., 310.

34. Adams to Livingston, October 31, 1782, in Wharton, *Revolutionary Diplomatic Correspondence,* V:839.

35. Comte de Vergennes to Géard de Rayneval, December 4, 1782, in Mary A. Giunta and J. Dane Hartgrove, eds., *The Emerging Nation: A Documentary History of the Foreign Relations of the United States Under the Articles of Confederation, 1780–1789,* 3 vols. (Washington, DC: National Historical Publications and Records Commission, 1996), I:706.

36. Vergennes to Rayneval, December 4, 1782, in Wharton, *Revolutionary Diplomatic Correspondence,* VI:107.

37. See Crout, "In Search of a 'Just and Lasting Peace,'" 396–98.

38. Adams to Jay, August 13, 1782, in *Works of John Adams,* VII:610.

39. Diary of John Adams, November 11, 1782, in Butterfield, *Diary and Autobiography of John Adams,* III:52.

40. Diary, November 18, 1782, Ibid., 61.

41. Adams to Warren, March 20, 1783, in *Warren-Adams Letters,* II:192.

42. Franklin to Samuel Cooper, December 26, 1782, in Smyth, *Writings of Franklin,* VIII:649.

43. Franklin to Mifflin, December 25, 1783, Ibid., IX:131.

44. Adams to Warren, March 20, 1 783, in *Warren-Adams Letters,* II:191–92.

45. Franklin to Livingston, July 22, 1783, in Smyth, *Writings of Franklin,* IX:61–62.

46. Adams to the president of Congress, February 10, 1784, in *Works of John Adams,* VIII:178.

CHAPTER 2

1. *Common Sense* (1776), in Moncure Daniel Conway, ed., *The Writings of Thomas Paine,* 4 vols. (New York, Putnam, 1894–1896), I:86.

2. Hamilton to William Floyd and George Clinton, March 17, 1783, in Harold C. Syrett, ed., *The Papers of Alexander Hamilton,* 27 vols. (New York: Columbia University, 1961–1987), III:290; Massachusetts newspaper quoted in Merrill Jensen, *The New Nation: A History of the United States During the Confederation, 1781–1789* (New York: Knopf, 1950), 154.

3. Franklin to the Comte de Vergennes, March 16, 1783, in Albert Henry Smyth, ed., *The Writings of Benjamin Franklin,* 10 vols. (New York: Macmillan, 1907), IX:19–20; Franklin to Livingston, April 15, 1783, Ibid., 30; Adams to Warren, April 12, 1783, in *Warren-Adams Letters: Being Chiefly a Correspondence Among John Adams, Samuel Adams, and James Warren,* 2 vols. (Boston: Massachusetts Historical Society, 1925), II:208; Report on the Treaty With Sweden, July 24, 1783, in William T. Hutchinson and William M.E. Rachal, eds., *The Papers of James Madison* 17 vols. (Chicago: University of Chicago Press, 1962–1991), VII:243–45.

4. Franklin to Livingston, April 13, 1783, in Smyth, *Writings of Franklin,* IX:31, 33; Franklin to Livingston, June 12, 1783, Ibid., p. 49; Franklin to Livingston, July 22, 1783, Ibid., 62, 70.

5. Franklin to Livingston, December 5, 1782, Ibid., 8:633.

6. Adams to the president of Congress, November 9, 1 783, in *The Works of John Adams,* 10 vols. (Boston: Little, Brown, 1851–1865),VIII:157; Adams to Livingston, February 5, 1783, in Francis Wharton, ed., *The Revolutionary Diplomatic Correspondence of the United States,* 6 vols. (Washington: Government Printing Office, 1889), VI:242–47.

7. Adams to Warren, March 21, 1783, in *Warren-Adams Letters,* II:194.

8. Sheffield quoted in Samuel Flagg Bemis, "John Jay," Bemis, ed., *The American Secretaries of State and Their Diplomacy,* 10 vols. (New York: Knopf, 1927–1929), I:223–24. See also Richard B. Morris, ed., *John Jay: The Winning of the Peace* (New York: Harper & Row, 1980), II:536–37.

9. Report on a Treaty of Commerce, May 1, 1783, in Syrett, *Papers of Hamilton,* III:344–45.

10. Franklin Jay, and Henry Laurens to Livingston, July 27, 1783, in Wharton, *Revolutionary Diplomatic Correspondence,* VI:600; Morris, *John Jay,* II:537–38; Jay to William Bingham, July 29, 1783, Ibid., 571–72; Edward Bancroft to Jay, August 1783, Ibid., 575–76; Adams to the president of Congress, November 13, 1783, in *Works of John Adams,* VIII:158–59.

11. Edmund Randolph to James Madison, May 24, 1783, in Hutchinson and Rachal, *Papers of Madison,* VII:73; Virginia Delegates to Benjamin Harrison, August 14, 1783, Ibid., 275; Madison to Randolph, August 18, 30, 1783, Ibid., 281, 295–96; Madison to Thomas Jefferson, September 20, 1783, Ibid., 353.

12. Adams to the president of Congress, September 5, 1783, Ibid., 145.

13. Hamilton to Jay, July 25, 1783, in Syrett, *Papers of Hamilton,* III:416–17.

14. "Jefferson to Randolph, February 15, 1783, in Julian P. Boyd et al., eds., *The Papers of Thomas Jefferson,* 33 vols. (Princeton, NJ: Princeton University Press, 1950–), VI:248.

15. Hamilton to Floyd and Clinton, March 17, 1783, in Syrett, *Papers of Hamilton,* III:291.

16. *The Continentalist,* no. 4, April 13, 1782, in Ibid., 76–77.

17. Madison to Randolph, September 13, 1783, in Hutchinson and Rachal, *Papers of Madison,* VII:315; Harrison to Virginia Delegates, October 3, 1783, Ibid., 366.

18. Hamilton to George Washington, September 30, *1783,* in Syrett, *Papers of Hamilton,* III:462.

19. Resolution of the New York Legislature Calling for a Convention of the States to Revise and Amend the Articles of Confederation, July 20, 1782, Ibid., 110–13; Washington to Hamilton, March 31, 1783, Ibid., 310.

20. Unsubmitted Resolution Calling for a Convention to Amend the Articles of Confederation, July 1783, Ibid., 420.

21. Report on the Public Credit, March 6, 1783, in Hutchinson and Rachal, *Papers of Madison,* VI:313–14.

22. Jefferson to Madison, May 8, 1784, in Hutchinson and Rachal, eds., *The Papers of James Madison,* VIII:29.

23. Resolutions to Strengthen Powers of Congress, May 19, 1784, Ibid., 38–39; Bill Granting Congress Limited Power to Regulate Commerce, June 5, 1784, Ibid., 57; Mercer to Madison, November 12, 1784, Ibid., 134–35; James Monroe to Madison, December 18, 1784, Ibid., 189–90.

24. Motion Respecting the Secretary of Foreign Affairs, June 4, 1783, in Syrett, *Papers of Hamilton,* III:374; Report on Peace Arrangements for the Department of Foreign Affairs, May 8, 1783, Ibid., 351.

25. Hamilton to Clinton, October 3, 1783, Ibid., 465; Virginia Delegates to Harrison, September 8, 1783, in Hutchinson and Rachal, *Papers of Madison,* VII:300–301.

26. Quoted in A. L. Burt, *The United States, Great Britain and British North America from the Revolution to the Establishment of Peace After the War of 1812* (New Haven, CT: Yale University Press, 1940), 87.

27. Johnson's speech quoted in Ibid., 88–91.

28. Madison to Jefferson, October 11, 1784, in Boyd, *Papers of Jefferson,* VII:440; Mercer to Madison, November 12, 1784, in Rutland and Rachal, *Papers of Madison,* VIII:134.

29. Joseph Jones to Madison, May 25, 1783, Ibid., 7:77; Livingston to Madison, July 19, 1783, Ibid., 235–37; Madison to James Madison, Sr., August 30, 1783, Ibid., 294; Virginia Delegates to Harrison, September 8, 1783, Ibid., 301. For a record of Carleton's actions in New York, see Hugh Hastings and J. A. Holden, eds., *The Public Papers of George Clinton,* 10 vols. (Albany, NY: State of New York, 1904), VIII:184–86, 203–4, 207–16.

30. Report on Measures to be Taken for Carrying Into Effect the Provisional Peace Treaty, May 30, 1783, in Syrett, *Papers of Hamilton,* III:366.

31. Hamilton to Clinton, June 1, 1783, Ibid., 370.

32. Ibid., p. 371; Jay to Hamilton, September 28, 1783, Ibid., p. 459; A Letter from Phocion to the Considerate Citizens of New York, January 1–27, 1784, Ibid., 492.

33. Monroe to Jefferson, November 1, 1784, in Boyd, *Papers of Jefferson,* VII:461; Monroe to Madison, November 15, 1784, in Rutland and Rachal, *Papers of Madison,* VIII:141.

34. Franklin to Elias Boudinot, November 1, 1783, in Smyth, *Writings of Franklin,* IX:110–11; Adams to Franklin, December 5, 1783, in *Works of John Adams,* VIII:164–65; Adams to Messrs. Willink and others, February 5, 1784, Ibid., 176; Franklin to Adams, February 5, 1784, Ibid., p. 177; Lyman H. Butterfield et al., eds., *Diary and Autobiography of John Adams,* 4 vols. (New York, 1964), III:148–49; Jefferson to Madison, February 20, 1784, in Boyd, *Papers of Jefferson,* VI:546.

35. Adams to the president of Congress, June 22, 1784, in *Works of John Adams,* VIII:204–5.

36. Monroe to Harrison, February 14, 1784, in Boyd, *Papers of Jefferson,* VI:539; Virginia Delegates to Harrison, May 13, 1784, Ibid, 7:248–49.

37. Franklin to Laurens, April 29, 1784, in Smyth, *Writings of Franklin,* IX:198.

38. Adams to Warren, June 30, 1 784, in *Warren-Adams Letters,* II:240; Franklin to Adams, July 4, 1784, in *Works of John Adams,* VIII:206–7; Franklin to Mifflin, June 16, 1784, in Smyth, *Writings of Franklin,* IX:226; American Commissioners to Jay, March 18, 1785, in Boyd, *Papers of Jefferson,* VIII:36.

39. Madison to Jefferson, May 15, 1784, in Rutland and Rachal, *Papers of Madison,* VIII:35; Adams to Warren, August 27, 1784, quoted in Boyd, *Papers of Jefferson,* VII:382n.

40. Jefferson to Adams, June 19, 1784, in Ibid., 7:309; Jefferson to Adams, July 24, 1784, Ibid., p. 382; Jefferson to Monroe, November 11, 1784, Ibid., p. 508.

41. Diaries of John and Abigail Adams in Butterfield, *Diary and Autobiography of John Adams,* III:166–67, 170–71.

42. Abigail Adams to Mercy Warren, September 5, 1784, in *Warren-Adams Letters,* II:243.

43. See Dumas Malone, *Jefferson and the Rights of Man* (Boston: Little, Brown, 1951), 6–7.

44. Franklin to Comte Dc Mercy Argenteau, July 30, 1784, in Smyth, *Writings of Franklin,* IX:248–49; Franklin to Adams, August 6, 1784, Ibid., 250; Commission for Negotiating Treaties of Amity and Commerce, May 12, 1784, in Boyd, *Papers of Jefferson,* VII:262–63. For Jefferson's treaty plans, see Ibid., 463ff.

45. Instructions to the Commissioners for Negotiating Treaties of Amity and Commerce, May 7, 1784, Ibid., 267.

46. Franklin to Adams, July 4, 1784, in *Works of John Adams,* VIII:207; Franklin to Hartley, September 6, 1783, in Smyth, *Writings of Franklin,* IX:88; Franklin to Mifflin, June 16, 1784, Ibid., 225–26; Hartley to Jay, March 2, 1784, in Morris, *John Jay,* II:700–701; John B. Church to Hamilton, September 25, 1784, in Syrett, *Papers of Hamilton,* III:579; aide-mémoire from Hartley, September 16, 1784, in Boyd, *Papers of Jefferson,* 7:422; American commissioners to Dorset, October 28, 1784, Ibid., 456, 457–58; American commissioners to the president of Congress, November 11, 1784, Ibid., 493–95; Jefferson to Monroe, November 11, 1784, Ibid., 509; Dorset to the American commissioners, November 24, 1784, Ibid., 547; Jefferson to Monroe, December 10, 1784, Ibid., 563; Franklin to Hartley, January 3, 1785, in Smyth, *Writings of Franklin,* IX:284–85.

47. Jefferson to Nathanael Greene, January 12, 1785, in Paul Leicester Ford, ed., *The Writings of Thomas Jefferson,* 10 vols. (New York: G. P. Putnam, 1892–1899), IV:25; Jefferson to Monroe, February 1785, Ibid., 30–31.

48. Franklin to Jay, February 8, 1785, in Smyth, *Writings of Franklin,* IX:287–88; Jefferson to Madison, March 18, 1785, in Boyd, *Papers of Jefferson,* VIII:39–40.

49. Adams to Jay, April 13, 14, 24, 1785, in *Works of John Adams,* VIII:234–37.

50. Franklin to Jay, February 8, 1785, in Smyth, *Writings of Franklin,* IX:287; Adams to Jay, March 9, 1785, in *Works of John Adams,* VIII:228–29. For this reason, Adams advocated the appointment of an American minister to London. See Adams to Jay, April 24, 1785, Ibid., 236–37.

51. Monroe to Jefferson, December 14, 1784, in Stanislaus Murray Hamilton, ed., *The Writings of James Monroe,* 7 vols. (New York: G. P. Putnam's Sons, 1898–1903), I:54–55; Franklin to Charles Thomson, May 13, 1784, in Smyth, *Writings of Franklin,* IX:213; Franklin to Mr. and Mrs. Jay, May 13, 1784, Ibid., 214; Franklin to William Franklin, August 16, 1784, Ibid., 253.

52. Jefferson to Monroe, August 28, 1785, in Ford, *Writings of Jefferson,* IV:87; Franklin to Benjamin Vaughn, July 24, 1785, in Smyth, *Writings of Franklin,* IX:365–66; Franklin to Jay, September 19, 1785, Ibid., 463.

CHAPTER 3

1. Jefferson to William Stephens Smith, February 19, 1787, in Julian P. Boyd, et al., eds., *The Papers of Thomas Jefferson,* 33 vols. (Princeton,

NJ: Princeton University Press, 1950–), XI:168; Jefferson to Madison, June 20, 1787, Ibid., 482; Adams's opinion of Jefferson is related several places in David McCullough's *John Adams* (New York: Simon & Schuster, 2001), 312, 328.

2. Monroe to Madison, March 6, 1785, in Stanislaus Murray Hamilton, ed., *The Writings of James Monroe*, 7 vols. (New York: G. P. Putnam's Sons, 1898–1903), I:64; Monroe to Jefferson, April 12, 1785, Ibid., 68–69; Elbridge Gerry to Jefferson, February 25, 1785, in Boyd, *Papers of Jefferson*, VII:652; Jay to the American commissioners, March 11, 1785, Ibid., 8:19; Jay to Jefferson, March 15, 1785, Ibid., 33; Adams to M. Dumas, May 11, 1785, in *The Works of John Adams*, 10 vols. (Boston: Little, Brown, 1851–1865), VIII:247; Adams to Jay, March 9, 1785, Ibid., 227; Jefferson to the Rev. William Smith, February 19, 1791, in Boyd, *Papers of Jefferson*, XIX:113.

3. Lyman H. Butterfield et al., eds., in *Diary and Autobiography of John Adams*, 4 vols. (Cambridge, MA: Belknap Press of Harvard University Press, 1961), III:176.

4. Adams to John Jay, May 13, 1785, in *The Works of John Adams*, VIII:248–49.

5. Adams to Jefferson, May 27, 1785, Ibid., VIII:252; *Public Advertiser* quoted in Abigail Adams to Jefferson, June 6, 1785, in Boyd, *Papers of Jefferson*, VIII:179–80.

6. Adams to Franklin and Jefferson, May 29, 1785, Ibid., VIII:170–71; Adams to Jay, June 1, 2, 1785, in *Works of John Adams*, VIII:254–56. Address to the king, June 1, 1785, Ibid., VIII:256–57.

7. Adams to Jay, June 2, 1785, Ibid., 257–58.

8. Adams to Jay, June 17, 1785, Ibid., VIII:268–72.

9. Jefferson to Monroe, June 17, 1785, in Boyd, *Papers of Jefferson*, VIII:252.

10. Boyd, *Papers of Jefferson*, VIII:231; Jefferson to Adams, October 3, 1785, Ibid., 579–80; Jefferson to Jay, January 27, 1786, Ibid., IX:235.

11. Patrick Henry to Jefferson, September 10, 1785, Ibid., VIII:509; Jefferson to Vergennes, December 1785, Ibid., IX:112.

12. Jefferson to Monroe, June 17, 1785, Ibid., VIII:228; Jefferson's report on conversations with Vergennes, December, 1787, Ibid., VIII:139; Merrill D. Peterson, "Thomas Jefferson and Commercial Policy, 1783–1795," *William and Mary Quarterly* XXII (October 1965): 596–97.

13. Jefferson to Montmorin, July 23, 1787, in Boyd, *Papers of Jefferson*, XI:617; Calonne, the French Comptroller General, to Jefferson, October 22, 1786, Ibid., X:474–78. For the French concessions see Ibid., X:474–78; final decree, dated December 29, 1787, Ibid., XII:468–70.

14. The Arret of December 7, 1788, Ibid., XIV:268–69; Jefferson to Izard, August 1, 1787, Ibid., XI:659; Rutledge to Jefferson, October 23, 1787, Ibid., XII:263–64; Brailsford and Morris to Jefferson, October 31,

1787, Ibid., 298–301; Brailsford and Morris to Jefferson, March 10, 1789, Ibid., XIV, 632–33; Rutledge to Jefferson, April 1, 1789, Ibid., XV:12–13.

15. Jefferson to Jay, December 31, 1787, Ibid., XII:479–82; Jay to Jefferson, April 24, 1788, Ibid., XIII:106.

16. Franklin and Jefferson to Adams, July 8, 1785, Ibid., VIII:273; Adams to Carmarthen, July 29, 1785, in *Works of John Adams,* VIII:288; Adams to Jay, July 29, 1785, Ibid., 288–89.

17. Adams to Jay, August 25, 1785, Ibid., VIII:303–5; Adams to Jay, November 4, 1785, Ibid., 337; Adams to Jay, December 3, 1785, Ibid., 350–51.

18. Adams to Jay, August 25, 1785, Ibid., VIII:309; Adams to Jay, October 15, 1785, Ibid., 521; Adams to Jay, October 21, 1785, Ibid., 326, 551; Adams to Jefferson, October 24, 1785, in Lester J. Cappon, ed., in *The Adams-Jefferson Letters: The Complete Correspondence between Thomas Jefferson and Abigail and John Adams* (Chapel Hill: University of North Carolina Press, 1959), 86.

19. Charles Francis Adams's *Life of John Adams,* in *Works of John Adams,* I:420; Jefferson to Madison, April 25, 1786, in William T. Hutchinson and William M. E. Rachal, eds., *The Papers of James Madison,* 17 vols. (Chicago: University of Chicago Press, 1962–1991), IX:26; Adams to Carmarthen, March 13, 1786, in Boyd, *Papers of Jefferson,* 5 vols., IX:327; American Commissioners to Jay, April 25, 1786, Ibid., 406; Jefferson to John Page, May 4, 1786, Ibid., 446; Jefferson to C.W.F. Dumas, May 6, 1786, Ibid., 462; Jefferson to David Humphreys, May 7, 1786, Ibid., 469.

20. Jefferson to Abigail Adams, August 9, 1785, in Paul Leicester Ford, ed., *The Writings of Thomas Jefferson,* 10 vols. (New York: G.P. Putnam's Sons, 1892–1899), IV:261; Jefferson to Smith, September 28, 1787, in Boyd, *Papers of Jefferson,* XII:193.

21. Jefferson to Madison, September 1, 1785, in Boyd, *Papers of Jefferson,* VIII:461.

22. Jefferson to Geismar, September 6, 1785, Ibid., VIII:499–500; Jefferson to James Currie, September 27, 1785, Ibid., 559.

23. Jefferson to Madison, September 1, 1785, Ibid., VIII:161; Jefferson to Jay, August 23, 1785, Ibid., 427.

24. Jefferson to G.K. van Hogendorp, October 13, 1785, Ibid., VIII:633; Jefferson to Jay, August 23, 1785, Ibid., 426.

25. Adams to Jay, May 5, 1785, in *Works of John Adams,* VIII:240–41; Adams to Jay, August 6, 1785, Ibid., 289–90; Adams to Jefferson, October 3, 1785, in Boyd, *Papers of Jefferson,* VIII:577.

26. Adams to Jay, October 17, 1785, in *Works of John Adams,* VIII, 323; Adams to Jay, October 21, 1785, Ibid., 527.

27. Adams to Jay, May 5, 1785, Ibid., VIII:241; Adams to Jay, December 6, 1785, Ibid., VIII:357.

28. Adams to Jay, May 5, 1785, Ibid., VIII:242; Adams to Jay, July 19, 1785, Ibid., 283; Adams to Jay, August 8, 1785, Ibid., 297; Adams to Jay, August 30, 1785, Ibid., 315.

29. Adams to Jefferson, August 7, 1785, in Boyd, *Papers of Jefferson,* VIII:554–55; Adams to Jefferson, September 4, 1785, Ibid., 477; Adams to Jefferson, October 3, 1785, Ibid., 577.

30. Adams to Jay, June 26, 1785, in *Works of John Adams,* VIII:273; Adams to Jay, July 19, 1785, Ibid., 282–83; Adams to Jay, October 21, 1785, Ibid., 332.

31. To review the negotiations with the Portuguese minister in London, see *Works of John Adams,* VIII:410–11; Adams to Jefferson, February 21, 1786, in Boyd, *Papers of Jefferson,* IX:295; Jefferson to Jay, March 12, 1786, Ibid., 525; Jefferson to David Humphreys, May 7, 1786, Ibid., 469.

32. Adams to Jay, October 15, 1785, in *Works of John Adams,* VIII:320; Adams to Jay, December 3, 1785, Ibid., 355.

33. Adams to Jay, November 5, 1785, Ibid., VIII:336–37; Adams to Jay, December 6, 1785, Ibid., 356.

34. Adams to Jay, December 9, 1785, in *Works of John Adams,* VIII:359–60; Adams to Jefferson, January 19, 1786, Ibid., 368.

35. Adams to Jay, May 25, 1786, Ibid., VIII:594–95.

36. Adams quoted in Monroe to Richard Henry Lee, May 24, 1786, in Stanislaus Murray Hamilton, ed., *The Writings of James Monroe,* 7 vols. (New York: G.P. Putnam's Sons, 1898–1903), I:130.

37. Adams to Jay, May 25, 1786, in *Works of John Adams,* VIII:595; Butterfield, *Diary and Autobiography of John Adams,* III:201.

38. Adams to Matthew Robinson, March 2, 1786, in *Works of John Adams,* VIII:383–85; Adams to James Bowdoin, May 9, 1786, Ibid., 589; Adams to Jay, May 16, 1786, Ibid., 391.

39. Jefferson to Madison, June 20, 1787, in Boyd, *Papers of Jefferson,* XI:482.

40. Butterfield, *Diary and Autobiography of John Adams,* III:201; Adams to Jay, January 25, 1787, in *Works of John Adams,* VIII:424; Adams to Jay, February 3, 1787, Ibid., 428–29; Adams to Jay, May 8, 1787, Ibid., 438–39; Messrs. Willink and Others to Adams, May 18, 1787, Ibid., 440–41; Jefferson to Madison, August 2, 1787, in Boyd, *Papers of Jefferson,* XI:664; Adams to Jefferson, August 25, 1787, Ibid., XII:55.

41. Jefferson to Adams, December 16, 1787, in Boyd, *Papers of Jefferson,* XI:429–30; Adams to Jefferson, February 12, 1788, Ibid., 582; Jefferson to Jay, March 16, 1788, Ibid., 671; Jefferson to the Commissioners of the Treasury, March 29, 1788, Ibid., 698–700.

42. Jay to Adams, July 25, 1787, in *Works of John Adams,* VIII:445–46; Adams to Jefferson, March 1, 1787, in Boyd, *Papers of Jefferson,* XI:189; Adams to Jay, February 14, 1788, in *Works of John Adams,* VIII:476.

43. Adams to Jay, February 21, 1788, in *Works of John Adams,* VIII:480.

44. Jefferson to Adams, February 20, 1787, in Boyd, *Papers of Jefferson,* XI:170; Jefferson to William Stephens Smith, February 19, 1787, Ibid., XI:168.

45. Dumas Malone, *Jefferson and the Rights of Man* (Boston: Little, Brown, 1951), 14, 15–16. For Shippen's observations of Paris, January 9, 1788, see Boyd, *Papers of Jefferson,* XII:502–4.

46. Jefferson to Madison, January 30, 1787, Ibid., XI:95–96; Jefferson to Adams, February 14, 1787, Ibid., 143; Jefferson to Lafayette, February 26, 1787, Ibid., 186; Carmichael to Jefferson, March 25, 1787, Ibid., 257.

47. Jay to Jefferson, August 18, 1786, see Boyd, *Papers of Jefferson,* X:271–72; Jay to Jefferson, March 9, 1789, Ibid., XIV:628; Jefferson to Jay, November 14, 1788, Ibid., XIV:56–57; for a history of the Consular Convention of 1788, see Ibid., 66–92.

CHAPTER 4

1. Franklin to Livingston, July 25, 1783, in Albert Henry Smyth, ed., *The Writings of Benjamin Franklin,* 10 vols. (New York: Macmillan, 1905–1907), IX:71–72; Franklin to Thomas Mifflin, December 25, 1783, Ibid., 133.

2. Adams to Jay, December 15, 1784, in *The Works of John Adams,* 10 vols. (Boston: Little, Brown, 1851–1865), VIII:218–19.

3. Jay to the American commissioners, March 11, 1785, Ibid., VIII:19; Jay to Jefferson, March 15, 1785, Ibid., 33; Adams to M. Dumas, May 11, 1785, in *Works of John Adams,* VIII:247; Adams to Jay, March 9, 1785, Ibid., 227.

4. Jefferson to Madison, September 1, 1785, in William T. Hutchinson and William M.E. Rachal, eds., *Papers* [of James Madison], 17 vols. (Chicago: University of Chicago Press, 1962–1991), VIII:361.

5. Jay to the American Commissioners, March 11, 1785, Julian P. Boyd et al., eds., *The Papers of Thomas Jefferson,* 33 vols. (Princeton, NJ: Princeton University Press, 1950–), VIII:19–21; Adams to Franklin and Jefferson, March 20, 1785, Ibid., VIII:46–47.

6. Jefferson to William Canichael, August 18, 1785, Ibid., VIII:410; Jefferson to Monroe, November 11, 1784, Ibid., VII:511–12.

7. Jefferson to Adams, July 7, 1785, Ibid., VIII:266; Adams to Jefferson, July 18, 1785, Ibid., 301; Jefferson to Adams, August 6, 1785, Ibid., 347.

8. Jefferson to Adams, September 4, 1785, Ibid., VIII:473; Adams to Jefferson, September 15, 1785, Ibid., 521.

9. Jefferson to Adams, September 19, 1785, Ibid., VIII:526.

10. Jefferson to Adams, September 24, 1785, Ibid., VIII:545.

11. Jefferson to Carmichael, November 4, 1785, Ibid., IX:14; Adams to Jefferson, October 2, 1785, Ibid., VIII:572; Monroe to Jefferson, January 19, 1786, Ibid., IX:187.

12. Adams to Jefferson, October 2, 1785, in Boyd, *Papers of Jefferson,* VIII:571–72; Monroe to Jefferson, January 19, 1786, Ibid., IX:187.

13. Adams to Jefferson, February 17, 1786, Ibid., IX:284–87.

14. Adams to Jay, February 20, 22, 1786, in *Works of John Adams,* VIII:374–79.

15. Jefferson to May, March 12, 1786, in Boyd, *Papers of Jefferson,* IX:325; Adams and Jefferson to Jay, March 28, 1786, Ibid., 558–59.

16. Quoted in Eugene Schuyler, *American Diplomacy and the Furtherance of Commerce* (New York: C. Scribner's Sons, 1886), 205–6.

17. Jefferson to Monroe, August 11, 1786, in Boyd, *Papers of Jefferson,* X:224; Adams to Jefferson, January 25, 1787, Ibid., XI:66.

18. Adams to Jefferson, May 25, 1786, in *Works of John Adams,* VIII:393; Jefferson to Adams, May 5, 1786, in Boyd, *Papers of Jefferson,* IX:595.

19. Adams to Jefferson, June 6, 1786, in Boyd, *Papers of Jefferson,* IX:611–12.

20. Adams to Jefferson, July 3, 1786, in Ibid., X:86–87.

21. Jefferson to Adams, July 11, 1786, Ibid., X:123–25; Jefferson's proposed convention against the Barbary States [Before July 4, 1786], Ibid., IX:566–68; Adams to Jefferson, July 31, 1786, Ibid., X:177–78.

22. Useful accounts include Ray W. Irwin, *The Diplomatic Relations of the United States with the Barbary Powers, 1776–1816* (Chapel Hill: University of North Carolina Press, 1931) and chapters in James A. Field, Jr., *America and the Mediterranean World, 1776–1882* (Princeton, NJ: Princeton University Press, 1969) and Luella J. Hall, *The United States and Morocco, 1776–1956* (Metchen, NJ: Scarecrow Press, 1971).

23. For background, see Arthur P. Whitaker, *The Spanish-American Frontier, 1783–1795: The Westward Movement and the Spanish Retreat in the Mississippi Valley* (Lincoln: University of Nebraska Press, 1927).

24. For a comprehensive treatment of these concepts and their origins, see Felix Glibert, *To the Farewell Address* (Princeton, NJ: Princeton University Press, 1961) and Gerald Stourzh, *Benjamin Franklin and American Foreign Policy* (Chicago: University of Chicago Press, 1954).

25. Oliver Pollock to Jay, June 3, 1785, in Mary A. Giunta and J. Dane Hartgrove, eds., *The Emerging Nation: A Documentary History of the Foreign Relations of the United States Under the Articles of Confederation, 1780–1789,* 3 vols. (Washington, DC: National Historical Publications and Records Commission, 1996), II:649–51.

26. Gardoqui to Jay, May 21, 1785, Ibid., II:641; Jay to Gardoqui, May 27, 1785, Ibid., II:645.

27. Journal of Congress, July 2, 1785, Ibid., II:692; Jay to Gardoqui, July 6, 1785, Ibid., II:692; Gardoqui to Jay, July 8, 1785, Ibid., II:693–94.

28. Thomson's Report on John Jay's Commission to Negotiate a Treaty with Spain, July 20, 1785, Ibid., II:705

29. Jay to the president of the Congress, August 15, 1785, Ibid., II:744–46; Congressional Resolution Changing John Jay's Instructions..., August 25, 1785, Ibid., II:768–69.]

30. Gardoqui to John Jay, September 23, 1785, Ibid., II:827–28; Congressional Resolution on Spanish Affairs, October 13, 1785, Ibid., II:183–84.

31. Gardoqui to Jay, May 25, 1786, Ibid., III:181; Jay to president of Congress, May 29, 1786, Ibid., III:190.

32. Gardoqui to Congress, June 30, 1786, Ibid., III:212–14; Jay's Report Regarding Negotiations with Spain, July 12, 1786, Ibid., III:225–26.

33. Jay to the president of Congress, August 3, 1786, Ibid., III:247–55.

34. Gardoqui to Jay, August 3, 1786, Ibid., III:255.

35. Jay's Report on the Mississippi River, August 17, 1786, Ibid., III:263–64.

36. See Congressional Resolutions Regarding the Spanish Negotiations, August 29 and August 31, 1786, Ibid., III:279–86, 286–88.

37. Assumptions and Draft Instructions for Gardoqui...., September 1, 1786, Ibid., III:288–90.

38. Instructions to the Virginia Delegates to Congress..., November 29, 1786, Ibid., III:370–71; Jefferson to Madison, January 20, 1787, Ibid., III:406.

39. Madison to Jefferson, March 19, 1787, Ibid. III:452–53; Congressional Order to John Jay...., April 4, 1787, Ibid., III:461.

40. Jay to the president of Congress, April 11, 1787, Ibid., III:466–68.

41. Jay' Report on George Rogers Clark's Seizure of Spanish Property, April 12, 1787, Ibid., III:469–72.

42. Jay to Gardoqui, October 17, 1788, Ibid., III:850.

43. The classic defense of Jay remains Frank Monaghan, *John Jay: Defender of Liberty* (Indianapolis: Bobbs-Merrill, 1935); also see Samuel Flagg Bemis, *Pinckney: America's Advantage from Europe's Distress, 1783–1800* (New Haven: Yale University Press, 1960).

CHAPTER 5

1. See editorial notes on Madison in Congress, February–May 1787, William T. Hutchinson and M.E. Rachal, eds., *Papers* [of James Madison], 17 vols. (Chicago: University of Chicago Press, 1962–1991), IX:263; Madison to Randolph, March 25, 1787, Ibid., 352; Notes on Debates, April 25, 1787, Ibid., 406; Views of the Political System of the United States, April, 1787, Ibid., 549.

2. Charles Thomson to Jay, Jan. 15, 1784, in Mary A. Giunta and J. Dane Hartgrove, eds., *The Emerging Nation: A Documentary History of the Foreign Relations of the United States Under the Articles of Confederation, 1780–1789,*

3 vols. (Washington, DC: National Historical Publications and Records Commission, 1996), II:277–78.

3. Adams to Jay, May 25, 1786, in Giunta and Hartgrove, eds., *The Emerging Nation,* III:179–81; Jay to Adams, November 1, 1786, Ibid., 362–63.

4. Washington to Jay, August 1, 1786, Jared Sparks, ed., *The Writings of George Washington,* 12 vols. (Boston: F. Andrews, 1838–1839), IX:188.

5. Jay's Report to Congress, October 12, 1786, in *Documentary History of the Constitution of the United States of America, 1786–1870,* 5 vols. (Washington, DC: Department of State, 1894–1905), IV:648.

6. Jay's Report on State Laws Contrary to the Treaty of Peace, October 13, 1786, in Giunta and Hartgrove, eds., *The Emerging Nation,* III:333–49; president of Congress to the State Governors, April 13, 1787, Ibid., III: 472–77.

7. Congressional Resolutions on State Observance of the Treaty of Peace, Ibid., III:454–55; Robert A. Rutland, ed., *The Papers of George Mason, 1725–1792,* 3 vols. (Chapel Hill: North Carolina Press, 1970), III:1019–20.

8. Adams to Franklin, January 24, 1784, in Giunta and Hartgrove, eds., *The Emerging Nation,* II:283.

9. Otto to Congress, November 30, 1785, Ibid., II:931–35; Otto to Comte de Vergennes, June 17, 1786, Ibid., III:204–5.

10. Jay to Jefferson, October 27, 1786, Ibid., III:358; John Temple to Lord Carmarthen, October 4, 1786, Ibid., III:325–26.

11. Richard B. Morris, *The Forging of the Union, 1781–1789* (New York: Harper & Row, 1987), 259; also see Leonard L. Richards, *Shay's Rebellion: The American Revolution's Final Battle* (Philadelphia: University of Pennsylvania Press, 2002) and Robert A. Freer, "Shay's Rebellion and the Constitution: A Study in Causation," *New England Quarterly* 42 (1969):388–410.

12. Madison to Monroe, June 21, 1786, Hutchinson and Rachal, eds., *Papers of James Madison,* IX:82–85; Gerry to Jefferson, February 25, 1785, in Edmund C. Burnett, ed., *Letters of Members of the Continental Congress,* 8 vols. (Washington: Carnegie Institution of Washington, 1921–1936), VIII:44; Monroe to Jefferson, January 19, 1786, in Julian P. Boyd et al., eds., *The Papers of Thomas Jefferson,* 33 vols. (Princeton, NJ: Princeton University Press, 1950–), IX:188.

13. Madison to Richard Henry Lee, July 7, 1785, in Hutchinson and Rachal, *Papers of Madison,* VIII:315.

14. Madison to Jefferson, March 18, 1786, Ibid., 502; Madison to Monroe, April 9, 1786, ibid., IX:25–26; Madison to Monroe, August 7, 1785, Ibid., VIII:334; Charles Pettit to Jeremiah Wadsworth, May 27, 1786, in Burnett, *Letters of Members of the Continental Congress,* VIII:370.

15. Congressional Resolutions Relating to Commercial Matters, Apr. 30, 1784, in Giunta and Hartgrove, eds., *The Emerging Nation,* II:354–56.

16. Congressional Resolutions on Expanding Control of Foreign Commerce, Oct. 23, 1786, in Giunta and Hartgrove, eds., *The Emerging Nation,* III:354–56.

17. Pierse Long to John Langdon, January 31, 1785, in Burnett, *Letters of Members of the Continental Congress,* VIII:18.

18. Madison to Monroe, August 7, 1785, in Hutchinson and Rachal, *Papers of Madison,* VIII, 333; Langdon to Jefferson, December 7, 1785, in Boyd, *Papers of Jefferson,* IX:84.

19. Rufus King to John Adams, November 2, 1785, in Burnett, *Letters of Members of the Continental Congress,* VIII:247–48.

20. Richard Henry Lee to Madison, August 11, 1785, in Hutchinson and Rachal, *Papers of Madison,* VIII:340.

21. Lee to Jay, September 11, 1785, in James Curtis Ballagh, ed., *The Letters of Richard Henry Lee* (New York: Macmillan, 1911–1914), II:389; Debates on Resolutions Related to the Regulation of Commerce…, Hutchinson and Rachal, *Papers of Madison,* VIII:407; Madison to Jefferson, January 22, 1786, Ibid., 476.

22. Samuel Osgood to John Adams, November 14, 1786, in Giunta and Hartgrove, eds., *The Emerging Nation,* III:366–67.

23. Jay to Jefferson, July 14, 1786, in Boyd, *Papers of Jefferson,* X:135.

24. Washington to Jay, August 1, 1786, in Sparks, ed., *The Writings of George Washington,* IX:187–88; Washington to Madison, November 6, 1786, in Hutchinson and Rachal, *Papers of Madison,* IX:161–62.

25. Madison to Monroe, March 14, 1786, Ibid., VIII:498; Madison to Jefferson, March 18, 1786, Ibid., 505.

26. Madison to Monroe, *Papers of Madison,* VIII:471; Jay to Adams, October 14, 1785, in Giunta and Hartgrove, eds., *The Emerging Nation,* II:862.

27. Jay's Report to Congress, January 31, 1786, Ibid., III: 83–84.

28. Jay to Washington, March 16, 1786, Ibid. III:127–28.

29. Address of the Annapolis Convention, September 14, 1786, in Harold C. Syrett, ed., *The Papers of Alexander Hamilton* 27 vols. (New York: Columbia University, 1961–1987), III:667.

30. *Documentary History of the Constitution of the United States of America, 1786–1870,* 5 vols. (Washington, DC: Department of State, 1894–1905), I:40.

31. Ibid., 688–89; Jefferson to Madison, December 16, 1786, in Rutland and Rachal, *Papers of Madison,* IX:210–11.

32. Discourses on Davila, in *The Works of John Adams,* 10 vols. (Boston: Little, Brown, 1851–1865), VI:280.

33. Letter quoted in Edmund Cody Burnett, *The Continental Congress: A Definitive History of the Continental Congress from Its Inception in 1774 to March 1789* (New York: Norton, 1964), 670.

34. In Worthington Ford et al., *Journals of the Continental Congress, 1774–1789,* 34 vols. (Washington, DC: Government Printing Office, 1904–1937), XXII:71–72.

35. Franklin to Jefferson, April 19, 1787, in Albert Henry Smyth, ed., *The Writings of Benjamin Franklin* (New York, 1907), IX:574; Monroe to Jefferson, July 27, 1787, in Boyd, *Papers of Jefferson,* XI:650–51.

36. See, for example, Clinton Rossiter, comp., *The Federalist Papers, Alexander Hamilton, James Madison and John Jay* (New York: New American Library, 1961).

CHAPTER 6

1. Sir John Temple to Lord Carmarthen, May 3, 1787, in Mary A. Giunta and J. Dane Hartgrove, eds., *The Emerging Nation: A Documentary History of the Foreign Relations of the United States Under the Articles of Confederation, 1780–1789,* 3 vols. (Washington, DC: National Historical Publications and Records Commission, 1996), III:493.

2. Franklin to Jefferson, April 19, 1787, in Albert Henry Smyth, ed., *The Writings of Benjamin Franklin,* 10 vols. (New York: Macmillan, 1905–1907), IX:574; Monroe to Jefferson, July 27, 1787, in Julian P. Boyd et al., eds., *The Papers of Thomas Jefferson,* 33 vols. (Princeton, NJ: Princeton University Press, 1950–), XI:630–31.

3. Adams to Jay, September 22, 1787, in *The Works of John Adams,* 10 vols. (Boston: Little, Brown, 1851–1865), VIII:451–52.

4. Otto to Comte de Montmorin, April 10, 1787, in Mary A. Giunta and Hartgrove, eds., *The Emerging Nation,* III:464; Richard B. Morris, *The Forging of the Union, 1781–1789* (New York: Harper & Row, 1987), 269.

5. Madison quoted in Irving R. Kaufman, "What Did the Founding Fathers Intend?," *The New Times Magazine,* Feb. 23, 1986, 60.

6. Max Farrand, ed., *The Records of the Federal Convention of 1787,* 3 vols. (New Haven, CT: Yale University Press, 1911), III:113, 548.

7. *Documentary History of the Constitution of the United States of America, 1786–1870,* 5 vols. (Washington, DC: Department of State, 1894–1905), IV:126–27.

8. Merrill Jensen, *The New Nation: A History of the United States During the Confederation, 1781–1789* (New York: Knopf, 1950), 43; Farrand, *Records of the Federal Convention,* I:21.

9. Farrand, *Records of the Federal Convention,* I:133.

10. John Jay to Thomas Jefferson, Aug. 18, 786, Henry Phelps Johnston, ed., *The Correspondence and Public Papers of John Jay,* 4 vols. (New York: B. Franklin, 1970), III:210; Farrand, *Records of the Federal Convention,* I:21.

11. Farrand, *Records of the Federal Convention,* I:64–65.

12. Ibid., I:65–66, 73–74.

13. Ibid., I:66–67, 70.

14. Ibid., I:292.

15. Ibid., II:85. 129–33, 183, 185. On the question of sending and receiving ambassadors, see especially Randolph's memorandum presented to the Committee of Detail, Ibid., IV:45–47.

16. Ibid., II:183, 185.

17. Ibid., I:426.

18. Ibid., II:297–98. For the compromise of July 16, see Ibid., II:13–14.

19. Ibid., II:538, 541.

20. Ibid., IV:53.

21. Ibid., II:297.

22. Ibid., II:392–94.

23. Ibid., II:392.

24. Ibid., II:481.

25. Ibid., III:210–11, 305, 333–35, 346.

26. Ibid., II:453, 498–99.

27. Ibid., III:624–25; Jonathan Elliot, ed., *The Debates of the Several Slate Conventions and the Adoption of the Federal Constitution,* 5 vols., 2nd ed. (Philadelphia: J.B. Lippincott, 1896), V:75. For Hamilton's remark of June 18, see Farrand, *Records of the Federal Convention,* I:292.

28. Farrand, *Records of the Federal Convention,* II:540.

29. Ibid., II:540–41, 549.

30. See James Iredell in Elliot, *Debates of the Several State Conventions,* IV:128.

31. Ibid., IV:119–20.

32. Ibid., IV:265, 269.

33. Ibid., IV:120, 258; Pierce Butler to Weedon Butler, May 5, 1788, Farrand, *Records of the Federal Convention,* III:302.

34. Elliot, *Debates of the Several State Conventions,* IV:264.

35. Edward Mead Earle, ed. [Alexander Hamilton, John Jay, and James Madison], *The Federalist* (New York, Tudor, 1937), 486–87.

36. Richard Henry Lee to Edmund Randolph, Oct. 16, 1787, Elliot, *Debates of the Several State Conventions,* I:503.

37. Ibid., II:288; IV:119.

38. Ibid., II:259.

39. Ibid., II:115, 118.

40. Ibid., I:493, 494–95; IV:263; George Mason to George Washington. Oct. 7. 1787, *Documentary History of the Constitution,* IV:316–18.

41. Elliot. *Debates of the Several State Conventions,* III:353–55, 504, 513.

42. Ibid., III:514, 650–51.

43. Ibid., II:459, 476–77, 504–55; Farrand, *Records of the Federal Convention,* III:162.

44. Elliot, *Debates of the Several State Conventions,* III:240, 359, 504, 507; IV:276.

45. Ibid., III:506.

46. Ibid., IV:278, 279.

47. Ibid., III:239; IV:18.

48. Ibid., III:270, 278.

49. Ibid., III:347–48, 510, 515; IV:279.

50. Ibid., III:265; see also Pierce Butler, Ibid., III:263.

51. Ibid., II:348; 3:510; IV:123–24.

52. Ibid., II:506.

53. Ibid., III:331; IV:127.

54. Ibid., III:225.

55. Ibid., IV:130, 276.

CHAPTER 7

1. The Pres of the Convention to the Pres of Congress, September 17, 1787, in Merrill Jensen et al., ed., *The Documentary History of the Ratification of the Constitution,* 23 vols. (Madison: Wisconsin Historical Society Press, 1976–2009), I:306; George Washington Diary, Monday, September 17, Ibid., I:319.

2. Washington to Madison, October 10, 1787, in John P. Kaminski and Gaspare J. Saladino, eds., *Commentaries on the Constitution, Public and Private,* 4 vols. (Madison: Wisconsin Historical Society Press, 1981–1986), I:358.

3. One of the People, *Pennsylvania Gazette* (Philadelphia), October 17, 1787; Jensen, *Documentary History,* II:187.

4. Federal Constitution, *Pennsylvania Gazette* (Philadelphia), October 10, 1787, in Kaminski and Saladino, eds., *Commentaries on the Constitution,* I:365; Daniel Clymer in Jensen, *Documentary History,* II:77; A Plain Citizen, *Independent Gazetteer* (Philadelphia), November 22, 1787, Ibid., II:289.

5. Charles Cotesworth Pinckney in Jonathan Elliot, ed., *The Debates of the Several State Conventions on the Adoption of the Federal Constitution,* 5 vols., 2nd ed. (Philadelphia: J.B. Lippincott, 1896), IV:282.

6. Tench Coxe in Kaminski and Saladino, eds., *Commentaries on the Constitution,* III:174; Hamilton quoted in Elliot, *Debates of the Several State Conventions,* II:231.

7. Federal Constitution, *Pennsylvania Gazette,* October 10, 1787, in Kaminski and Saladino, eds., *Commentaries on the Constitution,* I:365.

8. *Newport Herald,* October 25, 1787, Ibid., I:483.

9. Ibid., I:484.

10. John Jay's Address to the People of the State of New York, September 17, 1787, in Paul Leicester Ford, ed., *Pamphlets on the Constitution of the United States* (Brooklyn, 1888), 73; Social Compact, *New Haven Gazette,* October 4, 1787, Kaminski and Saladino, eds., *Commentaries on the Constitution,* I:310–11.

11. *Boston Independent Chronicle,* October 4, 1787, Kaminski and Saladino, eds., *Commentaries on the Constitution,* I:315; Oliver Ellsworth's speech in the Connecticut Convention, January 4, 1787, Ibid., III:247.

12. Ibid., I:244; Hugh Williamson's Remarks on the New Plan of Government, in Paul Leicester Ford, ed., *Essays on the Constitution of the United States, Published during its Discussion by the People, 1787–1788* (Buffalo, NY: W.S. Hein, 2003), 403.

13. Innes, Davie, and Hamilton in Elliot, *Debates of the Several State Conventions,* II:231; III:634–35; IV:18.

14. Edward Rutledge in Elliot, *The Debates of the Several State Conventions,* IV:274–75; Edmond Randolph, Ibid., III:196–97.

15. Ibid., II:431, II:526.

16. Ibid., II:230–31, II:189–90.

17. Ibid., II:209.

18. Ibid., III:227.

19. Washington to Jefferson, n.d., in Jensen, *Documentary History,* IV:429.

20. Washington to Knox, January 10, 1788, Ibid., IV:437.

21. Washington to Sir Edward Newenham, July 20, 1788, Ibid., IV:805–6; in William T. Hutchinson and William M.E. Rachal, eds., *Papers of James Madison,* 17 vols. (Chicago: University of Chicago Press, 1962–1991), III:249–50, 309.

22. A True American, Kaminski and Saladino, *Commentaries on the Constitution,* I:267.

23. Andrew Allen to Tench Coxe, November 13, 1787, Ibid., IV:123; *Newburyport Essex Journal,* October 10, 1787, Ibid., I:361.

24. James Wilson in Elliot, *Debates of the Several State Conventions,* II:527; Washington to Sir Edward Newenhan, July 20, 1788, Jensen, *Documentary History,* IV:805–6; William Samuel Johnson, speech in the Connecticut Convention, January 4, 1788, Kaminski and Saladino, *Commentaries on the Constitution,* III:249.

25. Patrick Henry in the Virginia convention, Elliot, *Debates the Several State Conventions,* III:150–51.

26. Melancthon Smith's Address to the People of the State of New York, Ford, *Pamphlets on the Constitution,* 94.

27. James Winthrop, *The Massachusetts Gazette,* November 27, 1787, Ibid., 57.

28. Richard Henry Lee to George Washington, October 11, 1787, Kaminski and Saladino, *Commentaries on the Constitution,* I:367; Mason in Elliot, *Debates of the Several State Conventions,* III:268.

29. Melancthon Smith in Ford, *Pamphlets on the Constitution,* 95; Alfred, *Independent Gazetteer* (Philadelphia), December 13, 1787, Kaminski and Saladino, *Commentaries on the Constitution,* II:434.

30. John Williams in Elliot, *Debates of the Several State Conventions,* II:240.

31. Ford, *Pamphlets on the Constitution,* 107.

32. Richard Henry Lee in Ibid., 281; Kaminski and Saladino, *Commentaries on the Constitution,* II:20.

33. Philadelphiensis, *Philadelphia Freeman's Journal,* December 12, 1787, Kaminski and Saladino, *Commentaries on the Constitution,* II:419; Centinel, *Independent Gazetteer,* January 2, 1788, Ibid., III:233.

34. Louis Guillaume Otto to Comte de Montmorin, November 26, 1787, Ibid., 230.

35. Luther Martin's address to the Constitutional Convention, probably June 19, 1787, in Max Farrand, ed., *The Records of the Federal Convention of 1787*, 4 vols. (New Haven: Yale University Press, 1911), IV:22.

36. William Gordon to George Washington, April 3, 1788, *Documentary History of the Constitution of the United States of America, 1786–1870*, 5 vols. (Washington, DC: Department of State, 1894–1905), IV:548.

37. Ford, *Pamphlets on the Constitution*, 95–96.

38. Lee's observations on the Constitutional Convention, Ibid., 282; James Winthrop, *The Massachusetts Gazette*, November 30, 1787, Ford, *Essays on the Constitution of the United States*, 62.

39. Brutus in the *New York Journal*, January 3, 1787, Kaminski and Saladino, *Commentaries on the Constitution*, III:238.

40. Patrick Henry in Elliot, *Debates of the Several State Conventions*, III:141.

41. Tyler's statement, Ibid., III:640. Italics added.

42. Winthrop in Ford, *Essays on the Constitution*, 104; Brutus in the *New York Journal*, January 3, 1788, Kaminski and Saladino, *Commentaries on the Constitution*, III:236.

43. Richard Henry Lee to James Gordon, Jr., February 26, 1788, Ibid., IV:211.

44. For James Monroe and James Bowdoin, see Elliot, *Debates of Several State Conventions*, II:129; III:212–13.

45. Oliver Ellsworth as A Landholder, *The Connecticut Courant*, 5, November 12, 1787, Ford, *Essays on the Constitution*, 141–43.

46. Ibid., 108–9.

47. Mason's objections to the Constitution, October 7, 1787, Kaminski and Saladino, *Commentaries on the Constitution*, I:350; Richard Henry Lee to Edmund Randolph, October 16, 1787, Ibid., 2; 325.

48. Robert A. Rutland, ed., *The Papers of George Mason, 1725–1792*, 3 vols. (Chapel Hill: North Carolina University Press, 1970), III:1056, 1117.

49. James Iredell's answers to Mason's objections to the Constitution, Ford, *Pamphlets on the Constitution*, 357.

50. Tench Coxe as An American, *Independent Gazetteer* (Philadelphia), December 28, 1787, *Commentaries*, 3:166–69.

51. The Landholder in *The Connecticut Courant*, December 10, 1787, Ford, *Essays on the Constitution*, 162; Kaminski and Saladino, *Commentaries on the Constitution*, II:402.

52. Edward Carrington to Thomas Jefferson, October 23, 1787, *Documentary History of Constitution*, IV:347.

53. Hugh Williamson's remarks on the new plan of government, Ford, *Essays on the Constitution*, 410; Civis, *Charleston Columbian Herald*, February 4, 1788, Kaminski and Saladino, *Commentaries on the Constitution*, IV:24.

54. One of the People, *Pennsylvania Gazette* (Philadelphia), October 17, 1787, Jensen, *Documentary History*, II:190.

55. Livingston in Elliot, *Debates of the Several State Conventions*, II:344; Noah Webster's examination into the leading principles of the Constitution, Ford, *Pamphlets on the Constitution*, 49.

56. Ford, *Pamphlets on the Constitution*, 49–51; John Jay in Elliot, *Debates on the Several State Conventions*, II:380.

57. Hamilton and Madison in Elliot, *Debates on the Several State Conventions*, II:351; III:393–94.

58. Alexander Hamilton, John Jay, and James Madison, *The Federalist*, ed. Edward Mead Earle (New York: The Modern Library, 1937), 185.

59. Richard Henry Lee, Letters of a Federal Farmer, Ford, *Pamphlets on the Constitution*, 301; Tyler's statement in Elliot, *Debates on the Several State Conventions*, III:641. See also Brutus in the *New York Journal*, January 3, 1788, Kaminski and Saladino, *Commentaries on the Constitution*, III:237–38.

60. Monroe and Smith in Elliot, *Debates of the Several State Conventions*, II:333; III:214.

61. Hamilton in Ibid., II:351; Madison's views, Ibid., III:249; *The Federalist*, No. 41, in William T. Hutchinson and William M. E. Rachal, eds., *Papers* [of James Madison], 17 vols. (Chicago: University of Chicago Press, 1962–1991), X:391.

62. Iredell in Elliot, *Debates of the Several State Conventions*, IV:96; Christopher Gore, the Massachusetts Federalist, Ibid., II:66–67. See also George Nicholas, February 16, 1788, Kaminski and Saladino, *Commentaries on the Constitution*, IV:124.

63. See Wilson's speech in Philadelphia, October 6, 1787, Kaminski and Saladino, *Commentaries on the Constitution*, I:341; Elliot, *Debates of the Several State Conventions*, II:521; Jensen, *Documentary History*, II:169.

64. Hutchinson and. Rachal, *Papers [of James Madison]*, X:392–93.

65. Elliot, *Debates of the Several State Conventions*, III:611; Benjamin Harrison to George Washington, October 4, 1787, *Documentary History of Constitution*, IV:313.

66. Elliot, *Debates of the Several State Conventions*, III:410; William Symmes to Peter Osgood, Jr., November 15, 1787, Kaminski and Saladino, *Commentaries on the Constitution*, II:112; Brutus in the *New York Journal*, January 24, 1788, Ibid., III:464.

67. See John Tyler in Elliot, *Debates of the Several State Conventions*, III:640.

68. Nathaniel Wythe in Ibid., III:620–21; Erutus, *New York Journal*, January 24, 1788; Kaminski and Saladino, *Commentaries on the Constitution*, III:465; Lee's Letters of a Federal Farmer, in Ford, *Pamphlets on the Constitution*, 306.

69. A Democratic Federalist, *Pennsylvania Herald*, October 17, 1787, Kaminski and Saladino, *Commentaries on the Constitution*, I:390; Henry in Elliot, *Debates of the Several State Conventions*, III:384–85.

70. Elliot, *Debates of the Several State Conventions*, II:502; 3:378–79; Rutland, *Papers of George Mason*, III:1073–74.

71. Samuel Bryan as Centinel, *Independent Gazetteer* (Philadelphia), October 5, 1787; Kaminski and Saladino, *Commentaries on the Constitution*, I:332–33.

72. Robert Whitehill's speech in Jensen, *Documentary History*, II:396, 426; Thomas B. Wait to George Thatcher, November 22, 1787, Kaminski and Saladino, *Commentaries on the Constitution*, II:168.

73. Richard Henry Lee to George Washington, October 11, 1787, Kaminski and Saladino, *Commentaries on the Constitution*, I:368; Rutland, *Papers of George Mason*, III:1067.

74. Samuel Bryan in Jensen, *Documentary History*, II:166; Kaminski and Saladino, *Commentaries on the Constitution*, I:336; II:5.

75. For this view from a French diplomat, see Louis Guillaume Otto to Comte de Montmorin, October 20, 1787, Kaminski and Saladino, *Commentaries on the Constitution*, I:425.

76. For a discussion of these factors, see Jensen, *Documentary History*, I:10–13.

77. Francis Hopkinson to Jefferson, July 17, 1788, in Julian P. Boyd et al., eds., *The Papers of Thomas Jefferson*, 33 vols. (Princeton, NJ: Princeton University Press, 1950–), XIII:370.

78. On Wilson, see Jensen, *Documentary History*, II:485; Noah Webster, *New York Daily Advertiser*, December 31, 1787, Kaminski and Saladino, *Commentaries on the Constitution*, III:195.

79. Jensen, *Documentary History*, II:404.

80. Hugh Williamson in Ford, *Essays on the Constitution*, 400; Foreign Spectator, *Independent Gazetteer* (Philadelphia), October 2, 1787; Kaminski and Saladino, *Commentaries on the Constitution*, I:291; George Washington to the Marquis de Lafayette, February 7, 1788, Ibid., IV:70; Pelatiah Webster as A Citizen of Philadelphia, *Pennsylvania Packet*, November 8, 1787, Ibid., II:67.

81. Wilson and McKean in Jensen, *Documentary History*, II:414, 496; Timothy Pickering to Charles Tillinghast, December 24, 1787, Kaminski and Saladino, *Commentaries on the Constitution*, II:204.

82. Adams to Jay, February 14, 1788, in *The Works of John Adams*, 10 vols. (Boston: Little, Brown, 1851–1865), VIII:475–76.

83. Wilson's statement in Jensen, *Documentary History*, II:172; Kaminski and Saladino, *Commentaries on the Constitution*, I:343.

EPILOGUE

1. Jack N. Rakove, "Making Foreign Policy—The View from 1787," in *Foreign Policy and the Constitution*, ed. Robert A. Goldwin and Robert A. Licht (Washington: The AEI Press, 1990), 18–19.

2. Jonathan Elliot, ed., *The Debates of the Several State Conventions on the Adoption of the Federal Constitution*, 5 vols. (Philadelphia, 1896), IV:264.

3. *The Federalist*, No. 75, in Alexander Hamilton, John Jay, and James Madison, *The Federalist*, ed. by Edward Mead Earle (New York: The Modern Library, 1937), 486–87.

4. U.S. Senate, *Executive Journal* (Washington, DC, 1828), I:3. For a superb discussion of Washington's efforts to conform to the "advice and consent" clause of the Constitution, see Royden J. Dangerfield, *In Defense of the Senate: A Study in Treaty Making* (Norman: University of Oklahoma Press, 1933), 11–17.

5. Norman A. Graebner, "Negotiating International Agreements," in George C. Edwards III and Wallace Earl Walker, eds., *National Security and the U.S. Constitution* (Baltimore: Johns Hopkins University Press, 1988), 210.

6. Dangerfield, *In Defense of the Senate*, 38–39.

7. Ibid., 41–42.

8. Edgar S. Maclay, ed., *Journal of William Maclay* (New York: Appleton, 1890), 122; Dangerfield, *In Defense of the Senate*, 44.

9. Ibid., 45–46; Charles Francis Adams, ed., *Memoirs of John Quincy Adams*, 12 vols. (Philadelphia: J.B. Lippincott, 1874–77), VI:427.

10. *Journal of William Maclay*, 132.

11. Dangerfield, *In Defense of the Senate*, 47–48.

12. Graebner, "Negotiating International Agreements," 212–14.

13. Max Farrand, ed., *The Records of the Federal Convention of 1787*, 3 vols. (New Haven: Yale University Press, 1911), II:465.

SELECTED REFERENCES

BIOGRAPHIES/MEMOIRS

Ammon, Harry. *James Monroe: The Quest for National Identity.* New York: McGraw-Hill, 1971.

Ben-Atar, Doron S. *The Origins of Jeffersonian Commercial Policy and Diplomacy.* New York: St. Martin's Press, 1993.

Brant, Irving. *James Madison.* 6 vols. Indianapolis: Bobbs-Merrill, 1941–1961. (See Vol. II: *James Madison: The Nationalist, 1780–1787.*)

Gottschalk, Louis R. *Lafayette Between the American and French Revolutions (1783–1789).* Chicago: University of Chicago Press, 1950.

Higginbotham, Don. *George Washington Reconsidered.* Charlottesville: University Press of Virginia, 2001.

Hutson, James H. *John Adams and the Diplomacy of the American Revolution.* Lexington: University Press of Kentucky, 1980.

Kaplan, Lawrence S. *Thomas Jefferson: Westward the Course of Empire.* Wilmington: SR Books, 1999.

Malone, Dumas. *Jefferson and His Time.* 6 vols. Boston: Little, Brown, 1948–1981.

Miller, John C. *Alexander Hamilton: Portrait in Paradox.* New York: Harper, 1959.

Mitchell, Broadus. *Alexander Hamilton.* 2 vols. New York: Macmillian, 1957–1962.

Monaghan, Frank. *John Jay.* Indianapolis: Bobbs-Merrill, 1935.

Morris, Richard B., ed. *John Jay: The Winning of the Peace.* 2 vols. New York: Harper & Row, 1980.

Puls, Mark. *Henry Knox: Visionary General of the American Revolution*. New York: Palgrave Macmillan, 2008.

Puls, Mark. *Samuel Adams: Father of the American Revolution*. New York: Palgrave Macmillan, 2006.

Smith, Page. *John Adams*. 2 vols. Garden City: Doubleday, 1962–1963.

Stahr, Walter. *John Jay: Founding Father*. New York: Hambledon, 2005. http://en.wikipedia.org/wiki/Special:BookSources/0826418791.

Stourzh, Gerald. *Alexander Hamilton and the Idea of Republican Government*. Stanford: Stanford University Press, 1970.

Stourzh, Gerald. *Benjamin Franklin and American Foreign Policy*. 2d ed. Chicago: University of Chicago Press, 1969.

BOOKS

Adams, Henry Mason. *Prussian-American Relations, 1775–1871*. Cleveland: Press of Western Reserve University, 1960.

Bernstein, R. B. *The Founding Fathers Reconsidered*. New York: Oxford University Press, 2009.

Brown, Roger H. *Redeeming the Republic: Federalists, Taxation, and the Origins of the Constitution*. Baltimore: Johns Hopkins University Press, 1993.

Burnett, Edmund Cody. *The Continental Congress: A Definitive History of the Continental Congress From Its Inception in 1774 to March 1789*. New York: Macmillan, 1941.

Chavez, Thomas E. *Spain and the Independence of the United States: An Intrinsic Gift*. Albuquerque: University of New Mexico Press, 2002.

Cummins, Light Townsend. *Spanish Observers and the American Revolution, 1775–1783*. Baton Rouge: Louisiana State University Press, 1991.

Dangerfield, Royden J. *In Defense of the Senate: A Study in Treaty Making*. Norman: University of Oklahoma Press, 1933.

Davis, Joseph L. *Sectionalism in American Politics, 1774–1789*. Madison: University of Wisconsin Press, 1977.

Dull, Jonathan R. *A Diplomatic History of the American Revolution*. New Haven: Yale University Press, 1985.

Dull, Jonathan R. *The French Navy and American Independence: A Study of Arms and Diplomacy, 1774–1787*. Princeton: Princeton University Press, 1975. (Excellent for Comte de Vergennes.)

Earle, Edward Mead, ed. *The Federalist*. New York: The Modern Library, 1937.

Flexner, James T. *George Washington: In the American Revolution, 1775–1783*. Boston: Little, Brown, 1968.

Gilbert, Felix. *To the Farwell Address: Ideas of Early American Foreign Policy*. Princeton: Princeton University Press, 1961.

Goldwin, Robert A. and Robert A. Licht, eds. *Foreign Policy and the Constitution*. Washington, DC: The AEI Press, 1990.

Greene, Jack and J.R. Pole, eds. *A Companion to the American Revolution.* Malden: Blackwell, 2000.

Gross, Robert A., ed. *In Debt to Shays: The Bicentennial of an Agrarian Rebellion.* Charlottesville: University Press of Virginia, 1993.

Hendrickson, David C. *Peace Pact: The Lost World of the American Founding.* Lawrence: University Press of Kansas, 2003.

Henkin, Louis. *Foreign Affairs and the Constitution.* 2d ed. New York: Oxford University Press, 1996.

Hoffert, Robert W. *A Politics of Tensions: The Articles of Confederation and American Political Ideas.* Niwot: University Press of Colorado, 1992.

Hoffman, Ronald and Peter J. Albert, eds. *Peace and the Peacemakers: The Treaty of 1783.* Charlottesville: University Press of Virginia, 1986.

Horgan, Lucille E. *Forged in War: The Continental Congress and the Origin of Military Supply and Acquisition Policy.* Westport: Greenwood Press, 2002.

Horsman, Reginald. *The Diplomacy of the New Republic, 1776–1815.* Arlington Heights: Harlan Davidson, 1985.

Hudson, Ruth Strong. *The Minister from France: Conrad-Alexander Gerard, 1729–1790.* Euclid: Lutz, 1994.

Jensen, Merrill. *The Articles of Confederation: An Interpretation of the Social-Constitutional History of the American Revolution, 1774–1781.* Madison: University of Wisconsin Press, 1970.

Jensen, Merrill. *The Making of the American Constitution.* Princeton: Van Nostrand, 1964.

Jensen, Merrill. *The New Nation: A History of the United States During the Confederation, 1781–1789.* New York: Knopf, 1950.

Jillson, Calvin C. *Congressional Dynamics: Structure, Coordination, and Choice in the First American Congress, 1774–1789.* Stanford: Stanford University Press, 1994.

Kaplan, Lawrence S., ed. *The American Revolution and "A Candid World."* Kent: Kent State University Press, 1977.

Kaplan, Lawrence S., ed. *Colonies into Nation: American Diplomacy, 1763–1793.* New York: Macmillan, 1972.

Maier, Pauline. *Ratification: The People Debate the Constitution, 1787–1788.* New York: Simon & Schuster, 2010.

Main, Jackson T. *Political Parties before the Constitution.* New York: Norton, 1974.

Marks, Frederick W., III. *Independence on Trial: Foreign Affairs and the Making of the Constitution,* 2d ed. Wilmington: Scholarly Resources, 1986.

Matson, Cathy D. and Peter S. Onuf. *A Union of Interests: Political and Economic Thought in Revolutionary America.* Lawrence: University of Kansas Press, 1990.

McDonald, Forrest. *Novus Ordo Seclorum: The Intellectual Origins of the Constitution.* Lawrence: University Press of Kansas, 1985.

Millican, Edward. *One United People: The Federalist Papers and the National Idea.* Lexington: University Press of Kentucky, 1990.

Morris, Richard. *The Forging of the Union, 1781–1789.* New York: Harper & Row, 1987.

Murphy, Orville T. *Charles Gravier, Comte de Vergennes: French Diplomacy in the Age of Revolution, 1719–1787.* Albany: State University of New York Press, 1982.

Onuf, Peter S. *The Origins of the Federal Republic: Jurisdictional Controversies in the United States, 1775–1787.* Philadelphia: University of Pennsylvania Press, 1983.

Onuf, Peter S., and Nicholas Onuf. *Federal Union, Modern World The Law of Nations in an Age of Revolution, 1776–1814.* Madison: Madison House, 1993.

Phillips, Paul Chrisler. *The West in the Diplomacy of the American Revolution.* Illinois Studies in the Social Sciences, 11:1–2. Urbana: University of Illinois, 1913.

Rakove, Jack N. *The Beginnings of National Politics: An Interpretive History of the Continental Congress.* Baltimore: Johns Hopkins University Press, 1982.

Rakove, Jack N. *Interpreting The Constitution: The Debate Over Original Intent.* Boston: Northeastern University Press, 1990.

Richards, Leonard L. *Shays' Rebellion: The American Revolution's Final Battle.* Philadelphia: University of Pennsylvania Press, 2002.

Rossiter, Clinton, comp. *The Federalist Papers, Alexander Hamilton, James Madison and John Jay.* New York: New American Library, 1961.

Saul, Norman E. *Distant Friends: The United States and Russia, 1763–1867.* Lawrence: University Press of Kansas, 1991.

Schulte Nordholt, Jan Willem. *The Dutch Republic and American Independence.* Chapel Hill: University of North Carolina Press, 1982.

Scott, H. M. *British Foreign Policy in the Age of the American Revolution.* New York: Oxford University Press, 1990.

Stinchcombe, William C. *The American Revolution and the French Alliance.* Syracuse: Syracuse University Press, 1969.

Szatmary, David. *Shays' Rebellion: The Making of an Agrarian Insurrection.* Amherst: University of Massachusetts Press, 1980.

Varg, Paul A. *Foreign Policies of the Founding Fathers.* East Lansing: Michigan State University Press, 1964.

Whitaker, Arthur Preston. *The Spanish American Frontier, 1783–1795: The Westward Movement and the Spanish Retreat in the Mississippi Valley.* Boston: Houghton Mifflin, 1927.

ARTICLES

Allen, Michael. "The Mississippi River Debate, 1785–1787." *Tennessee Historical Quarterly* 36 (Winter 1977): 447–67.

Bemis, Samuel Flagg. "John Jay." Bemis, ed. *The American Secretaries of State and Their Diplomacy.* 10 vols. New York: Knopf, 1927–1929.

Bernstein, R.B. "Parliamentary Principles, American Realities: The Continental and Confederation Congresses, 1774–1789," in *Inventing Congress: Origins & Establishment of First Federal Congress,* ed. by Kenneth R. Bowling and Donald R. Kennon. Athens: Ohio University Press, 1999, 76–108.

Brown, Richard D. "Shays' Rebellion and Its Aftermath: A View from Springfield, Massachusetts, 1787." *William and Mary Quarterly* 3d Ser., 40 (October 1983): 598–615.

Burnett, Edmund Cody. "The Committee of the States." Washington, DC: American Historical Association, *Annual Report, 1915,* 139–58.

Freer, Robert A. "Shays' Rebellion and the Constitution: A Study in Causation." *New England Quarterly* 42 (1969): 388–410.

Hutson, James H. "Intellectual Foundations of Early American Diplomacy." *Diplomatic History* I (Winter 1977): 1–19.

Jensen, Merrill. "The Idea of a National Government During the American Revolution." *Political Science Quarterly* 58:3 (1943): 356–79.

Ketcham, Ralph L. "France and American Politics, 1763–1793." *Political Science Quarterly* 78 (June 1963): 198–223.

LaFeber, Walter. "The Constitution and United States Foreign Policy: An Interpretation." *Journal of American History* 74 (December 1987): 695–717.

Marks, Frederick W., III. "Power, Pride, and Purse: Diplomatic Origins of the Constitution," *Diplomatic History* 11 (Fall 1987): 303–19.

Matson, Cathy D. and Peter S. Onuf. "Toward a Republican Empire: Interest and Ideology in Revolutionary America." *American Quarterly* 37 (Fall 1985): 496–531.

Merritt, Eli. "Sectional Conflict and Secret Compromise: The Mississippi Question and the United States Constitution." *American Journal of Legal History* 35 (April 1991): 117–71.

Pencak, William. "The Humorous Side of Shays' Rebellion." *Historical Journal of Massachusetts* 17 (Summer 1989): 160–76.

Powell, H. Jefferson. "The Founders and the President's Authority over Foreign Affairs." *William and Mary Law Review* 40 (May 1999): 1471–1537.

Rakove, Jack N. "The Collapse of the Articles of Confederation," in *The American Founding: Essays on the Formation of the Constitution,* ed. by J. Jackson Barlow, Leonard W. Levy and Ken Masugi. Westport: Greenwood Press, 1988, 225–45.

Rowe, G.S. and Alexander W. Knott. "The Longchamps Affair (1784–1786), The Law of Nations and the Shaping of Early American Foreign Policy." *Diplomatic History* 10 (Summer 1986): 199–220.

Warren, Joseph P. "The Confederation and the Shays' Rebellion." *American Historical Review* 11 (1905): 42–67.

Wehtje, Myron F. "Boston's Response to Disorder in the Commonwealth, 1783–1787." *Historical Journal of Massachusetts* 12 (January 1984): 19–27.

PUBLISHED COLLECTIONS

Burnett, Edmund C., ed. *Letters of Members of the Continental Congress.* 8 vols. Washington: Carnegie Institution of Washington, 1921–1936.

Documentary History of the Constitution of the United States of America, 1786–1870. 5 vols. Washington, DC: Department of State, 1894–1905.

Elliot, Jonathan, ed. *The Debates of the Several State Conventions on the Adoption of the Federal Constitution.* 5 vols., 2d ed. Philadelphia: J.B. Lippincott, 1896.

Farrand, Max, ed. *The Records of the Federal Convention of 1787.* 3 vols. New Haven: Yale University Press, 1911.

Ford, Paul Leicester, ed. *Essays on the Constitution of the United States, Published during its Discussion by the People, 1787–1788.* Buffalo: W.S. Hein, 2003. Reprint.

Ford, Paul Leicester, ed. *Pamphlets on the Constitution of the United States.* Brooklyn, 1888.

Ford, Worthington Chauncey and Gaillard Hunt, eds. *Journals of the Continental Congress, 1774–1789.* 34 vols. Washington, DC: Government Printing Office, 1904–1937.

Giunta, Mary A. and J. Dane Hartgrove, eds. *The Emerging Nation: A Documentary History of the Foreign Relations of the United States Under the Articles of Confederation, 1780–1789.* 3 vols. Washington, DC: National Historical Publications and Records Commission, 1996.

Jensen, Merrill et al., ed. *The Documentary History of the Ratification of the Constitution.* 23 vols. Madison: Wisconsin Historical Society Press, 1976–2009.

Kaminski, John P. and Gaspare J. Saladino, eds. *Commentaries on the Constitution, Public and Private.* 4 vols. Madison: Wisconsin Historical Society Press, 1981–1986.

Sparks, Jared, ed. The *Diplomatic Correspondence of the American Revolution.* 6 vols. Washington, DC: J.C. Rives, 1857.

Wharton, Francis, ed. *The Revolutionary Diplomatic Correspondence of the United States.* 6 vols. Washington: Government Printing Office, 1889.

Worthington Ford et al. *Journals of the Continental Congress, 1774–1789.* 34 vols. Washington, DC: Government Printing Office, 1904–1937.

INDIVIDUALS

Adams, John. *The Works of John Adams,* 10 vols. Boston: Little, Brown, 1851–1865.

Ballagh, James Curtis, ed. *The Letters of Richard Henry Lee.* 2 vols. New York: Macmillan, 1911–1914.

Boyd, Julian P. et al., eds. *The Papers of Thomas Jefferson,* 33 vols. Princeton, NJ: Princeton University Press, 1950-.

Butterfield, Lyman H. et al., eds., in *Diary and Autobiography of John Adams,* 4 vols. Cambridge, MA: Belknap Press of Harvard University Press, 1961.

Cappon, Lester J., ed. *The Adams-Jefferson Letters: the complete correspondence between Thomas Jefferson and Abigail and John Adams.* Chapel Hill: University of North Carolina Press, 1959.

Conway, Moncure Daniel, ed. *The Writings of Thomas Paine.* 4 vols. New York: G. P. Putnam's Sons, 1894–1896.

Ford, Paul Leicester, ed. *The Writings of Thomas Jefferson.* 10 vols. New York: G. P. Putnam's Sons, 1892–1899.

Hamilton, Stanislaus Murray, ed. *The Writings of James Monroe.* 7 vols. New York: G. P. Putman's Sons, 1898–1903.

Hastings, Hugh and J.A. Holden, eds. *The Public Papers of George Clinton.* 10 vols. Albany: 1899–1914.

Hutchinson, William T. and William M.E. Rachal, eds. *Papers* [of James Madison]. 17 vols. Chicago: University of Chicago Press, 1962–1991.

Johnston, Henry Phelps, ed. *The Correspondence and Public Papers of John Jay.* 4 vols. New York: B. Franklin, 1970. Reprint

Rutland, Robert A., ed. *The Papers of George Mason, 1725–1792.* 3 vols. Chapel Hill: North Carolina Press, 1970.

Smyth, Albert Henry, ed. *The Writings of Benjamin Franklin.* 10 vols. New York: Macmillan, 1905–1907.

Sparks, Jared, ed. *The Writings of George Washington.* 12 vols. Boston: F. Andrews, 1838–1839.

Syrett, Harold C., ed. *The Papers of Alexander Hamilton.* 27 vols. New York: Columbia University, 1961–1987.

Warren-Adams Letters: Being Chiefly a Correspondence Among John Adams, Samuel Adams, and James Warren. 2 vols. Boston: Massachusetts Historical Society, 1925.

INDEX

About the Authors

NORMAN A. GRAEBNER, Randolph P. Compton Emeritus Professor of History, University of Virginia, was an internationally acknowledged authority on the United States and American diplomacy, as well as the author and coauthor of 30 books, among them *Reagan, Bush, Gorbachev: Revisiting the End of the Cold War* and *America and the Cold War, 1941–1991: A Realist Interpretation* (both Praeger).

RICHARD DEAN BURNS is Emeritus Professor and former chair of the History Department, California State University, Los Angeles, as well as the author and coauthor of more than a dozen books, among them *Reagan, Bush, Gorbachev: Revisiting the End of the Cold War* and *America and the Cold War, 1941–1991: A Realist Interpretation* (both Praeger).

JOSEPH M. SIRACUSA is Professor of Human Security and International Diplomacy and Associate Dean of International and Justice Studies at the Royal Melbourne Institute of Technology, Melbourne, Australia, and the author and coauthor of 25 books, among them *Reagan, Bush, Gorbachev: Revisiting the End of the Cold War* and *America and the Cold War, 1941–1991: A Realist Interpretation* (both Praeger).